NEW MERM

General Editors
William C. Carroll, Boston University, USA
Tiffany Stern, Shakespeare Institute, University of Birmingham, UK

Reconstruction of an Elizabethan
Theatre by C. Walter Hodges

NEW MERMAIDS

NEW MERMAIDS

BEN JONSON

VOLPONE

Revised Edition

Edited by Robert N. Watson

methuen | drama

LONDON • NEW YORK • OXFORD • NEW DELHI • SYDNEY

METHUEN DRAMA
Bloomsbury Publishing Plc
50 Bedford Square, London, WC1B 3DP, UK
1385 Broadway, New York, NY 10018, USA

BLOOMSBURY, METHUEN DRAMA and the Methuen Drama logo are
trademarks of Bloomsbury Publishing Plc

First published in Great Britain 2003
This revised edition published 2019

Cover design: Louise Dugdale
Cover image © ilbusca / Getty images

A catalogue record for this book is available from the British Library.

A catalog record for this book is available from the Library of Congress.

ISBN: PB: 978-1-350-00779-6
          ePDF: 978-1-350-00776-5
          eBook: 978-1-350-00777-2

Series: New Mermaids

Typeset by RefineCatch Limited, Bungay, Suffolk
Printed and bound in India

To find out more about our authors and books visit www.bloomsbury.com
and sign up for our newsletters.

CONTENTS

ACKNOWLEDGEMENTS

I am deeply indebted to previous editors of *Volpone*, especially Alvin Kernan (who illuminates the metatheatrical aspect of the play), Brian Parker, and Philip Brockbank, as well as to the great edition of Jonson's complete works by C. H. Herford, Percy Simpson and Evelyn Simpson. My debts to the cumulative work of other learned commentators on the play are also immense. This project has been supported by conscientious research assistants from the Center for Medieval and Renaissance Studies and the Clark Center for Seventeenth and Eighteenth Century Studies at UCLA, the wisdom and learning of Brian Gibbons and my UCLA colleagues, and research funds from the Faculty Senate at UCLA.

LIST OF ILLUSTRATIONS

INTRODUCTION

Preface

Ben Jonson's *Volpone* – the sharpest, funniest comedy about money and morals in the seventeenth century – is still the sharpest and funniest about those things in the twenty-first. *Volpone* depicts total selfishness thinly covered by sanctimonious speeches, lust and possessiveness poorly disguised as love and marriage, cynical legalism passing itself off as pure justice, boastful name-dropping that pretends to be cultural sophistication, and avarice deluding itself that it is really prudence and even piety. Aided by his wily servant Mosca, the greedy Volpone pretends to be dying so he can trick other greedy people into giving him lavish gifts in hopes of becoming his heir, but poetic justice awaits them all.

This edition provides a carefully edited text of the play in modern spelling, with many explanatory notes for students, and images accompanied by discussion questions, as well as analysis of the play in historical context, in performance, and in literary criticism.

Plot Summary

Volpone, a childless nobleman in Renaissance Venice, worships his hoard of gold. With the aid of his crafty servant Mosca, he pretends to be dying so he can trick other greedy people – the unctuous lawyer Voltore, the elderly, half-deaf Corbaccio, the sexually jealous merchant Corvino, and the talkative, flirtatious, social-climbing Englishwoman Lady Would-Be – into bringing him expensive presents that they hope will provoke Volpone to name them as heir to his fortune.

Mosca eventually convinces Corbaccio to disinherit his virtuous son Bonario, naming Volpone as his heir instead, and convinces the jealous Corvino to send his beautiful wife, the virtuous Celia, to Volpone's bed as a cure that will surely win the inheritance. As that assignation approaches, Mosca rescues his master from the tenacious Lady Would-Be by claiming to have seen her husband, Sir Politic Would-Be, sharing a gondola ride with a local prostitute, and she rushes out to catch them in the act.

Against his own possessive tendencies and against her will, Corvino leaves Celia alone with the supposed invalid in his bedroom. Dropping his pretence of feeble senility, Volpone leaps up, declaring himself healthy, lusty, and willing to grant her the most expensive and exotic pleasures if she will become his mistress. When she reacts with chaste horror and prayers, Volpone attempts to rape her. Bonario – whom Mosca had invited into the house so he could overhear his father turning his legacy over to Volpone – instead overhears the sexual assault, and leaps out to strike down Volpone and rescue Celia. In the resulting court hearing, however, Voltore – still seeking Volpone's favour, and supported by perjury that the other legacy-hunters offer for the same reason – uses his audacious lawyerly skill to make Volpone (carried into court acting mortally ill again) seem the victim, and the innocent pair seem the criminals.

Meanwhile, in the sub-plot, Lady Would-Be insists that the person talking with Sir Politic – another Englishman named Peregrine – must be the prostitute Mosca had warned her about, disguised as a man. Tired of Sir Politic Would-Be's ridiculous pretence of being a seasoned traveller, shrewd entrepreneur, and sophisticated geopolitical insider, the clever Peregrine tricks Sir Pol into thinking that his ideas about how Venice could be conquered have been overheard by Venetian authorities, causing Sir Pol to burn all his self-important papers and hide in a tortoise-shell where Peregrine's allies mock and torment him. When the prank is revealed, Sir Politic flees Venice in disgrace.

Volpone finally overplays his hand by authorizing Mosca to announce his death, so he can (in disguise) torment the vultures with a will that names Mosca himself as heir to the entire fortune. This news provokes Voltore to begin telling the court the truth about what happened between Volpone and Celia, but the disguised Volpone whispers to Voltore that he is actually still alive; so Voltore – in a renewed effort to win Volpone's favour and hence his fortune – pretends that his truth-telling was a lie produced by a demon that had briefly possessed him.

Mosca seizes the chance to claim the fortune permanently, and now that he is supposedly wealthy, the judges fawn over him and hope to marry him to their daughters. But he, too, overplays his hand, assuming Volpone can hardly afford to come back from supposed death to accuse him. When Mosca refuses the disguised Volpone's whispered offer of half the estate, and supports the court's ruling that Volpone should be taken from the court and whipped, Volpone has nothing left to lose and throws off his disguise. All the greedy schemers are thus exposed, and condemned to punishments fitting their crimes – and fitting their social class, since Mosca receives the most brutal sentence.

The Play in Performance

Volpone opened at the famous Globe Theatre in 1606. The same cast that performed Shakespeare's masterpieces of that period had recently performed Shakespeare's *Othello*, also set in Venice. For 180 years following *Volpone*'s successful debut (except when the Puritans closed the theatres from 1642 to 1660), it was frequently in performance – long after most other Jacobean plays had been forgotten. In 1733, there were twelve productions of *Volpone* by England's leading companies. After a mid-century lull, it regained prominence in the later eighteenth century, though it began to suffer decorous cuts to its lower-comic parts (such as Volpone's servants and the Politic Would-Be sub-plot). Performances became rare after the retirement of Garrick in 1776, and the play finally fell into disuse after a 1785 Drury Lane production, while more senti-mental comedies and puritanical attitudes – the very attitudes the play itself made fun of – dominated nineteenth-century English theatre.

Since its revival at the Lyric Theatre Hammersmith in 1921 (which won a rave review from T.S. Eliot), *Volpone* has been produced more often than any other non-Shakespearean play of the period, and more often than several of Shakespeare's. It has also inspired adaptations such as a 1940 French film, scripted by Jules Romains, which begins with a back-story resembling Shakespeare's *Merchant of Venice*, then follows a 1926 socialist reworking of the play by Stefan Zweig that allows Mosca to share the hoarded wealth with the poor. Joan Littlewood's superb 1955 production, reflecting the leftist values of the Theatre Workshop, also gave Mosca the final triumph. Larry Gelbart's 1976 hit Broadway play *The Sly Fox*, set in San Francisco during the Gold Rush, also drew on Zweig, but left the Fox less mortified ('volpone' is Italian for 'fox', and Jonson's subtitle provided that translation). Originally starring the gruff George C. Scott as Foxwell J. Sly, it returned to Broadway in 2004 with Richard Dreyfuss in the title role and a celebrity cast, but the revival was weak. The 1967 feature film 'The Honey Pot' starred Rex Harrison as a Mr. Fox testing three money-hungry mistresses. The 1960s also produced opera and musical-comedy versions of the play, and a commissioned opera at Wolf Trap in 2004, with rhyming libretto, that won much praise and a Grammy nomination. If these adaptations have anything in common, it is the effort to make *Volpone* a more conventional comedy, softening the cruelty, allowing at least a glimmer of romance and the possibility of a happy ending.

Staging the play in its original form seems to require at least some kind of upper balcony (from which Celia can throw her handkerchief out a window, and Bonario can later observe Volpone's attack on her), a large curtained bed (where Volpone can rest and conceal his treasure, and from which he can partly emerge to whisper to Mosca or the audience), and a court bench large and dignified enough for the four *Avocatori* in the trial scenes. Otherwise, directors have great leeway, and they have used it.

A crucial question in staging the play, as in reading it, is how to balance the beast-fable allegory – drawn from Aesop and suggested by the names and behaviour of many of the characters – with realistic human psychology. Many productions have costumed Volpone in vulpine furs, and the legacy-hunters at least partly as the birds their names suggest, giving Voltore a long 'vulture'-like beak, Corbaccio the stooped posture and croaking voice of a raven, and making a black-robed Corvino chase, crow-like, the disguised Volpone away from his nest. Sometimes (as in Donald Wolfit's landmark productions) the *Avocatori* become owls, though the text does not propose it; Wolfit stretched Jonson's fable further by making the diabolical Mosca snake-like (though his name is Italian for 'fly') and the pugnacious, sexually obsessed Corvino bullish. In the 1952 RSC production, Anthony Quayle's fabulously unctuous Mosca not only wore shiny black clothes and rubbed his hands together like a fly, but emitted a strange buzzing laugh, and (thanks to matching table legs) appeared to have six black legs as he took inventory of Volpone's treasures.

Though the tendency early in the twentieth century was to keep the play nimble (and affordable) with simple traditional costumes and minimal sets, subsequent major productions were designed to emphasize the beast-fable. For the 1968 National Theatre version, Tyrone Guthrie sent his actors to study animals at London Zoo, and aptly extended the avian repertoire by costuming the mindless mimic Sir Pol and his garishly dressed Lady as parrots, as their names suggest. In 1972, the Bristol Old Vic – which had successfully emphasized the animal aspects in voice and movement in a 1955 production – pursued the same idea through its sets, allowing the bird-characters to swoop down from on high, and Volpone to emerge from a kind of burrow. A delightful 1998 version at the Noise Within in California featured a raucous chorus of crows.

'The animalistic side to the play enables you to develop a very visual, sensuous way of delineating the characters. By drawing on both their animal qualities and the *commedia dell'arte* tradition you can create a rather alarming, exotic, fun kind of world for both the characters and the audience. The animalistic side in the play encourages actors to explore their characters' obsessional drive and the ways in which they are both blinkered in what they want and the way in which they prey on each other.'

—Greg Hersov, Director of the 2004 production of *Volpone* at the Royal Exchange Theatre in Manchester; https://www.royalexchange.co.uk/164-volpone-greg-hersov/file (accessed 17 October 2018)

Other sets have ranged from traditional simplicity, such as Wolfit's basic proscenium stage that used the front curtain to divide venues, to the opulence of the 1952 RSC version, which featured functional gondolas and an elaborate background depiction of the ornate Piazza di San Marco, thus highlighting the Venetian materialism the play criticizes. Like all major Renaissance plays, *Volpone* has also been modernized, as in the 1971 Stratford, Ontario production that (like Thomas Mann's story 'Death in Venice') evoked the city's 1890s decadence, and turned the Politic Would-Be couple into Ugly American tourists from Texas. The lively 1990 English Shakespeare Company version – which cleverly suggested comparisons between Volpone's three servants and his three male legacy-hunters, and hinted at the depravity of late capitalism – gave Volpone an invalid's IV drip and had donations arrive in shopping trolleys.

The pre-eminent modern Volpone was Wolfit, who for over twenty years played Volpone as an almost Falstaffian force of playfulness and appetite, cutting Volpone's weaker moments to assure the audience's admiration, though this Volpone was also like Falstaff in his ruthless exploitation of others. To keep Volpone as the commanding figure, Wolfit also cut lines suggesting Mosca's readiness to mock and betray Volpone long before Volpone's fatal decision to play dead; how early and eagerly Mosca considers such betrayal is crucial for that role. Wolfit trimmed the Sir Pol sub-plot, too, thereby keeping the focus more on greed and cruelty than on lighter social follies.

Others (such as Ralph Richardson, whose 1952 RSC Volpone was condemned as meek, and William Hutt's nastier 1971 portrayal) depicted Volpone more coolly, as a decadent aristocrat merely battling his own boredom (with the servants usually reflecting that decadence grotesquely); several more recent productions have begun the play with Mosca rousting prostitutes – female and sometimes male – from Volpone's bed, or starting Volpone's day with a cocktail. The implicit blasphemy in the opening scene's worship of gold has been heavily emphasized, to the point that (in the 1968 National Theatre production) Volpone's 'take of my hand' became the offering of a golden coin, in place of a Communion wafer, to the kneeling Mosca; the 1971 Stratford production began with mass responses from a procession of monks who then stripped for an orgy. Modern productions have occasionally underscored the play's distorted sexuality by having a man in drag play Lady Pol (as would necessarily have happened in the all-male Jacobean theatre).

Celia has sometimes been performed as a meek little victim, other times as a strident moralist, and even occasionally as a hypocritical temptress, more vixen than victim. A lot depends on how one stages her encounters with Volpone, from the mountebank scene – where her body-

Figure 1 Celia (Morag Hood), with Nano (David Rappaport, left) and Castrone (John-Angelo Messan, right) below her, as they introduce Volpone for his performance as a mountebank in the 1977 National Theatre production, directed by Peter Hall. © Donald Cooper/Photostage.

language can answer many questions that the text leaves open – to the attempted-rape scene.

Fig. 1 Teaching Question: In hopes of making contact with the attractive Celia, Volpone takes a break from playing a dying man to playing a doctor selling miracle cures. What do those roles have to do with each other? Why do you think Celia throws her handkerchief down to him?

The mixed tone of the ending of this play – a comedy that culminates with harsh sentences and no winners – has troubled directors as much as it has critics. The Bristol Old Vic production changed the ending several times during its run, unable to decide whether to suggest that Volpone (like Reynard the Fox in the fable) would finally escape. Guthrie, having played up the light comic pleasures of the story, tried adding a madrigal between the sentencing and the epilogue to overcome the closing bitterness; in later stagings Guthrie surrendered by eliminating the epilogue and letting the *Avocatori* lead sadistic laughter at the prisoners. A production in New York in 1985 ducked the problem by keeping the atmosphere morally sombre from the start, and the 1999 RSC Swan production, though funny, was effectively dark and menacing throughout. Many other productions (including the Wolfit and the Ontario versions) have sought to emphasize the separation between the defeated exit of Volpone and the potentially triumphant return, in the Epilogue, of the actor who played him.

A 2012 *Volpone* at the Red Bull in New York thrived on its energy, especially in the secondary roles, but at moments defanged the play's satiric bite. The most recent major production was directed by Trevor

Figure 2 Celia (Rhiannon Handy) is admonished by her husband Corvino (Matthew Kelly), who despite his extreme jealousy is trying to talk her into climbing into the sickbed with Volpone (Henry Goodman), in the 2015 Royal Shakespeare Company production, directed by Trevor Nunn. Photo by Manuel Harlan, copyright RSC.

Nunn at the Swan in Stratford-upon-Avon in 2015, starring Henry Goodman in the title role. Other than some insect-like tics of Mosca, it abjured the beast-fable in favour of modern dress, and featured selfies, twenty-first-century medical equipment, an electronic stock-ticker, and various quips on current events added to the text. The production was criticised, however, for dulling Jonson's sharpness by slowing the pace and by rendering Volpone sympathetic.

Fig. 2 Teaching Questions:
What is the effect of having video screens that alternate between medical monitors and stock-market tickers in Volpone's house, while the complications of human life play out in front of them?
What is the relationship between financial greed and sexual possessiveness in the play?

Collectively, the stage history seems to warn against trying – perhaps misled by Jonson's Prologue – to hide the tough, sinister side of the play behind cheerful laughter, or trying to hide the essential theatricality of the play and of the plays within it. Evidently *Volpone* needs to be savage and stagy. Efforts to conceal what are assumed to be Jonson's incompatibilities with modern sensibilities do him more harm than good (this is true on the page as well as the stage, I will now argue). The man may often have been difficult for no good reason, but there are usually very good reasons for the difficulty of his works.

The Author

Ben Jonson was an astonishing character: a passionate man with no apparent interest in love, a working-class child who became the exemplar of high court culture, a decorous classicist given to extreme drunkenness and murderous violence, a self-proclaimed Stoic driven by violent appetites for praise and pleasure, a dedicated social climber who stubbornly sabotaged his own advancement, a moralistic writer who always seems to side with his rogues, and a genius of comic drama who repeatedly withdrew bitterly from the theatre. Jonson is a victim of his own success: having systematically used the mantles of classical literature and royal employment to conceal his common origins and wild tendencies, Jonson has convinced many potential modern readers that he is yet another formal snob in the literary establishment.

Jonson's father, a minister, died before his son was born in 1572; his stepfather was a bricklayer. Intelligence and diligence won the boy a scholarship to the prestigious Westminster School in London as a day-student, where he met his lifelong mentor, William Camden. After apprenticing unhappily to his stepfather's trade, Jonson volunteered for the wars in Flanders, where – evidently not deeming that slow campaign dangerous enough – he reportedly challenged an enemy soldier to single combat, and killed him.

In his early twenties, Jonson married and had several children; the deaths of his first daughter and first son are lamented movingly in his *Epigrams*, and there is no evidence that any of his legitimate offspring survived to adulthood. By 1597 he was acting and writing in the nascent theatre industry – and heading for jail. He had played the lead in Thomas Kyd's *Spanish Tragedy*, and was designated one of England's best tragic playwrights in Francis Meres's 1598 *Palladis Tamia* (though neither Jonson nor anyone else preserved any of the plays on which that judgement must have been based). In August 1597, however, he was imprisoned for his part in finishing a satiric play called *The Isle of Dogs* (also now lost). The next year, within a few days of the opening performance of his *Every Man in His Humour*, with William Shakespeare in the cast, Jonson killed another fellow-actor (Gabriel Spencer, who had been in prison with him) in a duel; he escaped execution – any man able to read Latin could claim exemption as a clergyman – but had his thumb branded and his belongings confiscated. To make things worse, he announced his conversion to Catholicism, which was then essentially illegal. After his release, his characteristic pugnacity (already evolving into its adult guise of scholarly arrogance) propelled him into a prolonged literary brawl – now hyperbolically known as the War of the Theatres – with Thomas Dekker and John Marston, a brawl that carries over into the Prologue to *Volpone*; he also boasted (in his revealing 'Conversations with Drummond') of battering Marston physically and taking his pistol. He dined with the conspirators only weeks before the Gunpowder Plot, and was secretly enlisted in the subsequent investigation.

Despite disgrace and debt – or perhaps because of them – Jonson used his literary skills and scholarly reputation to gain the patronage of powerful aristocrats, whom he followed to their country houses, leaving his family back in London, to endure the bubonic plague, which killed his first son. He wrote intricate elegies of praise to anyone who supported him, and brutally nasty epigrams against anyone who crossed him. When verse satires were made illegal, he (along with Chapman and Marston) invented the 'comical satire' mode of drama. When the Scottish King James succeeded Queen Elizabeth in 1603, Jonson co-authored a play called *Eastward Ho* that satirized Scots and landed him again in prison.

Jonson emerged to write a series of great and popular comedies, including *Volpone, Epicoene, The Alchemist*, and *Bartholomew Fair*, as well as the best of his surviving tragedies (*Sejanus*, based on ancient Roman history) and a number of his great lyric poems. During the same time period, having worked his way back into favour, he became James's leading author of masques: elaborately produced ceremonial allegories designed to instruct and flatter the high-ranking persons who watched and often performed them. But he feuded bitterly with the renowned set designer of these productions, Inigo Jones; and James's successor as king, his son Charles I, turned to other authors. Jonson was even hired by Sir Walter Raleigh to tutor Raleigh's son in Paris – until the drunken Jonson (nearly three hundred pounds of him by this time) was carted mockingly through the streets by his tutee. Virtually every claim to glory brought with it a threat of disgrace: along with the instances already mentioned, the early *Poetaster*, the mid-career *Sejanus* and *Epicoene*, and the late *Devil is an Ass* each somehow landed him in trouble with the authorities.

Jonson's lifelong struggle to construct and project a dignified self through his literary art culminated in the 1616 Folio of his *Works*. Despite some mockery of the idea of presenting mere plays under the grand traditional title of 'Works', Jonson had become a revered figure, a kind of poet laureate, winning honorary degrees, state employment, and a pension (including an annual barrel of wine). The 'Tribe of Ben', a loose association of leading Cavalier poets, worshipped him as their 'father' at many bibulous occasions. Still, disasters befell him, including a fire that destroyed his books and papers in 1623, and a stroke in 1628 that rendered him paraplegic – and a far less successful comic playwright – until his death in 1637.

Analysis

Money and Morality

Volpone likes to be flattered that he is not like the misers despised in medieval literature, but this evasion only casts him as a more modern version of that figure – the modern billionaire unaccountably determined to acquire further billions, whatever the ethical and social costs, if only to assert his superiority to his fellow-billionaires. This modern self is defined by its performances and its acquisitions, with no stable or satisfactory person at the centre of it, surrounded by a sterile caricature of family, and protected by the illusion that wealth can claim priority even over death.

Figure 3 Volpone (Michael Gambon) in the 1995 National Theatre production, directed by Matthew Warchus. Photo by Robbie Jack/Corbis via Getty Images.

It is a game for the man who has everything except a life or a heart, and Volpone plays it well. He feigns sickness to get riches, unaware that his riches have themselves becomes a disease.

Fig. 3 Teaching Question: A skeleton is never mentioned in this play, so why would the director have put this one on stage, holding an hourglass and touching Volpone this way?

The legacy hunters have prominent sources in classical literature (Horace, Petronius, Lucian, Juvenal), but they emerge here as venture-capitalists, investing more and more of their considerable wealth in flattering Volpone, in hopes of inheriting even greater wealth when he dies. As this new economic system came to predominate in the late Renaissance, the old feudal rules of social order collapsed; money became the primary measure of status, in contrast to the older prestige of lineage. Yet the limited imagination of some people who succeed financially, then and now, leaves them with little idea of what to do with their fortunes other than try to make them into larger fortunes, and to mimic the style and seek the power of a feudal aristocracy – to become (at best) high-brow patrons and (more often) petty barons. In this sense, Jonson's *Volpone* conveys the same warning as Marlowe's *Doctor Faustus*: that the modern world – though it may lack the explicitly diabolical tempters of the old morality-plays – offers to buy our souls in exchange for some superficial power and glory that never really transcends the banal and the mundane. Gold replaces God, as it does for Volpone in the opening lines, even if it brings nothing except more gold. Opulent possessions become the new form of demonic possession.

This most praised and most performed of Jonson's brilliant comedies is, paradoxically, a moral story in which every character is wrong (or at least extremely naïve); and, despite the extremely wide moral spectrum they seem to represent, they are wrong in some deeply similar ways. The play's primary satiric target is greed, but it also recognises that greed is merely one facet of the insatiable human desire to continue desiring (even, perhaps especially, where there is no pressing need), and of the fundamental human tendency (which Jonson exposes throughout his comedies) to live in grandiose egoistical fantasies rather than in the real world.

English authors liked to depict their maritime rival Venice as a scene of immorality, but this city-state is also apt (as in Shakespeare's *Merchant of Venice*) as a place where there is only mediated value; in the absence of land and other natural resources, Venice built its economy and identity entirely around exchange. So it provides a perfect setting for a sophisticated understanding of greed as desire that has broken loose from real objects and real needs – an apt lesson for Jacobean London, which was rapidly moving from a feudal system toward a capitalist one. As among the wealthy in many major twenty-first century cities, money in *Volpone* becomes (like Celia for the men who seek to control her) more a symbolic marker than a substantial instrument, in a costly competition for personal pride rather than mere survival. Nobody in this story is obliged to any manual labour, at least until Mosca is finally sentenced to the galleys. Neither Volpone nor the three men pursuing his inheritance lack anything that more money could buy, but they still compete for extreme wealth. Unlike a lifespan, money can be multiplied without limit, like the sensual adventures Volpone vainly offers to Celia.

That sexual offer also involves costumes and roles: all of Jonson's Venice is a stage, a world of plays superseding reality, as well as of play superseding work. In an eyewitness travel book called *Coryats Crudities*, for which Jonson wrote a commendatory poem, Venetian mountebanks match Volpone's showmanship as Scoto, and Venetian courtesans match Lady Would-Be's equally ill-fated attempt to seduce Volpone with heavy make-up and elegant rhetoric; Jonson's actors would have been performers imitating performers imitating performers. As in the 'humours' plays Jonson had been writing during the preceding years, various characters in *Volpone* are led astray largely by over-confidence in the flattering scripts they have adopted or adapted for themselves. What is new here is the degree to which the satiric manipulators delude and injure themselves in the process of deluding and injuring their victims. Jonson's audience, meanwhile, is rebuffed for confidently awaiting either the victory of goodness which concludes most popular comedies, or else the victory of satiric wit that concludes so many other Jonsonian comedies. Behind his ostensible purpose in punishing the rogues, which (his Epistle asserts) is to disarm the moral critics of the theatre, Jonson may also intend to unsettle any spectator who complacently believes he or she has caught onto Jonson's comic formula. Much of the play's remarkable tautness and energy comes from Jonson simultaneously spurring on and reining in his own roguish impulses.

Eventually Volpone will become truly as sick and immobile as he had pretended to be, Mosca is sentenced to the total servility he had feigned, the legacy-hunters reveal themselves as essentially the animals after which they are named, and Sir Pol becomes a victim of his own grandiose paranoid politics. So acting controls reality in this play, but (as in fairytales) not in the way the wishers had hoped. The characters each have ingenious plans, all of which backfire. The joke is finally on everyone, including the audience.

But, while the narcissistic aspect of theatre is mortified, the pleasure of theatre is thereby reborn. Here – as usual in his comedies, which work deliciously on stage – Jonson offers the thrill of watching swift, death-defying manoeuvres in a tight space, of watching the protagonists improvize and integrate an ever-increasing number of sub-plots, each reflecting some deluded character's egoistic fantasy. Mosca must keep all these incompatible story lines running on the same stage, without collisions; it is a bold juggling act that earns gasps of admiration as it endures through mounting complications and several near falls, and provides a satisfying series of crashes when Jonson brings it all tumbling to earth at the end.

Sources and Analogues

One unrecognised basis for Jonson's plot is the tradition of moot cases at the Inns of Court. These were mixtures of festivity and pedagogy, testing legal scholars with scenarios designed to generate hilariously complex disputes about the rights to inherited property. The playlet staged by

Figure 4 Against the backdrop of many golden treasures, Androgyno (Ankur Bahl) sits on the lap of Volpone (Henry Goodman), with Castrone (Julian Holt) behind them and Nano (Jon Key) just to their left, as Mosca (Orion Lee) looks on from the doorway, in the 2015 Royal Shakespeare Company production, directed by Trevor Nunn. © Donald Cooper/ Photostage.

Volpone's servants about the Pythagorean re-incarnations of a soul provides a perfect overture to this topic. Jonson then replicates many favourite conundrums of the moot cases by giving Volpone so many potential heirs, each with different claims and different disqualifications – including the rumour that his servants are his children and the implication that those children are sterile, Voltore's status as his lawyer, Sir Politic's status as a foreigner and possible traitor, the exchange of wills with Corbaccio, the questions about women's eligibility to inherit property, proposed forfeitures to the state or to charity, and Volpone's own temporary death.

> **Fig. 4 Teaching Question:** Why do you think Jonson makes Volpone a father-figure for this strange but merry household?

Volpone also leans heavily on the tradition of Aesopian beast-fables, especially the legends of Reynard the Fox, many of whose adventures – extremely popular in Renaissance European folklore – suggest parallels to Volpone. As Parker observes, Reynard too is tried by a corrupt court, first for attempted rape, then for feigning death in an attempt to capture the crow's wife. He pretends to be a doctor, and is often depicted preaching from a platform like the one Volpone uses to play Scoto of Mantua. Like Volpone (and like some real foxes), Reynard often plays dead in order to trap the predatory birds who gather to feed on his corpse. The vulture (here, the lawyer Voltore) is a notorious carrion-seeker. The raven was a long-lived bird whose croaking voice was associated with death, and who was thought sometimes to abandon its offspring (as old Corbaccio disowns Bonario). The crow (the jealous merchant Corvino) is another scavenger, and ironically a bird traditionally associated with marital fidelity. Flies also feed on the dead, and were associated (as Mosca is here) with demonic possession. Sir Pol displays the parrot's devotion to loud, mindless mimicry, and is hunted down by the sharper hawk Peregrine. The fable thus conjoins with the overall ethical thrust of the play: as traditional social and religious principles yield to the avaricious appetite, human beings inevitably sink to the level of beasts.

Jonson combines this bestiary tradition with the popular tradition of Italian improvisational theatre known as the *commedia dell'arte*, in which stock roles (such as the cuckold Pantalone with whom Corvino explicitly associates himself, and the nattering Punchinello with whom Jonson associates Sir Pol) were reflected by exaggerated masks and plumes that could easily have doubled as bird costumes (Parker). Suitors in the *commedia* often try (as Volpone does) to woo a sequestered woman by playing a mountebank or apothecary under her window, assisted by zanies, until the master of the house chases them away; Volpone's speeches here add another meta-theatrical level by suggesting an ironic commentary on Jonson's own turbulent career as a playwright (see the note to 2.2.33 ff.).

Volpone and Mosca

Discussions of Volpone often begin at the beginning, with Volpone's famous panegyric to gold (1.1.1–27). Critics and editors sift through the variety of literary echoes the speech offers, seeking evidence that the play is essentially another condemnation of greed, that it is a subversive celebration of appetite, or that Volpone suffers from a perversion of his religious or sexual instincts. Perhaps, instead, the flood of conventional motifs suggests a man searching for a satisfactory role in which to cast himself. The fate of miserly characters in literature is so unappealing that Volpone tries (with temporary success) to translate it into the more exalting roles of worshipful saint and devoted romantic lover, with gold as his deity and paramour. He also leans on a wide range of classical allusions to give his avarice the dignity it so conspicuously lacks in literature (see H&S, IX, 689).

Mosca amplifies Volpone's interest in Celia with the most hackneyed sort of romantic imagery (1.5.107–22), as if he knew that Volpone could not resist writing himself wholeheartedly into this sort of bodice-ripping love-story. Volpone consciously assumes the role of Scoto of Mantua in order to make contact with Celia, but his subsequent seductive song to her, when he gets her into his bedroom, betrays a carelessness about the interplay of literature and life: the song is lovely in its way, but dangerously second-hand. The literary precedent from Catullus foreshadows the ill-fatedness of Volpone's corrupt schemes, sexual as well as financial. Even when expressing his most powerful private desires, Volpone thus remains a puppet to conventions.

Furthermore, he has miscast his play: he assumes that Celia will prove to be like Lucrezia in Machiavelli's play *La Mandragola*, a typical wife in the world of Italian satire, quite willing to be seduced away from her worthless husband. Like the manipulators in Jonson's earlier comedies, Volpone promises Celia a set of participatory literary allusions which they will consciously control to maximize their own pleasure (3.7.220–34). Unluckily for him, the play drifts out of the gravitational field of satiric comedy, and temporarily into that of sentimental melodrama. When, as a result, he lies uncomfortably trapped in the courtroom, Volpone momentarily fears that his role as an invalid will become real and permanent (5.1.1–10), a fear that soon proves prophetic, in the court's poetically just sentence (5.12.117–24). He had mistakenly assumed that he inhabited a genre that favours cynical exploitation, rather than an equally familiar (but less Jonsonian) genre that enforces poetic justice.

Just as Volpone imagines himself the triumphant fox of the several ancient beast-fables, so Mosca envisions himself as the all-conquering wily servant of the ancient mode still known as New Comedy, and of the satiric city-comedies Jacobean playwrights based on that classical model. As his plot progresses, Mosca asks his master to 'applaud my art', even while hoping to avoid the kind of 'epilogue' that punished Volpone's strategic role-playing as Scoto of Mantua (2.4.32–8). Preparing to turn against his long-time master and ally, Mosca declares, 'this is called the fox-trap' (5.5.18), which may remind us of the dramatic 'mouse-trap' trick Hamlet uses to expose King Claudius. But by pursuing a plan merely because it seems to fit a dramatic precedent, Mosca virtually assures his doom in the context of Jonson's iconoclastic comedy; Jonson would never let a Shakespearean plot triumph within his own.

What makes Mosca's fate particularly bitter is that the pattern he relies on is essentially Jonson's own, in which the keenest predatory wit – often a wily servant – ends up triumphant. Like Volpone, Mosca is finally defeated less through his own weakness than through betrayal by his creator, who is experimenting with a sternly moralistic conclusion. When Volpone calls an end to all the playing by throwing off his disguise as the sergeant, all the other roles – Volpone as a dead or dying man, Voltore as a victim of diabolical possession, Corvino as an upstanding husband, Mosca as a *magnifico* – collapse too. In Jonson's other plays, characters who try to end the play by casting off their own masks fail to crush the theatrical and picaresque spirit; when Surly in *The Alchemist* and Justice Overdo in *Bartholomew Fair* throw off their disguises, they succeed neither in ending the play, nor in punishing the rogues. If Jonson does manage (as his Epistle promises) 'to put the snaffle in their mouths who cry out, We never punish vice in our interludes', it is only by putting the irons on the legs of the characters who assumed that such critics were right, and that theirs would prove to be another amoral Jonsonian world.

Through most of the play, Volpone and Mosca control their gulls by the same principle that functions in the other comedies: they exploit the fact that people would rather misperceive reality than surrender their self-aggrandizing fantasies. Like Clement and Brainworm in *Every Man In His Humour* or Lovewit and Face in *The Alchemist*, they are exploiters of cognitive dissonance. Mosca comments that each of the legacy-hunters

> Is so possessed, and stuffed with his own hopes
> That anything unto the contrary,
> Never so true, or never so apparent,
> Never so palpable, they will resist it –

> (5.2.24–7)

While Voltore daydreams happily about the new title, role, and costume he supposes he is about to acquire, Volpone and Mosca delight themselves (as do the schemers and the audience alike in the earlier plays) by envisioning the moment when this inflated image will collide with the degrading reality of the situation (1.2.97–113).

When Volpone's performance as Scoto enrages Corvino by threatening to cast him as the humiliated Pantalone of the *commedia* (2.3.2–9), Mosca distracts him by offering to cast him as (in effect) the understudy to the role of *magnifico* now played by the supposedly dying Volpone. The prostitution of his wife suddenly becomes, in Corvino's eyes, merely a piece of stage-business peripheral to this grand transformation. Volpone will get what he wants, not through his virtuosity as an actor in the role of mountebank, but through Mosca's virtuosity as a reviser of old plays: Corvino can only stumble from one script to another. Even when he finds out the truth, his impulse is to resort to a standard emblematic expression of his despair, 'with a rope and dagger / To visit all the streets' (5.2.93–4). But finally, in yet another facet of the play's pattern of poetic justice, Volpone and Mosca fall into the trap of literary formulas they had set for their victims.

Celia and Bonario

Celia and Bonario provoke the greatest confusion among the critics of *Volpone*, and generate a remarkable instance of Jonson's manipulation of genres. The extreme and apparently authentic virtue of these characters makes them anomalous in the world of satiric city-comedy. Are we to take them as the sole remaining locus of true virtue, or as yet another naïve and pretentious target of ridicule? The question is impossible to resolve, as the protracted critical disagreements suggest, because these characters are one thing on their own terms, and another within the dramatic context Jonson imposes on them, much as they are transformed from heroes to villains by the little play of demonic possession in the Venetian courtroom. What critics have tried to resolve by analysing personality traits can be understood only by analysing literary conventions: these are exiles from the world of sentimental melodrama, which is the one place their sort of virtue has any real relevance or force.

The fate of these characters has disturbed readers of *Volpone* in revealing ways. William Butler Yeats found these innocents poignant in their isolation. The oblique objection of another great poet, Samuel Taylor Coleridge, took the form of a suggestion that 'a most delightful comedy might be produced, by making Celia the ward or niece of Corvino, instead of his wife, and Bonario her lover'. Since then, scholars have repeatedly puzzled over the fact that Jonson neglects to propel Celia and Bonario into the romantic union that would conventionally have been their lot. It often seems as if the pair themselves expect their life-trials to be resolved as they would be in such a comedy. But those who call on the heavens for aid in *Volpone* (as even more grimly in Shakespeare's *King Lear*) will meet some rude surprises; and though they may survive, they will never be allowed to fulfil the roles that they proudly assign themselves. Jonson thus again turns our conventionalised expectations of romantic theatre against themselves, in favour of his own realism. If we try to perceive Celia and Bonario entirely as heroes, the play calls us fools; if we try to perceive them entirely as fools, the play calls us rogues. The discomfort felt by readers is natural under such circumstances, and we can escape the dilemma only by recognising the novelty of Jonsonian comedy.

Celia is not simply a simpleton; that would dull the edge of the parody. She is guilty, not (as critics have asserted) of stupidity exactly, but (like so many of Jonson's victims) merely of misunderstanding the nature of the play-world she inhabits. The eccentric perspective of her extreme and conventional virtue causes her to misread the plot repeatedly. Because she is constitutionally incapable of fathoming the greed and cynicism of the schemes enmeshing her, Celia misinterprets her husband's urgings as evidence that this is in fact a conventional ploy to test her doubted fidelity, though Corvino's actual plot is virtually the opposite (3.7.24).

As Volpone attempts to rape her, Celia's pleas for divine rescue sound very much like an actor repeating a cue waiting for a saving entrance – which is very much what they are. She keeps calling upon heaven to stand up for the right (Bonario joins in this practice at the trial), because that is what would happen in a traditional maudlin tale of threatened innocence. But here, as in *King Lear*, the lack of any divine response to these repeated calls is an exploitation of the audience's desires and expectations, used to remind us yet again that the real world does not work in the reassuring manner of the play-worlds we are used to witnessing.

Celia begs to be allowed to 'take down poison, / Eat burning coals, anything', rather than submit to sexual dishonour. She tells Volpone that she is his 'martyr', and goes on spouting – with perfect sincerity – the classic clichés of female virtue (3.7.93–107). Celia behaves, in other words, just as a conventional heroine should behave. But no one – not her seducer, her husband, her God, or her author – seems to be impressed. The world of satiric city-comedy is like the world of the Venetian court: a place 'Where multitude and clamor overcomes', and where calling as witnesses 'Our consciences' and 'Heaven which never fails the innocent' is therefore equivalent to having 'no testimonies' at all (4.6.15–19). What would become of the archetypal tragic rape victim, Lucrece, in a cynical comic universe?

'Although Jonson frequently draws the ire of feminist scholars, the court proceedings in *Volpone* have a strikingly feminist slant, critiquing legal institutions that put the victim on trial. . . . the innocent victim is currently being discredited by a pack of liars and a shrewd lawyer. Called a "whore", "harlot" and "prostitute", Celia is forced to look on silently as others call into question her chastity and integrity by inventing an alternate sexual history for her'.
—Marshall Botvinick, *Jonson,* Volpone (Macmillan, 2015), p. 62.

Bonario looks at Mosca's outrageously insincere show of sad humility, and tells himself, 'This cannot be a personated passion', probably because it is exactly the sort of behaviour that occurs sincerely in the sort of senti-mental melodramas that populate Bonario's mind. The rhetoric of Bonario's dramatic entrance to prevent the rape can only be characterized as clichéd:

> Forbear, foul ravisher, libidinous swine!
> Free the forced lady, or thou diest, impostor.
> But that I am loath to snatch thy punishment
> Out of the hand of justice, thou shouldst yet
> Be made the timely sacrifice of vengeance,
> Before this altar, and this dross, thy idol.
> Lady, let's quit the place: it is the den
> Of villainy. Fear nought, you have a guard;
> And he, ere long, shall meet his just reward.

(3.7.266–74)

This play is not an allegory, nor do its speeches begin in alliteration and end in rhyme; these anomalous signals of more exalted genres involving heroic Anglo-Saxon warriors or heroic couplets reinforce the impression that the virtuous couple and their sentiments are badly out of place. A morality-play tradition in which Good Conscience had to rescue Innocent Humanity from the clutches of the Vice rings deliberately hollow on Jonson's stage.

The Would-Be Plot

One other aspect of *Volpone* that has long troubled critics, editors, and directors is the questionable integration of the Sir Politic Would-Be subplot into the play as a whole. But the follies of this English couple often generate useful parallels to the Venetian vices in the main plot; and, as their name suggests, the Would-Be family provides further occasions for Jonson to attack self-aggrandising literary delusions. If at times their story seems irrelevant to the centre of the play, that may itself be Jonson's point. The Would-Be subplot is a would-be main plot.

Lady Politic acknowledges that she derives her behaviour from Castiglione's famous handbook for aristocrats *The Courtier* (4.2.35), but she ends up seeming more like a courtesan, and her speech is an obsessive chain of literary allusions (3.4.75–95). Characteristically, Jonson attacks this affectation indirectly, through the framing of the plot, as well as by direct ridicule. Lady Politic's ability to mistake the Englishman Peregrine for a Venetian courtesan, because she believes Mosca's hints that her life is becoming a standard story of Italianate sexual connivance, typifies her self-dramatizing tendencies. She is too enthralled with her role as the righteous detective to notice how little Peregrine resembles such a courtesan, and there is no way for her to recognise that Mosca's advice is merely a ploy in the main line of Jonson's story, to which her marital problems remain extremely peripheral.

Sir Politic, too, feeds his melodramatic fantasies on discarded scraps from the main plot. He is obsessed with clothing and scripted behaviour (4.1.8), and his grandiose schemes resemble those generated by 'projectors' – mostly mere con-men in Jonson's comedies, but heroic entrepreneurs in other stories and histories of the period. Sir Pol is absorbed in such outlandish schemes and tales that Peregrine is left wondering, 'Does he gull me, trow? or is gulled?' (2.1.24). The answer, of course, is both: Sir Pol becomes so enthralled with his imaginary intrigues that he starts believing his own lies. What his diary reveals is that he takes the painfully banal events of his daily life – such as replacing shoelaces and urinating – and writes them down in books ('quotes' them) as if they were indeed the makings of an international spy-thriller (4.1.128–47). In letting us know that we would not be interested in reading Pol's closely-guarded diary, Jonson is partly letting us know why he has forestalled Pol's efforts to make the play into a political melodrama and to cast himself as its Machiavellian protagonist. The opposite of the cruel and clever isolate Volpone, this genial and sociable idiot who repeatedly flees from petty brawls is unlikely to star in that genre.

That does not, however, preclude Sir Pol from proving useful in another genre. Peregrine concludes that Pol 'would be a precious thing / To fit our English stage', except that everyone would dismiss him as an exaggeration (2.1.56–60). He finally decides to punish Pol by pretending that these dangerous plots are actually occurring: that Pol's spy-fantasies have been misread as real by real spies. Pol's reaction is to confess, too late, that he drew all his politic schemings 'Out of the play-books' (5.4.41–2). His fate (analogous to that of Volpone) is to find the world all too willing to play along with his role, in a way that makes him confront its costs and limitations. He tries to cloak himself in cleverness, as in the tortoise-shell which was a Renaissance symbol of Polity, but in both cases the put-on cover-story finally serves only to hurt and humiliate him.

Peregrine wonders whether his 'counter-plot' (4.3.24) will end up causing Pol's 'Adventures' to be 'put i' the *Book of Voyages*? And his gulled story registered for truth?' (5.4.3–6). Such punishment would ironically fit the crime. After Pol is humiliated, one witness compares the scene to a puppet-show: 'a rare motion to be seen in Fleet Street' (5.4.77), and Pol moans that he 'shall be the fable of all feasts; / The freight of the *gazetti*; ship-boys' tale; / And, which is worst, even talk for ordinaries' (5.4.82–4). He will become, as he had hoped, renowned, but not at all in the way he had hoped: this master of gossip about prodigies has himself become a prodigious subject of gossip. In Jonson's comedies, the effort to play an exalted literary role remains the surest path to humiliation.

Peregrine's uncertainty about whether Pol is a clever exploiter or a gullible victim arises from the formulaic fervour of Pol's self-important fantasies. But Peregrine's fear that he is being tricked enmeshes him in this same pattern of error: he, too, ends up misreading Jonson's plot. Commentators often assume that Peregrine is the wise hero of the play, but his one decisive action is a misreading of a misreading, rather than a perfect moral insight: when Lady Would-Be mistakes him for her husband's supposed courtesan, Peregrine misinterprets her behaviour as evidence that she is a courtesan, and Pol her pander. So Peregrine's punishment of Pol for this supposed outrage is hardly the triumph of an all-knowing satirist exploiting folly, but instead the delusion of another victim (however witty) of Jonson's control of the plot. The gallant Peregrine, even more clearly than Mosca, is a plausible version of Jonson's usual triumphant satiric wit, and English audiences were clearly invited to identify with him; but these clever characters eventually become the prey of the very devices that had empowered them in earlier Jonsonian comedies, and earlier in this comedy. Peregrine is the least wrong, perhaps, of all the characters in *Volpone*, but also probably the least interesting.

The critics who see Peregrine as a Jonsonian hero may thus be missing an important point. Even the role of punitive satirist – one Jonson has usually exalted, as a surrogate of the role he claims for himself – fails in Volpone. Peregrine is finally a marginal character, so much so that productions have often cut him, and his battle of errors with Sir Pol, completely.

The Ending

Several objections have commonly been raised to the harshly moralistic conclusion of this play. Except for the attempted rape of Celia (which is stylized toward farce), Volpone's and Mosca's crimes are really poetic justice against loathsome and over-privileged scavengers, and audiences generally find themselves quite ready to forgive both lead characters 'for the wit o' the offence' (as the scheming servant is forgiven at the end of *Every Man In His Humour* and *The Alchemist*). Audiences are further discomforted by the way the severe sentences jumble the genre of the play, which Northrop Frye's classic *Anatomy of Criticism* cites as an anomaly in being 'a kind of comic imitation of a tragedy'; and it certainly seems like a satire as well. Why does Jonson insist on wedging a severe sentence against Volpone in the few lines between his delicious performance as the exploiter of vices and his applause-winning appearance as the Epilogue?

Perhaps the strain we feel at the end of *Volpone* is Jonson pulling back on the bridle of his own satiric spirit; he projects into the audience his own dilemma as a comic moralist. The surprisingly blunt exposure and punishment in Volpone pits the indulgent conventions of satiric comedy, in which wit is the sole criterion for success, against the forces of conventional morality that were, through the Puritans, exerting renewed pressure against the popular theatre. What is imprisoned at the end of the play, but escapes into the Epilogue, is an aspect of comedy that conspires with the cruel, selfish, cynical exuberance of the spectators. Volpone and Mosca betray each other, but in a deeper sense they are both betrayed by Jonson. The lead characters and the audience alike confidently await the vindication of the clever exploitative plot, only to have it explode as badly as the more naïve plots.

Audiences understandably wonder why Mosca refuses to accept half of Volpone's fortune, insisting instead on a total triumph that practically forces Volpone to seek out vengeful counter-measures; or why Volpone chooses a counter-measure that essentially assures him of a fate far worse (even for such a greed-driven personality) than poverty. Perhaps neither of them can conceive that their play could really end so bluntly and brutally, any more than the audience can, because they all share the same set of expectations about Jonsonian comedy. Volpone's announcement of his true identity at the end of the play may indeed be 'a flourish of defiance' like those of Webster's Duchess of Malfi or Shakespeare's Richard III (Leggatt), but the result is a long, dull, painful penance, not a glorious final conflagration. Editors and critics have long striven to identify the many literary sources of *Volpone* and to understand how Jonson translates them into Volpone's speeches and schemes. They have also struggled to explain why someone as clever and generally disillusioned as Volpone makes such grave errors in predicting the reactions of Celia and Mosca at crucial points in the plot. Combining the questions offers some plausible answers: Volpone, deluding himself by expecting his story to conform in full to its literary precedents, becomes yet another Jonsonian character defeated when his world stubbornly refuses to imitate conventional art.

Volpone apparently believes exactly what many commentators now believe: that his story is essentially a retelling of old beast-fables about the clever fox who outwits the birds of prey and finally entraps them by feigning death. These parables resemble the typical satiric city-comedy, with the cleverest creature feeding himself fat on gulls whose overconfidence has made them vulnerable. Volpone, disguised as a court-sergeant to taunt Corvino further, evidently understands himself as the moralizing spokesman at the end of such a fable:

Methinks
Yet you, that are so traded i' the world,
A witty merchant, the fine bird Corvino,
That have such moral emblems on your name,
Should not have sung your shame, and dropped your cheese,
To let the fox laugh at your emptiness.

(5.8.9–14)

If only Volpone had the option of ringing down the final curtain right then, as he gloats about fulfilling a familiar little literary piece in which he plays the triumphant role. He does not (cannot) recognise that Jonson may choose to abandon the parallel at the last minute. The mouldy tale in which Volpone has cast himself with too much confidence, vanity, and literary-mindedness becomes instead a different story, 'called mortifying of a fox' (5.12.125), as Volpone himself ruefully acknowledges. It is as if Volpone – despite having robbed so many others by indulging their dreams of glory – starts to believe that he himself is the hero of the Reynard tales, who ends up escaping from such a similar series of accusations. Jonson out-foxes that belief by importing the variant on the story – best known in Chaucer's 'Nun's Priest's Tale' – in which Reynard squanders his victory by insisting on jeering at his victims.

If Peregrine had exposed Sir Pol's schemes as mere self-inflation, exposed the fraud of Volpone and his co-conspirators, punished them merely with shame and impoverishment, and bestowed the ill-gotten fortune on Celia and Bonario, the play would have been much more conventionally satisfying. The Jonsonian hero would achieve his usual moral and practical sovereignty, the two plots would be unified, the fate of the evil-doers would be just without marring the comic atmosphere, and the romantic couple would be vindicated. But Jonson chooses to challenge us, rather than merely satisfy us. Specifically, he challenges the preachy critics mentioned in the Epistle (here printed at the end of the play-text), telling them that a strictly ethical conclusion in Jonsonian comedy will not take the customary and comfortable form envisioned by Celia and Bonario, because the real world seldom works that way. If his critics demand a moral ending, they will receive it only in the harsh discordant form of the court's official sentences, where power and money crush playfulness, and those critics will have to decide whether they really prefer that to the comic spirit that survives in Volpone's epilogue and in Jonson's other comedies.

The striking oddities of *Volpone* make sense as part of Jonson's struggle to keep his audience ethically and theatrically alert. Things that do not seem to fit are, for the most part, not intended to fit. The Would-Be subplot is, in this sense, not nearly so superfluous as it might have seemed. The characters of Celia and Bonario are indeed anomalous, but it is an anomaly that forces us to confront our assumptions about both comedy and morality. The ending may seem too sternly punitive as a response to the plotters who, for the most part, merely allowed the wickedness of the fortune-hunters to punish itself; the play, as a result, may give confusing signals about its genre. But that confusion allows Jonson, characteristically, to undermine the complacencies of his audience, including any assumption that the victory in Jonson's comedies must always go to the most clever cynic.

Several things thus happen simultaneously, even synergistically, in *Volpone*:

1) a critique, at once extremely bitter and extremely funny, of decadent human greed;
2) an extended parable that echoes ancient and popular fables about the crafty fox;
3) an indirect critique of the literary conventions accepted by Jonson's competitors;
4) a series of satiric depictions of other follies epidemic in Jonson's society.

Together they make *Volpone* the most wickedly delightful piece of comedy produced by Elizabethan and Jacobean England – the greatest dramatic culture (with the possible exception of the Greeks of two thousand years earlier) in the history of the world.

The Text

This edition is a modern-spelling text based on facsimiles of Jonson's 1607 Quarto *Volpone* and 1616 Folio *Works*, both of which I believe he supervised carefully, though not fanatically. F appears to be based on a copy of Q marked, presumably by Jonson, with minor revisions. Ordinarily this would lend greatest weight to F, which is how editors of *Volpone* (with the exception of Henry de Vocht's little-known 1936 version) have tended to proceed. But revisions are not always improvements, and Jonson was surely a sharper playwright around 1606, as he began his string of great comedies, than he was approaching 1616, with *Bartholomew Fair* his only recent play, and no theatrical successes in his remaining decades.

Some of F's corrections are indeed corrections, its punctuation is often more expressive, and some changes may have emerged from performance, as the collaborative theatrical wisdom of the period asserted itself. But the fresh wisdom of the genius at the start of his remarkable comic period deserves more respect than Jonson himself or his editors have given it. Furthermore, some changes apparently arose from tightened censorship rather than artistic reconsideration.

The differences between Q and F (about a hundred substantive changes, not counting small corrections and shifts in punctuation) are quite minor anyway, and do not suggest any differences in intention – except perhaps for re-punctuation in the rape scene that renders Celia commandingly rational in F, rather than breathlessly desperate as in Q (in performance, Siobhan McKenna's defiance of Ralph Richardson epitomized the implications of F, whereas Rosalind Iden's panic over Donald Wofit's attack epitomized the implications of Q). Not even the myopia of an editor, and the accompanying narcissism of small differences among editions, can justify an absolute preference between the Q and F texts of *Volpone*, which are here therefore conflated to provide the best possible communication of this biting and hilarious play, with all its verbal and moral complexities, to a general modern audience.

With that goal in mind, I have worked as Jonson evidently did, using Q as a basis susceptible to small revisions: mostly modernization of spelling and punctuation, along with selective endorsements of revisions Jonson himself offered in F, and a few emendations (especially where authorized by the 1640 Second Folio) of what appear to be minor errors that slipped through both editions. Unlike previous editors, I have favoured the Q text of Jonson's Dedicatory Epistle, since it presumably reflects his thoughts at the time the play was composed, and certainly reflects the date at the end of the letter, more accurately than the F revision. The showy and archaic complexity of Jonson's syntax (in either version), evidently designed to flatter the university audience to whom he was dedicating the first publication of *Volpone*, makes this Epistle so difficult that I have placed it at the end of the text, rather the beginning, to avoid discouraging modern readers before they reach the delights of the play proper.

I have also replaced Jonson's continental practice of marking a new scene at each significant entrance with the modern practice that does so only when all characters have exited. At the beginning of each scene, the original texts list all the characters who appear in that scene; I have replaced that group listing with individual entrances at the likeliest moment in the text. These and other added stage directions appear in square brackets, and readers and performers should feel free to question them. Stage directions from the Folio version of the play are not in brackets, but there were none in in the Quarto, and it is unclear whether they were added by Jonson himself.

I have sought to retain some impression of Jonson's characteristic verbal rhythms, which he conveyed by elisional apostrophes and heavy punctuation. Modern usage generally dictates exchanging Jonson's colons and semicolons, as when Mosca remarks, 'There, he is far enough; he can hear nothing: / And, for his father, I can keep him off' (F, 3.7.17–18); occasionally the original texts use a colon in place of a modern exclamation point. Otherwise, however, this edition retains (to an unusual degree) Jonson's elaborate punctuation, which provides a valuable guide at times to sense for the reader, at other times to performance for the actor. A comma often represents the space, the lightly emphatic pause (between a predicate and its objective or subjective clause), in which a modern speaker would insert 'that', as when Corbaccio offers a drug by claiming to 'know, it cannot but most gently work' (Q, 1.4.16), or when Mosca describes Celia's 'soft lip, / Would tempt you to eternity of kissing!' (Q, 1.5.112).

At other times the comma provides a pause for dramatic effect: modern writers – indeed, most modern editors – would remove at least the second of the commas in Mosca's almost pornographic description of Celia as 'a beauty, ripe, as harvest' (Q, 1.5.109); but Jonson's commas suggest the provocative pauses that give Mosca's description the quality of a cumulative, developing series of thoughts; 'ripe' works by itself, before becoming subsumed into the conventional comparison. The same effect explains the even more peculiar insistence of commas when Mosca evokes, for Voltore, the wealth supposedly awaiting him upon Volpone's death: 'When you do come to swim, in golden lard, / Up to the arms, in honey' (Q, 1.3.70); for an editor to decide, merely for the sake of eliminating commas, that the swimming should be associated only with the lard, and the immersion separately with the honey, is a waste of Mosca's mesmerising artistry, and Jonson's behind it.

The mid-sentence question marks of Mosca's 'Am not I here? whom you have made? your creature?' (Q, 1.5.78) demand preservation for similar reasons: the phrases are each separate expressive units, as well as finally blending into a single sentence that, normally punctuated, would be less than the sum of its parts. Ironically, modernizing editors have inadvertently made Jonson seem old-fashioned by over-eagerly modernizing the oddities of his syntax and punctuation which, in their original form, reveal exactly the process of a human subjectivity spontaneously and realistically developing from moment to moment that Jonson is commonly accused of lacking.

'One of the interesting things we sometimes do in rehearsal and I enjoy is to take all the punctuation out. What would you do? You'd seek punctuation, you'd seek shape and phrasing . . . you'd go, oh, there's a change of thought there, or, that thought leads to that thought. . . . Punctuation is not a pain in the neck, it's a liberation in theatre.'
—Henry Goodman, star of the 2015 *Volpone* at the RSC Swan Theatre, in a 2016 interview with Prof. Mike Cordner of the University of York

ABBREVIATIONS

Brockbank	*Volpone*, ed. Philip Brockbank, New Mermaids (London: A&C Black, 1968)
F	Jonson, Ben, *Works*, First Folio edition, London, 1616.
F2	Jonson, Ben, *Works*, Second Folio edition, London, 1640.
H&S	Herford, C. H., Simpson, Percy and Simpson, Evelyn, eds., *Ben Jonson*, Oxford: Clarendon Press, 1925–52.
Kernan	*Volpone*, ed. Alvin Kernan, New Haven: Yale University Press, 1962.
Parker	*Volpone*, ed. Brian Parker, revised edition, Revels Plays, Manchester: Manchester University Press, 1999.
Q	*Volpone*, first Quarto edition, London, 1607.

Citations of Shakespeare are based on *The Riverside Shakespeare*, ed. G. B. Evans, Boston: Houghton Mifflin, 1974.

FURTHER READING

Barton, Anne, *Ben Jonson, Dramatist*, Cambridge: Cambridge University Press, 1984; the most helpful and perceptive modern study of Jonson's plays.

Bloom, Harold, *Ben Jonson's* Volpone, or the Fox: *Modern Critical Interpretations*, New York: Chelsea House, 1988; a selection of essays by major critics.

Donaldson, Ian, *Ben Jonson: A Life*, Oxford: Oxford University Press, 2011; this deeply researched biography links *Volpone* with Jonson's dangerous proximity to the Gunpowder Plot, and suggests the play may obliquely satirise Sir Robert Cecil.

Empson, William, '*Volpone*', *The Hudson Review* 21 (1968–9), 651–66; a characteristically lively and combative introduction to the play's effects in performance.

Gibbons, Brian, *Jacobean City Comedy*, 2nd ed., London: Methuen, 1980; the best overview of the play's genre, which Jonson would bequeath to the wittiest playwrights of subsequent decades.

Harp, Richard and Stewart, Stanley, eds., *The Cambridge Companion to Ben Jonson*, Cambridge: Cambridge University Press, 2000; an excellent introduction to the author and his contexts.

Hawkins, Harriet, 'Folly, Incurable Disease, and *Volpone*', *Studies in English Literature* 8 (1968), 335–48; explores links between characters' mental and physical failings.

Jonson, Ben, *The Cambridge Edition of the Works of Ben Jonson* (7 Vols.), ed. David Bevington, Martin Butler, and Ian Donaldson, Cambridge: Cambridge University Press, 2012; a massive and masterful updating of the text and relevant scholarship on *Volpone* and the rest of Jonson, including an extensive performance history.

Leggatt, Alexander, 'The Suicide of Volpone', *University of Toronto Quarterly* 39 (1969–70), 19–32; denies that Volpone's decision to confess is a break in his character, seeing it instead as a culmination of dangerous devotion to theatrical art.

Maus, Katharine Eisaman, 'Idol and Gift in *Volpone*', *English Literary Renaissance* 35 (2005), 429–53; links Volpone's greed to idolatry through the anthropologist Marcel Mauss's influential theory of gifts.

Paster, Gail Kern, *The Idea of the City in the Age of Shakespeare*, Athens, Georgia: University of Georgia Press, 1985; includes a perceptive study of Jonson's Venice.

Redwine, James D., 'Volpone's "Sport" and the Structure of Jonson's *Volpone*', *Studies in English Literature, 1500–1900*, 34 (1994), 301–21; argues that the last Act of the play is justified as a condemnation of Volpone's sadistic enjoyment of the suffering of others.

Riggs, David R., *Ben Jonson: A Life*, Cambridge: Harvard University Press, 1989; a brilliant biography, rich in historical detail and psychoanalytic insight; Riggs sees Jonson struggling with his personal failings through Volpone, and convincingly suggests that Jonson is mocking his own theatrical career through Volpone's performance as a mountebank.

Teague, Frances Nicol, 'Seeing to Things in "Volpone"', *Mediterranean Studies* 19 (2010), 112–26; explores the relationship of the visual and imagistic aspects of the play with animal-emblem traditions.

Vinter, Maggie, '"This is called mortifying of a fox": *Volpone* and How To Get Rich Quick by Dying Slowly', *Shakespeare Quarterly* 65 (2014), 140–63; sees Volpone trying and ultimately failing to escape the individual's traditional moral obligations to a community, allowing Jonson to propose a new kind of community through theatre.

Watson, Robert N., *Ben Jonson's Parodic Strategy: Literary Imperialism in the Comedies*, Cambridge: Harvard University Press, 1987; provides a more extended application, to this play and others, of the argument outlined in this Introduction.

Original Quarto title page:
Simul & iucunda, & idonea dicere vitae. Jonson is quoting a line from one of his favourite
   works, Horace's *Ars Poetica* (333–4), which asserts that poets wish 'to say things that are
   pleasing and, at the same time, useful for life'.

BEN: IONSON

his

VOLPONE

Or

THE FOXE.

— *Simul & iucunda, & idonea dicere vitæ.*

Printed for *Thomas Thorppe.*
1607.

VOLPONE, a Magnifico Volpone meant 'an old fox' and hence 'an old craftie, slie, subtle companion, sneaking lurking wily deceiver' (according to a popular 1598 dictionary, *A Worlde of Wordes*, by John Florio, to whom Jonson sent a copy of Q thanking him for 'the aid of his Muses'). *A Magnifico* was a name for a Venetian magnate or plutocrat, and also an alternative name for the Pantalone character in the *commedia dell'arte*. Though Jonson's Epistle warns against such 'applications', and editors have generally dismissed this one, several commentators in Jonson's own time suspected that Volpone was based on Thomas Sutton, the wealthiest commoner in London, and a controversial figure whose lack of direct heirs apparently allowed him to profit by manipulating those who were scheming to gain his legacy, which eventually founded the Charterhouse hospital (as Volpone's wealth finally goes to 'the hospital of the *Incurabili*' at 5.12.120).

MOSCA, his Parasite Mosca meant a kind of fly, and became thereby a term for human parasites, those who live and feed on others (usually by servile flattery); as references to demonic possession accumulate later in the play, we may also suspect a reference to Beelzebub, 'Lord of the Flies'.

VOLTORE, an Advocate Voltore meant 'a ravenous bird called a vultur' (Florio), and – because vultures feed on dead animals – the name was applied to legacy-hunters. It was also applied to persuasive lawyers; an Advocate was the equivalent of an English barrister or American defence attorney.

CORBACCIO Italian for a raven, a bird believed (as in Psalm 147, Proverbs 30.17, and Luke 12.24) to neglect its offspring, who (like Bonario) therefore had to rely on heaven for protection; its croaking was thought to signal death.

CORVINO Italian for a small crow – an emblem of marital fidelity, and an enemy of the fox.

NANO Italian for dwarf; dwarves were popular as court jesters.

CASTRONE 'a gelded man' (Florio), one who has been castrated, often to preserve a high singing voice or to preclude sexual intercourse.

ANDROGYNO 'he that is both male and female' (Florio)

POLITIC WOULD-BE a would-be schemer in affairs of state, one who wishes (like many English Renaissance travellers) to be thought important, clever, prudent and worldly. Shortened to Pol, his name links him to the parrot, which suits his mindless efforts to mimic the fashionable phrases and sophisticated schemes of those around him.

PEREGRINE a traveller; also a kind of hawk, birds which Jonson's Epigram LXXXV says 'strike ignorance' and 'make fools their quarry'; an emblematic tradition made them the opposite of the tortoise.

CELIA literally, 'heavenly one', celestial; sometimes the name of the heroine in the *commedia dell'arte*

BONARIO 'debonaire, honest, good, uncorrupt' (Florio), though it can also thereby imply 'naïve'

FINE MADAM WOULD-BE cf. Jonson's satiric Epigram LXII 'To Fine Lady Would-Be'; she probably has a large red beak of a nose that emphasizes her kinship to Pol the parrot

AVOCATORI Venetian officials who served as prosecutors and sometimes (as in Jonson's version) as judges

COMMANDATORI lower officials who enforced subpoenas summoning witnesses and malefactors to court hearings

2

THE PERSONS OF THE COMEDY

[in order of appearance]

VOLPONE, *a Magnifico*
MOSCA, *his Parasite*
VOLTORE, *an Advocate*
CORBACCIO, *an old Gentleman*
CORVINO, *a Merchant*
NANO, *a Dwarf*
CASTRONE, *an Eunuch*
ANDROGYNO, *a Hermaphrodite*
POLITIC WOULD-BE, *a Knight* [*from England*]
PEREGRINE, *a Gentleman-traveller* [*from England*]
CROWD
CELIA, *the Merchant's wife*
SERVATOR[I], *Servant*[*s*]
BONARIO, *a young Gentleman*, [Corbaccio's *son*]
FINE MADAM WOULD-BE, *the Knight's wife*
WOMEN, [*Attendants waiting on* Lady Would-Be]
AVOCATORI, *four Magistrates*
NOTARIO, *the Court clerk*
COMMANDATORI, *Officers*
MERCATORI, *Merchants*

The Scene: Venice

3

THE ARGUMENT

V *olpone, childless, rich, feigns sick, despairs,*
O *ffers his state to hopes of several heirs,*
L *ies languishing; his parasite receives*
P *resents of all, assures, deludes; then weaves*
O *ther cross-plots, which ope' themselves, are told.*   5
N *ew tricks for safety are sought; they thrive; when, bold,*
E *ach tempts th'other again, and all are sold.*

As in the comedies of Plautus, the first letters form an acrostic of the play's title.
  2   *state* estate, property
  5   *ope'* open
        told exposed
  7   *sold* betrayed, ruined

PROLOGUE

Now, luck God send us, and a little wit
    Will serve, to make our play hit,
According to the palates of the season:
    Here is rhyme, not empty of reason.
This we were bid to credit, from our poet,   5
    Whose true scope, if you would know it,
In all his poems, still, hath been this measure:
    To mix profit, with your pleasure;
And not as some (whose throats their envy failing)
    Cry hoarsely, 'All he writes, is railing',   10
And, when his plays come forth, think they can flout them,
    With saying, 'He was a year about them'.
To these there needs no lie, but this his creature,
    Which was, two months since, no feature;
And, though he dares give them five lives to mend it,   15
    'Tis known, five weeks fully penned it,
From his own hand, without a co-adjutor,
    Novice, journeyman, or tutor.
Yet, thus much I can give you, as a token
    Of his play's worth: no eggs are broken;   20

Prologue This Prologue may be spoken by Nano, Androgyno, and/or Castrone, since it shares the clunky poetic meter of their show in 1.2, and Mosca and Volpone will be needed onstage in character as soon as the Prologue ends.

1   *God* This word was changed to a meaningless 'yet' in F, probably because of the 1606 Act against Blasphemy.

5   *credit* believe, understand

6   *scope* intention

8   *profit* didactic value, as in Horace's formula of *utile dolci*; but perhaps quipping also on the playwright's financial motive in writing for the public theatre.

10 *railing* a tirade of abuse, complaint, and criticism; theatrical rivals such as Dekker and Marston voiced this objection to Jonson.

12 *about them* in writing them; Jonson proudly contrasted his careful workmanship with the hasty play-writing of his competitors, including Shakespeare, but here he boasts that he can also outdo them in writing quickly.

13 *To these . . . creature* To refute these critics requires no lie, only this play he has created; or, he does not need to call them liars – 'give the lie' – only show this play

17–18 *co-adjutor . . . tutor* Various kinds of assistant, each common in the play-factory that was the Elizabethan public theatre, ranging from a full collaborator to an apprentice, a hack assistant and scene-doctor, or a mentor and corrector.

Nor quaking custards with fierce teeth affrighted,
　Wherewith your rout are so delighted;
Nor hales he in a gull, old ends reciting,
　To stop gaps in his loose writing,
With such a deal of monstrous, and forced action,　　　25
　As might make Bedlam a faction;
Nor made he his play for jests stol'n from each table,
　But makes jests, to fit his fable.
And so presents quick comedy, refined,
　As best critics have designed:　　　30
The laws of time, place, persons he observeth,
　From no needful rule he swerveth.
All gall, and copp'ras, from his ink he draineth,
　Only, a little salt remaineth;
Wherewith, he'll rub your cheeks, till, red with laughter,　　　35
　They shall look fresh, a week after.

21　*quaking custards* the stock cowards of comedy, with reference also to pie-in-the-face slapstick and the fool's leap into a giant custard at the Lord Mayor's banquet; here, as in *Poetaster*, 5.3.525, Jonson mocks the phrase 'Let custards quake' from his rival Marston's *Scourge of Villainy* (1599), an example of what was called 'biting satire'.

22　*your rout* the rabble, 'your basic mob'

23–4　*Nor hales . . . writing* Nor will this playwright haul in a gullible fool reciting stock phrases or bits from other plays

26　*make Bedlam a faction* add a new group to the madhouse, or competitor to the show people went to see there, or possibly, gain the endorsement of madmen; Bedlam was the common name of the insane asylum of St Mary of Bethlehem in London.

27　*jests stol'n from each table* jokes stolen like random leftovers from a feast, or picked up as table-talk, or plagiarized from a jest-book

29　*quick* lively

31　*The laws of time, place, persons* Sixteenth-century Italian critics developed precepts from Aristotle's *Poetics* into an insistence on the Dramatic Unities, which lent verisimilitude and thus believability to a play by having it all occur in a single day and area, with suitable and consistent character-types (since *Volpone* has a distinct subplot, Jonson conveniently omits the law governing unity of action here); Jonson often used his adherence to these laws to attack his theatrical rivals, who generally did not observe them.

33　*gall, and copp'ras* substances used to make ink, but standing here for animosity (attributed to the gall-bladder) and bitterness (ferrous sulphate, known as copperas, tastes extremely harsh)

34　*salt* sediment; edible salt was a metaphor for pungent wit, and was also used in cleaning and food preservation, leading to 'fresh' in line 36.

VOLPONE
OR THE FOX

ACT 1, SCENE 1

[*Enter*] MOSCA, [*pulling back the curtains to reveal*]
VOLPONE [*in bed*]

VOLPONE

Good morning to the day; and, next, my gold:
Open the shrine, that I may see my saint.

[MOSCA *uncovers the treasure*]

Hail the world's soul, and mine. More glad than is
The teeming earth, to see the longed-for sun
Peep through the horns of the celestial Ram,   5
Am I, to view thy splendour, darkening his;
That, lying here, amongst my other hoards,

---

0   s.d. Though his entrance could be delayed until just before he speaks, Mosca prob-
    ably enters here, perhaps opening the curtains around Volpone's bed, or opening
    curtains to admit the morning sun.
1   This opening reflects Jonson's determination to preserve the 'unity of time' recom-
    mended by Aristotle's *Poetics*: the play all takes place in a single day, making it seem
    more real for the audience.
2   *shrine . . . saint* Volpone asks Mosca to open curtains concealing the gold, to which
    Volpone then addresses a kind of matins prayer, which would normally have been
    addressed to God in praise of the morning sun. His subsequent speeches are
    permeated with religious language blasphemously redirected toward gold.
3   *world's soul* the Platonic *anima mundi*, but punning on *sol* – the French word for
    the sun; Volpone sees gold (which alchemists called 'the son of Sol', as at line 10
    below) as the soul of worldly desires; *sol* was also the name of a French coin (as at
    4.5.97 below).
4   *teeming* full of life, and ready to give birth
5   *horns . . . Ram* Aries in the zodiac, the beginning of spring, when the increasing
    sunlight nurtures renewed life
6   *thy splendour . . . his* the gold's splendour making the sun seem dim by
    comparison
7   *hoards* secret treasures, presumably including jewels and silver plate

9

Show'st like a flame by night; or like the day
Struck out of chaos, when all darkness fled
Unto the centre. O thou son of Sol,   10
But brighter than thy father, let me kiss,
With adoration, thee, and every relic
Of sacred treasure in this blessèd room.
Well did wise poets, by thy glorious name,
Title that age which they would have the best,   15
Thou being the best of things, and far transcending
All style of joy, in children, parents, friends,
Or any other waking dream on earth.
Thy looks when they to Venus did ascribe,
They should have giv'n her twenty thousand Cupids;   20
Such are thy beauties, and our loves! Dear saint,
Riches, the dumb god that giv'st all men tongues;
That canst do nought, and yet mak'st men do all things;
The price of souls; even hell, with thee to boot,
Is made worth heaven! Thou art virtue, fame,   25
Honour, and all things else! Who can get thee,
He shall be noble, valiant, honest, wise –

9–10   *Struck ... centre* Established amid the primal Chaos, driving all darkness to the
centre of the earth (described in the opening of Genesis)

10   *son of Sol* in alchemy, the sun was described as the father of gold

14–15   *thy glorious name ... best* The great poets called the first and best period in human
history 'the Golden Age' – the classical equivalent of the Christian Garden of Eden;
e.g. Ovid's *Metamorphoses*, I.89–112 and XV.96 ff.

16–20   When Seneca translated the portion of Euripides's *Danae* on which this passage is
based (*Epistles* CXV.14), he reported that Euripides had to placate the original
audience by assuring them that this impious greedy speaker would be punished –
very much the same promise Jonson makes in the Epistle accompanying *Volpone*
(lines 121–4) (Parker).

19–20   *Venus ... Cupids* the goddess often called golden – *aurea Venus* – by Homer and
classical Latin poets would need to have many supplementary beauties (typified by
the son she produced, the god of love) to be worthy of that adjective; but Volpone
is also unwittingly confessing that he has perverted the love inspired (in the
classical tradition) by Cupid into the greed defined (in the Christian tradition) as
cupiditas.

22   *dumb* mute; Compare the proverbs 'when gold speaks every tongue is silent' (Tilley
G295) and 'silence is golden'.

23   *That ... things* Recalling Aristotle's definition of divinity as the unmoved mover
(Parker)

24   *with thee to boot* with gold as a compensation (playing perhaps also on 'booty',
stolen treasure); where Christ's sacrifice had paid 'the price of souls', gold can buy
them back for damnation.

MOSCA

    And what he will, sir. Riches are in fortune

    A greater good than wisdom is in nature.

VOLPONE

    True, my belovèd Mosca. Yet, I glory   30

    More in the cunning purchase of my wealth,

    Than in the glad possession, since I gain

    No common way: I use no trade, no venture;

    I wound no earth with ploughshares; fat no beasts

    To feed the shambles; have no mills for iron,   35

    Oil, corn, or men, to grind 'em into powder;

    I blow no subtle glass; expose no ships

    To threat'nings of the furrow-facèd sea;

    I turn no monies, in the public bank;

    Nor usure private.

MOSCA   No, sir, nor devour   40

    Soft prodigals. You shall ha' some will swallow

    A melting heir, as glibly as your Dutch

    Will pills of butter, and ne'er purge for't;

    Tear forth the fathers of poor families

    Out of their beds, and coffin them, alive,   45

    In some kind, clasping prison, where their bones

    May be forthcoming, when the flesh is rotten.

    But your sweet nature doth abhor these courses:

    You loathe, the widow's, or the orphan's tears

---

28   *what he will* whatever he desires

28–9   *Riches . . . nature* It is better to be wealthy than wise (playing on a conventional debate about the relative importance of nature and fortune).

33   *venture* speculative business scheme

35   *shambles* slaughterhouse

37   *subtle glass* Venice was (and still is) famous for its artistic glass-blowers.

38   *furrow-facèd* covered with dangerous waves

39   *turn* exchange

40   *usure private* loan-sharking; as Shakespeare also shows, Venice was a hot-bed of usury in the Renaissance.

41   *Soft prodigals* Gullible spend-thrifts; foolish heirs are often cheated by clever urban operators in the plays of this period, especially Jonson's.

42   *melting* wasteful (continuing also the play on their 'soft' edibility, one of countless cannibalistic metaphors in the play)

42–3   *Dutch . . . butter* The Dutch appetite for butter was notorious.

43   *purge* suffer diarrhoea or vomiting, or possibly, need a laxative

44–7   *Tear . . . rotten* Hold men in debtors' prison, letting them out only when they have been reduced to mere bones

Should wash your pavements; or their piteous cries 50
Ring in your roofs, and beat the air for vengeance.

VOLPONE

Right, Mosca, I do loathe it.

MOSCA   And besides, sir,
You are not like a thresher, that doth stand
With a huge flail, watching a heap of corn,
And, hungry, dares not taste the smallest grain, 55
But feeds on mallows, and such bitter herbs;
Nor like the merchant, who hath filled his vaults
With *Romagnía*, and rich Candian wines,
Yet drinks the lees of Lombard's vinegar;
You will not lie in straw, whilst moths, and worms 60
Feed on your sumptuous hangings and soft beds.
You know the use of riches, and dare give, now,
From that bright heap, to me, your poor observer,
Or to your dwarf, or your hermaphrodite,
Your eunuch, or what other household trifle 65
Your pleasure allows maint'nance.

VOLPONE   Hold thee, Mosca,
Take, of my hand: [*Gives him money*] thou strik'st on truth,
    in all;
And they are envious, term thee parasite.
Call forth my dwarf, my eunuch, and my fool,
And let 'em make me sport.

                                        [*Exit* MOSCA]
                              What should I do, 70
But cocker up my genius, and live free
To all delights my fortune calls me to?
I have no wife, no parent, child, ally,

---

56   *mallows* a common plant family which Pliny (among others) believed to be
     medicinal. Cf. Horace's *Satires* II.3.111–21: 'If beside a huge corn-heap a man were
     to lie outstretched, keeping ceaseless watch with a big cudgel, yet never dare,
     hungry though he be and owner of it all, to touch one grain thereof, but rather feed
     like a miser on bitter herbs' (Parker).
58   *Romagnía . . . wines* sweet wines from Greece and Crete
59   *Lombard's vinegar* The wines of Lombardy were notoriously harsh.
63   *observer* lowly, worshipful follower
66   *Hold thee* Stop talking, and/or, You may hold this coin or jewel
68   *term* [who] call
71   *But cocker up my genius* Except indulge my natural talents and tendencies (with a
     suggestion of rousing his genital powers to pleasure)

To give my substance to; but whom I make,
Must be my heir; and this makes men observe me,   75
This draws new clients, daily, to my house,
Women, and men, of every sex, and age,
That bring me presents, send me plate, coin, jewels,
With hope, that when I die, which they expect
Each greedy minute, it shall then return   80
Tenfold upon them; whilst some, covetous
Above the rest, seek to engross me, whole,
And counterwork, the one, unto the other,
Contend in gifts, as they would seem, in love;
All which I suffer, playing with their hopes,   85
And am content to coin 'em into profit,
And look upon their kindness, and take more,
And look on that; still, bearing them in hand,
Letting the cherry knock against their lips,
And draw it by their mouths, and back again.   90
How now!

ACT 1, SCENE 2

[*Enter* MOSCA,] NANO, ANDROGYNO, CASTRONE

NANO
    Now, room for fresh gamesters, who do will you to know,

---

74   *substance* wealth
       whom I make whomever I designate
75   *observe me* treat me reverently
76   *clients* persons depending on patronage, as in the decadent phase of ancient Rome
78   *plate* gold or silver dishes
82–4   *engross me . . . love* take over my wealth wholesale, and undermine each other, competing in gifts that masquerade as true affection
85   *suffer* allow
88   *bearing them in hand* leading them on
89   *cherry knock against their lips* This refers to a tantalizing game called chop-cherry, much like bobbing for apples.
 0   Like many Renaissance play-texts, the printed *Volpone* seems too long to have been acted in two hours; this scene is often cut by modern directors who favour rapid plot-development over arcane set-pieces.
 1   *room* make room

13

They do bring you neither play, nor university show;
And therefore do entreat you, that whatsoever they rehearse,
   May not fare a whit the worse, for the false pace of the verse.
If you wonder at this, you will wonder more, ere we pass,   5
   For know, here [*Indicating* ANDROGYNO] is enclosed the
      soul of Pythagoras,
That juggler divine, as hereafter shall follow;
   Which Soul (fast, and loose, sir) came first from Apollo,
And was breathed into Aethalides, Mercurius his son,
   Where it had the gift to remember all that ever was done.   10
From thence it fled forth, and made quick transmigration
   To goldy-locked Euphorbus, who was killed, in good fashion,
At the siege of old Troy, by the cuckold of Sparta.
   Hermotimus was next (I find it, in my charta)

---

2   *neither play, nor university show* neither from the public theatre, nor from the academic pastimes or classical revivals performed by the Cambridge and Oxford students Jonson addresses in his Epistle. The cluster of learned references in this scene seem better suited to a university than a general audience.

4   *whit* the slightest bit (with a pun on 'wit', on which the academic plays especially depended)
     false pace Nano is speaking in an awkward old-fashioned type of verse, familiar from medieval drama: rhymed tetrameter couplets, with varying numbers of unstressed syllables.

5   *ere we pass* before we are finished

6   *Pythagoras* a famous ancient Greek philosopher, whose followers believed in reincarnation, including across species. The cynical version Volpone's freakish servants perform here echoes Lucian's parody of those beliefs in *The Dream, or The Cock* – a parody which warns against worshipping wealth. So there is a warning for Volpone here, especially since people degrade themselves into lower animals throughout this play. The rest of the speech echoes many Pythagorean doctrines, including the musical order of the cosmos, and the silence and bean-free vegetarianism he demanded from his followers (lines 26–40) (Parker).

7   *juggler* Often a pejorative term for any kind of cheater in this period, though juggling in the modern sense would fit the tricky series of hand-offs that follows.

8   *fast, and loose* hard to pin down; based on a tricky game of guessing whether a belt was actually knotted around a dagger, and hence held fast, or could simply be pulled loose.

9   *Aethalides, Mercurius his son* the herald for Jason's argonauts, Mercury's son (Jonson liked this form of the possessive, though it is based on a false etymology).

12   *goldy-locked Euphorbus* According to *The Iliad*, the Trojan Euphorbus bound up his hair with gold, wounded Patroclus, and was killed by the Spartan king Menelaus (the theft of whose wife provoked the Trojan wars).

14   *Hermotimus* ancient Greek philosopher who probably lived shortly after Pythagoras
     charta charter, written script or history

To whom it did pass, where no sooner it was missing,   15
    But with one Pyrrhus of Delos, it learned to go a-fishing:
And thence did it enter the Sophist of Greece.
    From Pythagore, she went into a beautiful piece,
Hight Aspasia, the meretrix; and the next toss of her
    Was, again, of a whore, she became a philosopher,   20
Crates the Cynic (as itself doth relate it);
    Since, kings, knights, and beggars, knaves, lords and fools gat it,
Besides, ox, and ass, camel, mule, goat, and brock,
    In all which it hath spoke, as in the cobbler's cock.
But I come not here to discourse of that matter,   25
    Or his one, two, or three, or his great oath, 'by quater',
His musics, his trigon, his golden thigh,
    Or his telling how elements shift; but I
Would ask, how of late, thou hast suffered translation,
    And shifted thy coat, in these days of reformation?   30

ANDROGYNO

Like one of the reformèd, a fool, as you see,
    Counting all old doctrine heresy.

NANO

But not on thine own forbid meats hast thou ventured?

16   *Pyrrhus* perhaps the Greek philosopher who was 'a fisherman of Delos' (Parker)
17   *Sophist of Greece* Pythagoras
19   *Hight Aspasia, the meretrix* Called Aspasia the courtesan; she was the mistress of the ancient Greek king Pericles.
20   *again* This may refer ahead syntactically to becoming again a philosopher.
21   *Crates* a student of Diogenes, who disdained material pleasures
      itself The neuter pronoun here may refer to the soul itself, the source text, the cock narrator in Lucian, or Androgyno, whose name indicates mixed gender.
22   *gat it* temporarily held this soul
23   *brock* badger
24   *the cobbler's cock* In the Lucian text, a rooster tells its tale to a greedy shoe-maker.
26   *quater* Pythagoras's musical and mathematical model of the universe was based on symmetrical permutations of the numbers 1–4, as in the balanced triangle (the 'trigon' of the next line).
27   *golden thigh* a legend about Pythagoras's body
30   *shifted . . . reformation* changed allegiance (hence the expression 'turn-coat' for a traitor) since Protestantism gained power
31   *reformèd, a fool* One of Jonson's many attacks on the radical Protestants, now known as Puritans, whom he would have hated as enemies of three things very important to him at this time: theatre, bodily pleasures, and Catholicism.
32   *Counting* Considering

ANDROGYNO

    On fish, when first a Carthusian I entered.

NANO

    Why, then thy dogmatical silence hath left thee?   35

ANDROGYNO

    Of that an obstreperous lawyer bereft me.

NANO

    O wonderful change! When Sir Lawyer forsook thee,

      For Pythagore's sake, what body then took thee?

ANDROGYNO

    A good dull mule.

NANO   And how! by that means,

    Thou wert brought to allow of the eating of beans?   40

ANDROGYNO

    Yes.

NANO But, from the mule, into whom didst thou pass?

ANDROGYNO

    Into a very strange beast, by some writers called an ass;

    By others, a precise, pure, illuminate brother,

      Of those devour flesh, and sometimes one another,

    And will drop you forth a libel, or a sanctified lie,   45

      Betwixt every spoonful of a Nativity pie.

NANO

    Now quit thee, for heaven, of that profane nation;

      And gently report thy next transmigration.

ANDROGYNO

    To the same that I am.

NANO   A creature of delight?

    And (what is more than a fool) an hermaphrodite?   50

    Now 'pray thee, sweet soul, in all thy variation,

      Which body wouldst thou choose, to take up thy station?

---

34   *Carthusian* an austere order of monks, forbidden meat and speech, but allowed fish
39   *how!* an exclamation of surprise and inquiry
43   *precise, pure, illuminate brother* a Puritan, one who claims to have seen the light
44   *those* those who; cf. Galatians 5.14–15
46   *Nativity* an alternative term for Christmas used by Puritans, who mistrusted any
      residue of the term 'Mass'
47   *quit thee* get out
      for heaven for heaven's sake
51   *'pray thee* [I] prithee tell me
52   *take up thy station* stay in

ANDROGYNO
Troth, this I am in, even here would I tarry.
NANO
  'Cause here, the delight of each sex thou canst vary?
ANDROGYNO
Alas, those pleasures be stale, and forsaken;   55
  No, it is your fool wherewith I am so taken,
The only one creature that I can call blessed,
  For all other forms I have proved most distressed.
NANO
Spoke true, as thou wert in Pythagoras still.
  This learnèd opinion we celebrate will,   60
Fellow eunuch, as behooves us, with all our wit, and art,
  To dignify that, whereof ourselves are so great, and special a
    part.
VOLPONE
Now very, very pretty! Mosca, this
Was thy invention?
MOSCA   If it please my patron,
  Not else.
VOLPONE   It doth, good Mosca.
MOSCA   Then it was, sir.   65

Song

        Fools, they are the only nation
        Worth men's envy, or admiration;
        Free from care, or sorrow-taking,
        Themselves, and others merry making;
        All they speak, or do, is sterling.   70
        Your Fool, he is your great man's dearling,
        And your lady's sport, and pleasure:
        Tongue and bable are his treasure.
        His very face begetteth laughter,
        And he speaks truth, free from slaughter;   75

53 *Troth* I swear by my honesty
62 *that* the folly
65 s.d. *Song* probably sung by Nano and Castrone in high-pitched eunuch voices
70 *sterling* excellent, valuable
73 *bable* both the fool's sceptre (called a bauble) with its clear phallic suggestions, and
    babble, rapid meaningless speech
75 *free from slaughter* immune from punishment; Jonson's rival Marston mocked this
    eye-rhyme in *The Fawn*, 4.1 (Brockbank).

He's the grace of every feast,
And, sometimes, the chiefest guest;
Hath his trencher, and his stool,
When wit shall wait upon the Fool:
　　O, who would not be　　　　　　　　　　　　　　　　80
　　　　He, he, he?

One knocks without

VOLPONE
Who's that? Away, look Mosca.

　　　　　　　　　　　　　[*Exit* NANO *and* CASTRONE]
MOSCA　　　　　　　　　　　　Fool, be gone,

　　　　　　　　　　　　　　　　[*Exit* ANDROGYNO]

'Tis Signior Voltore, the advocate,
I know him by his knock.
VOLPONE　　　　　　　　　Fetch me my gown,
My furs, and night-caps. Say, my couch is changing,　　　85
And let him entertain himself, awhile,
Within i'th' gallery.

　　　　　　　　　　　　　　　　[*Exit* MOSCA]

　　　　　　Now, now, my clients
Begin their visitation! Vulture, kite,
Raven, and gorcrow, all my birds of prey,
That think me turning carcass, now they come;　　　　90
I am not for 'em yet.

　　　[*Enter* MOSCA *carrying* VOLPONE's *disguise*]

　　　　　　How now? The news?

MOSCA
　A piece of plate, sir.
VOLPONE　　　　　　　Of what bigness?
MOSCA　　　　　　　　　　　　　Huge,
Massy, and antique, with your name inscribed,

78　　*trencher* plate for eating
79　　*wait upon* several simultaneous meanings: serves as a food-waiter for, acts as a
　　　subservient courtier to, and waits for his turn after
81　　s.d. *without* outside, offstage
85　　*couch is changing* bed is being made
89　　*gorcrow* flesh-eating crow
91　　*not for* not ready for – not yet disguised, but also, not yet decayed
93　　*Massy* Massive, heavy

And arms engraven.

VOLPONE   Good! And not a fox
Stretched on the earth, with fine delusive sleights,   95
Mocking a gaping crow? ha, Mosca?

MOSCA   Sharp, sir.

VOLPONE
Give me my furs. Why dost thou laugh so, man?

MOSCA
I cannot choose, sir, when I apprehend
What thoughts he has within now, as he walks:
That this might be the last gift he should give;   100
That this would fetch you; if you died today,
And gave him all, what he should be tomorrow;
What large return would come of all his ventures;
How he should worshipped be, and reverenced;
Ride, with his furs, and foot-cloths; waited on   105
By herds of fools, and clients; have clear way
Made for his mule, as lettered as himself;
Be called the great and learnèd advocate:
And then concludes, there's nought impossible.

VOLPONE
Yes, to be learnèd, Mosca.

MOSCA   O no: rich   110
Implies it. Hood an ass with reverend purple,
So you can hide his two ambitious ears,
And he shall pass for a cathedral doctor.

VOLPONE
My caps, my caps, good Mosca, fetch him in.

94–6   *And not . . . crow?* Volpone jokes that the coat of arms engraved on the plate ought
        to refer to the tactics (such as playing dead) by which the fox consumes the crow
        who was hoping to consume him.

98   *choose* resist

103   *What large . . . ventures* What a profit he would make on his investment in expen-
        sive gifts designed to win the dying man's favour

105   *foot-cloths* richly ornamented fabric draped over an aristocrat's horse

107   *lettered* learned

111–13 Erasmus's famous *Praise of Folly* mocks those 'who arrogate to themselves the
        appearance and title of wise men and walk like asses in scarlet hoods, though after
        all their hypocrisy Midas' ears will discover their master' (trans. John Wilson,
        1668). Doctors of Divinity wore red hoods, and 'purple' and 'red' were often
        synonyms in Jonson's time.

114   *caps* nightcaps; but perhaps with an unwitting ironic resemblance to the ass's hood
        in the previous lines

MOSCA
Stay, sir, your ointment for your eyes.

VOLPONE   That's true;   115
Dispatch, dispatch: I long to have possession
Of my new present.

MOSCA   That, and thousands more,
I hope, to see you lord of.

VOLPONE   Thanks, kind Mosca.

MOSCA
And that, when I am lost in blended dust,
And hundred such as I am, in succession –   120

VOLPONE
Nay, that were too much, Mosca.

MOSCA   You shall live,
Still, to delude these harpies.

VOLPONE   Loving Mosca,
'Tis well, my pillow now, and let him enter.

                                                        Exit MOSCA

Now, my feigned cough, my phthisic, and my gout,
My apoplexy, palsy, and catarrh,   125
Help, with your forcèd functions, this my posture,
Wherein, this three year, I have milked their hopes.
He comes, I hear him – uh, uh, uh, uh – oh.

ACT 1, SCENE 3

MOSCA [*brings in*] VOLTORE [*clutching the plate*]

MOSCA
You still are, what you were, sir. Only you,
Of all the rest, are he, commands his love;

116   *Dispatch* Hurry
122   *harpies* mythological creatures with the face of a woman and the body of a fierce
      bird of prey
124   *phthisic* tuberculosis, or possibly asthma
125   *apoplexy, palsy, and catarrh* stroke or seizure, paralysis or quivering, and mucus flow
126   *forcèd* feigned
      posture imposture, deluding performance (though perhaps referring directly to his
      sickly sprawl in the bed)
128   *uh* Jonson probably intended the 'h' to sound like the German guttural 'ch', simu-
      lating a shallow cough (Parker).
  2   *he . . . love* the man who has Volpone's favour

And you do wisely to preserve it, thus,
With early visitation, and kind notes
Of your good meaning to him, which, I know,   5
Cannot but come most grateful. [*To* VOLPONE] Patron, sir.
Here's Signior Voltore is come –
VOLPONE   What say you?
MOSCA
Sir, Signior Voltore is come, this morning,
To visit you.
VOLPONE   I thank him.
MOSCA   And hath brought
A piece of antique plate, bought of St Mark,   10
With which he here presents you.
VOLPONE   He is welcome.
Pray him, to come more often.
MOSCA   Yes.
VOLTORE   What says he?
MOSCA
He thanks you, and desires you see him often.
VOLPONE
Mosca.
MOSCA   My patron?
VOLPONE   Bring him near, where is he?
I long to feel his hand.
MOSCA [*Guiding his hand*] The plate is here, sir.   15
VOLTORE
How fare you, sir?
VOLPONE   I thank you, Signior Voltore.
Where is the plate? Mine eyes are bad.
VOLTORE [*Putting the plate in* VOLPONE'*s hands*] I am sorry,
To see you still thus weak.
MOSCA   [*Aside*] That he is not weaker.
VOLPONE
You are too munificent.
VOLTORE   No, sir, would to heaven
I could as well give health to you, as that plate.   20
VOLPONE
You give, sir, what you can. I thank you. Your love

---

6   *Cannot . . . grateful* Must be very welcome
10   *St Mark* Venice's Piazza di San Marco was famous for its goldsmiths.

Hath taste in this, and shall not be unanswered.
I pray you see me often.

VOLTORE   Yes, I shall, sir.

VOLPONE
Be not far from me.

MOSCA [*Aside to* VOLTORE] Do you observe that, sir?

VOLPONE
Hearken unto me, still. It will concern you.   25

MOSCA
[*Aside to* VOLTORE] You are a happy man, sir, know your good.

VOLPONE
I cannot now last long.

MOSCA [*Aside to* VOLTORE] You are his heir, sir.

VOLTORE
[*Aside to* MÓSCA] Am I?

VOLPONE   I feel me going – uh,uh,uh,uh –
I am sailing to my port – uh,uh,uh,uh! –
And I am glad I am so near my haven.   30

MOSCA
Alas, kind gentleman, well, we must all go.

VOLTORE
But, Mosca.

MOSCA   Age will conquer.

VOLTORE   'Pray thee hear me.
Am I inscribed his heir, for certain?

MOSCA   Are you?
I do beseech you, sir, you will vouchsafe
To write me i' your family. All my hopes   35
Depend upon your worship: I am lost,
Except the rising sun do shine on me.

VOLTORE
It shall both shine, and warm thee, Mosca.

MOSCA   Sir.
I am a man that have not done your love
All the worst offices: here I wear your keys,   40

22   *Hath taste* Can be sensed
35   *write ... family* include me in your household (when Volpone's death ends my
       employment there)
37   *rising sun* This plays on Voltore's hope to become an inheriting 'son' to Volpone,
       and Mosca's hope to become 'son' to Voltore (as well as recalling the play's opening
       lines).
39–40 *that have ... offices* who has not rewarded your kindness with such bad services

See all your coffers, and your caskets locked,
Keep the poor inventory of your jewels,
Your plate, and monies, am your steward, sir.
Husband your goods here.

VOLTORE   But am I sole heir?

MOSCA

Without a partner, sir, confirmed this morning;   45
The wax is warm yet, and the ink scarce dry
Upon the parchment.

VOLTORE   Happy, happy me!
By what good chance, sweet Mosca?

MOSCA   Your desert, sir;
I know no second cause.

VOLTORE   Thy modesty
Is loath to know it; well, we shall requite it.   50

MOSCA

He ever liked your course, sir: that first took him.
I oft have heard him say, how he admired
Men of your large profession, that could speak
To every cause, and things mere contraries,
Till they were hoarse again, yet all be law;   55
That, with most quick agility, could turn,
And return; make knots, and undo them;
Give forkèd counsel; take provoking gold
On either hand, and put it up. These men,
He knew, would thrive, with their humility.   60
And (for his part) he thought, he should be blest
To have his heir of such a suffering spirit,
So wise, so grave, of so perplexed a tongue,

44   *Husband* Manage prudently
46   *wax* the stamped sealing wax that marked the will as legitimate
51   *He ever . . . him* He always liked your manner, or path of life; that was what first
      won his affection
53   *large profession* As so often from Mosca, this is probably an insult – 'There are too
      many lawyers, and they profess to believe whatever is convenient at the moment'
      – that is disguised as a compliment: 'An important profession generously serving
      the public good'.
54   *mere contraries* totally contradictory
58   *forkèd* ambiguous; but the term has diabolical associations. Mosca keeps thinly
      disguising his insults.
59   *On . . . up* From both sides, and pocket it (as if for safe-keeping)
62   *suffering* patiently enduring
63   *perplexed* intricate, with an implication of double-dealing

And loud withal, that would not wag, nor scarce
Lie still, without a fee; when every word   65
Your worship but lets fall, is a chequin.

> *Another knocks*

Who is that? One knocks, I would not have you seen, sir.
And yet – pretend you came, and went in haste;
I'll fashion an excuse. And, gentle sir,
When you do come to swim, in golden lard,   70
Up to the arms, in honey, that your chin
Is borne up stiff with fatness of the flood,
Think on your vassal; but remember me:
I have not been your worst of clients.

VOLTORE   Mosca –

MOSCA

When will you have your inventory brought, sir?   75
Or see a copy of the will? [*More knocking, and* MOSCA *shouts
    toward the door*] Anon!
[*To* VOLTORE] I'll bring 'em to you, sir. Away, be gone,
Put business i' your face.

> [*Exit* VOLTORE]

> [VOLPONE *sits up in bed*]

VOLPONE   Excellent, Mosca!
Come hither, let me kiss thee.

MOSCA   Keep you still, sir.
Here is Corbaccio.

VOLPONE   Set the plate away,   80
The vulture's gone, and the old raven's come.

ACT 1, SCENE 4

MOSCA

[*To* VOLPONE] Betake you to your silence, and your sleep;
[*To the silver plate*] Stand there, and multiply. Now shall we see

---

66   *chequin* a gold coin used in Renaissance Venice
76   *Anon!* In just a moment (to the person knocking)
78   *Put . . . face* Look hurried, and/or look as if you were here on business
2   *multiply* Mosca encourages the precious metal to breed more like itself, as he is
     about to make it do; the way greed replaces natural human reproduction with
     unnatural or perverted reproduction is a persistent theme of the play.

A wretch, who is, indeed, more impotent,
Than this can feign to be; yet hopes to hop
Over his grave.

[*Enter* CORBACCIO]

Signior Corbaccio   5
You're very welcome, sir.
CORBACCIO   How does your patron?
MOSCA
Troth, as he did, sir, no amends.
CORBACCIO   What? Mends he?
MOSCA
No, sir: he is rather worse.
CORBACCIO   That's well. Where is he?
MOSCA
Upon his couch sir, newly fall'n asleep.
CORBACCIO
Does he sleep well?
MOSCA   No wink, sir, all this night,   10
Nor yesterday, but slumbers.
CORBACCIO   Good! He should take
Some counsel of physicians: I have brought him
An opiate here, from mine own doctor –
MOSCA
He will not hear of drugs.
CORBACCIO   Why? I myself
Stood by while't was made; saw all th' ingredients;   15
And know, it cannot but most gently work.
My life for his, 'tis but to make him sleep.
VOLPONE
[*Aside*] Ay, his last sleep, if he would take it.
MOSCA   Sir,
He has no faith in physic.
CORBACCIO   Say you? Say you?
MOSCA
He has no faith in physic: he does think   20

4   *this* Volpone
11   *but slumbers* only dozes
19   *physic* medicine

Most of your doctors are the greater danger,
And worse disease, t' escape. I often have
Heard him protest that your physician
Should never be his heir.

CORBACCIO   Not I his heir?

MOSCA
Not your physician, sir.

CORBACCIO   O, no, no, no,   25
I do not mean it.

MOSCA   No sir, nor their fees
He cannot brook: he says, they flay a man,
Before they kill him.

CORBACCIO   Right, I conceive you.

MOSCA
And then, they do it by experiment,
For which the law not only doth absolve them,   30
But gives them great reward; and, he is loath
To hire his death so.

CORBACCIO   It is true, they kill
With as much licence as a judge.

MOSCA   Nay, more;
For he but kills, sir, where the law condemns,
And these can kill him, too.

CORBACCIO   Ay, or me;   35
Or any man. How does his apoplex?
Is that strong on him, still?

MOSCA   Most violent.
His speech is broken, and his eyes are set,
His face drawn longer, than 'twas wont –

CORBACCIO   How? how?
Stronger, than he was wont?

MOSCA   No, sir: his face   40

---

21   *your doctors* doctors in general (a common Renaissance construction); the
      complaints against this profession that follow, like those against lawyers in the
      previous scene, were familiar from classical as well as Renaissance commentators.
27   *brook* tolerate
      flay take the skin off
28   *conceive* understand
29   *by experiment* by trying out medicines on their patients
35   *these can kill him* doctors can safely kill a judge
40   *wont* formerly accustomed to being
40   *stronger . . . wont?* Spoken by Mosca in Q, clearly an error and corrected by F.

Drawn longer, than 'twas wont.
CORBACCIO   O, good.
MOSCA   His mouth
  Is ever gaping, and his eyelids hang.
CORBACCIO   Good.
MOSCA
  A freezing numbness stiffens all his joints,
  And makes the colour of his flesh like lead.
CORBACCIO   'Tis good.
MOSCA
  His pulse beats slow, and dull.
CORBACCIO   Good symptoms, still.   45
MOSCA
  And, from his brain –
CORBACCIO   Ha? How? Not from his brain?
MOSCA
  Yes, sir, and from his brain –
CORBACCIO   I conceive you, good.
MOSCA
  Flows a cold sweat, with a continual rheum,
  Forth the resolvèd corners of his eyes.
CORBACCIO
  Is't possible? Yet I am better, ha!   50
  How does he, with the swimming of his head?
MOSCA
  O, sir, 'tis past the scotomy: he now
  Hath lost his feeling, and hath left to snort;
  You hardly can perceive him, that he breathes.
CORBACCIO
  Excellent, excellent, sure I shall outlast him: 55
  This makes me young again, a score of years.
MOSCA
  I was a-coming for you, sir.
CORBACCIO   Has he made his will?

---

46   *from his brain* Though the hard-of-hearing Corbaccio again misunderstands at
      first, thinking perhaps Mosca is talking about whether Volpone is out of his mind,
      he soon gleefully recognizes that Mosca is describing the final stages of apoplexy,
      in which the drainage of brain fluid was thought to lead to death.
49   *resolvèd* drooping and/or watery
50   *Yet I am better* I am even better off (because Volpone is even worse)
52   *scotomy* dizziness, accompanied by dimness of sight (OED)
53   *left* ceased

What has he giv'n me?

MOSCA   No, sir.

CORBACCIO   Nothing? ha?

MOSCA

He has not made his will, sir.

CORBACCIO   Oh, oh, oh.

But what did Voltore, the lawyer, here?   60

MOSCA

He smelled a carcass, sir, when he but heard

My master was about his testament;

As I did urge him to it, for your good –

CORBACCIO

He came unto him, did he? I thought so.

MOSCA

Yes, and presented him this piece of plate.   65

CORBACCIO

To be his heir?

MOSCA   I do not know, sir.

CORBACCIO   True,

I know it too.

MOSCA   By your own scale, sir.

CORBACCIO   Well,

I shall prevent him, yet. See, Mosca, look,

Here, I have brought a bag of bright chequins,

Will quite weigh down his plate.

MOSCA   Yea, marry, sir.   70

This is true physic, this your sacred medicine,

No talk of opiates, to this great elixir.

CORBACCIO

'Tis *aurum palpabile*, if not *potabile*.

MOSCA

It shall be ministered to him, in his bowl?

---

62   *about his testament* working on composing his will
70   *weigh down* outweigh
      marry indeed (a common form of the oath, '[I swear by the Virgin] Mary')
72   *No talk . . . elixir* Opiates can't compare to this great medicine, gold, which is like
      the alchemists' elixir, the 'philosopher's stone', that was rumoured to bestow eternal
      life
73   *'Tis . . . potabile* It is gold which can be felt, if not drunk. A liquid solution of gold
      was widely believed to be a health-giving miracle drug.

CORBACCIO
Ay, do, do, do.

MOSCA   Most blessed cordial,   75
This will recover him.

CORBACCIO   Yes, do, do, do.

MOSCA
I think, it were not best, sir.

CORBACCIO   What?

MOSCA   To recover him.

CORBACCIO
O, no, no, no; by no means.

MOSCA   Why, sir, this
Will work some strange effect if he but feel it.

CORBACCIO
'Tis true, therefore forbear; I'll take my venture: 80
Give me't again.

MOSCA   At no hand, pardon me;
You shall not do your self that wrong, sir. I
Will so advise you, you shall have it all.

CORBACCIO
How!

MOSCA All, sir, 'tis your right, your own; no man
Can claim a part; 'tis yours, without a rival,   85
Decreed by destiny.

CORBACCIO   How? How, good Mosca?

MOSCA
I'll tell you, sir. This fit he shall recover –

CORBACCIO
I do conceive you.

MOSCA   And, on first advantage
Of his gained sense, will I re-importune him
Unto the making of his testament;   90
And show him this. [*Indicates the money*]

CORBACCIO   Good, good.

MOSCA   'Tis better yet,

75   *cordial* medicine for the heart
80   *venture* speculative investment, in this case the gold he brought Volpone
81   *At no hand* By no means
84   *How!* Perhaps a question, as two lines later, but probably here an exclamation, much like the modern 'What!'
88–9 *advantage . . . sense* opportunity of Volpone's recovering consciousness

If you will hear, sir.

CORBACCIO   Yes, with all my heart.

MOSCA
Now, would I counsel you, make home with speed;
There, frame a will; whereto you shall inscribe
My master your sole heir.

CORBACCIO   And disinherit   95
My son?

MOSCA   O, sir, the better: for that colour
Shall make it much more taking.

CORBACCIO   O, but colour?

MOSCA
This will, sir, you shall send it unto me.
Now, when I come to enforce (as I will do)
Your cares, your watchings, and your many prayers,   100
Your more than many gifts, your this day's present,
And, last, produce your will; where – without thought,
Or least regard, unto your proper issue,
A son so brave, and highly meriting –
The stream of your diverted love hath thrown you   105
Upon my master, and made him your heir;
He cannot be so stupid, or stone dead,
But, out of conscience, and mere gratitude –

CORBACCIO
He must pronounce me, his?   It is true.

CORBACCIO   This plot
Did I think on before.

MOSCA   I do believe it.   110

CORBACCIO
Do you not believe it?

MOSCA   Yes, sir.

CORBACCIO   Mine own project.

MOSCA
Which when he hath done, sir –

CORBACCIO   Published me his heir?

---

93   *make* go

96–7   *that colour . . . taking* that pretence will make your overall pretence toward Volpone
       much more convincing; a similar trick appears in Lucian's *Dialogues of the Dead*,
       XVIII (Parker).

99   *enforce* emphasize, impress on Volpone

103   *proper issue* own true offspring

MOSCA
  And you so certain to survive him.
CORBACCIO   Ay.
MOSCA
  Being so lusty a man.
CORBACCIO   It is true.
MOSCA   Yes, sir.
CORBACCIO
  I thought on that too. See, how he should be   115
  The very organ to express my thoughts!
MOSCA
  You have not only done yourself a good –
CORBACCIO
  But multiplied it on my son?
MOSCA   It is right, sir.
CORBACCIO
  Still, my invention.
MOSCA   'Las, sir, heaven knows,
  It hath been all my study, all my care –   120
  I e'en grow grey withal – how to work things –
CORBACCIO
  I do conceive, sweet Mosca.
MOSCA   You are he,
  For whom I labour, here.
CORBACCIO   Ay, do, do, do:
  I'll straight about it.
MOSCA   Rook go with you, raven.
CORBACCIO
  I know thee honest.
MOSCA   You do lie, sir.
CORBACCIO   And –   125
MOSCA
  Your knowledge is no better than your ears, sir.
CORBACCIO
  I do not doubt, to be a father to thee.

114   *lusty* healthy, robust, energetic
115   *he* Mosca
116   *very organ* true instrument
119   *Still, my invention* This, too, is what I had planned
124   *straight* immediately
       Rook . . . raven May you be cheated (with a pun on 'rook', which means both 'swindle' and 'a kind of raven')

MOSCA

   Nor I, to gull my brother of his blessing.

CORBACCIO

   I may ha' my youth restored to me, why not?

MOSCA

   Your worship is a precious ass –

CORBACCIO   What say'st thou?   130

MOSCA

   I do desire your worship, to make haste, sir.

CORBACCIO

   'Tis done, 'tis done, I go.   [*Exit*]

VOLPONE   O, I shall burst;

   Let out my sides, let out my sides –

MOSCA   Contain

   Your flux of laughter, sir: you know, this hope

   Is such a bait, it covers any hook.   135

VOLPONE

   O, but thy working, and thy placing it!

   I cannot hold; good rascal, let me kiss thee;

   I never knew thee in so rare a humour.

MOSCA

   Alas, sir, I but do as I am taught:

   Follow your grave instructions; give 'em words;   140

   Pour oil into their ears; and send them hence.

VOLPONE

   'Tis true, 'tis true. What a rare punishment

   Is avarice, to itself!

MOSCA   Ay, with our help, sir.

VOLPONE

   So many cares, so many maladies,

   So many fears attending on old age,   145

   Yea, death so often called on, as no wish

---

128   *Nor I . . . blessing* And I intend to steal, by trickery, this father's legacy. Mosca is
      alluding to Jacob's theft of the paternal blessing from his brother Esau in Genesis.

134   *flux* flood

      this hope the hope of inheriting Volpone's estate

137   *hold* hold back

138   *so rare a humour* so excellent a state of inspired wit

140   *grave* wise

141   *Pour . . . ears* Flatter them with pleasing words (from a Latin proverb) (Parker)

142   *'Tis true* Even while laughing at Corbaccio for believing Mosca's flattery, Volpone
      here believes an almost identical flattery: that he is really the one who conceived
      the plots he sees Mosca executing, supposedly on his behalf.

Can be more frequent with 'em, their limbs faint,
Their senses dull, their seeing, hearing, going,
All dead before them; yea, their very teeth,
Their instruments of eating, failing them: 150
Yet this is reckoned life! Nay, here was one,
Is now gone home, that wishes to live longer!
Feels not his gout, nor palsy, feigns himself
Younger, by scores of years, flatters his age,
With confident belying it, hopes he may   155
With charms, like Aeson, have his youth restored,
And with these thoughts so battens, as if fate
Would be as easily cheated on, as he,
And all turns air!

                                                    Another knocks
              Who's that, there, now? A third?

MOSCA

Close, to your couch again; I hear his voice.   160
It is Corvino, our spruce merchant.

VOLPONE   [*Lying down*] Dead.

MOSCA

Another bout, sir, with your eyes. [*Applies more ointment*]
                                            Who's there?

ACT 1, SCENE 5

[*Enter*] CORVINO

MOSCA

Signior Corvino! Come most wished for! O,
How happy were you, if you knew it, now!

148   *going* walking
155   *belying* denying
156   *Aeson* The evil magic of Medea restored the youth of Aeson, the father of Jason (see
      the note to I.ii.9 above).
157   *battens* feeds himself into fatness
159   *And all turns air* Though all his hopes will turn out to be empty; or perhaps, As if
      the material fact of Corbaccio's decaying body meant nothing.
160   *Close* Hush, resume your secrecy
161   *spruce* trim, dapper
162   *bout* dose (of the substance used to make Volpone's eyes appear sickly)
  1   *Come* You have come when you were

CORVINO
  Why? What? Wherein?

MOSCA   The tardy hour is come, sir.

CORVINO
  He is not dead?

MOSCA   Not dead, sir, but as good;
  He knows no man.

CORVINO   How shall I do then?

MOSCA   Why, sir?   5

CORVINO
  I have brought him, here, a pearl.

MOSCA   Perhaps he has
  So much remembrance left, as to know you, sir;
  He still calls on you: nothing but your name
  Is in his mouth. Is your pearl orient, sir?

CORVINO
  Venice was never owner of the like.   10

VOLPONE
  [*Faintly*] Signior Corvino.

MOSCA   Hark.

VOLPONE   Signior Corvino.

MOSCA
  He calls you, step and give it him. [*Aloud to* VOLPONE] He's here, sir,
  And he has brought you a rich pearl.

CORVINO   How do you, sir?
  Tell him, it doubles the twelfth carat.

MOSCA   Sir,
  He cannot understand, his hearing's gone;   15
  And yet it comforts him, to see you –

CORVINO   Say,
  I have a diamond for him, too.

MOSCA   Best show't, sir,
  Put it into his hand: 'tis only there
  He apprehends; he has his feeling, yet.

                    [VOLPONE *seizes the pearl*]

---

8   *still* always

9   *orient* The most lustrous and hence valuable pearls came from the East. Since 'stones' was common slang for testicles, the fact that Corvino here gives Volpone two stones may foreshadow the sexual advantage he will give Volpone later.

14   *doubles … carat* The pearl measures twenty-four carats, hence extremely valuable.

See, how he grasps it!

CORVINO   'Las, good gentleman!   20

How pitiful the sight is!

MOSCA   Tut, forget, sir.

The weeping of an heir should still be laughter,

Under a visor.

CORVINO   Why, am I his heir?

MOSCA

Sir, I am sworn, I may not show the will,

Till he be dead. But, here has been Corbaccio,   25

Here has been Voltore, here were others too,

I cannot number 'em, they were so many,

All gaping here for legacies; but I,

Taking the vantage of his naming you –

[*Mimicking* VOLPONE] 'Signior Corvino, Signior Corvino' –

took   30

Paper, and pen, and ink, and there I asked him,

Whom he would have his heir? Corvino. Who

Should be executor? Corvino. And,

To any question he was silent to,

I still interpreted the nods he made   35

Through weakness for consent; and sent home th' others,

Nothing bequeathed them, but to cry, and curse.

CORVINO

O, my dear Mosca.

                               They embrace

              Does he not perceive us?

MOSCA

No more than a blind harper. He knows no man,

No face of friend, nor name of any servant,   40

Who't was that fed him last, or gave him drink;

Not those he hath begotten, or brought up

Can he remember.

CORVINO   Has he children?

MOSCA   Bastards,

Some dozen, or more, that he begot on beggars,

Gypsies, and Jews, and black-moors, when he was drunk.   45

---

23   *visor* mask – in this case, of feigned mourning
39   *blind harper* Proverbial for insensibility: cf. Tilley H175, 176.

Knew you not that, sir? 'Tis the common fable.
The dwarf, the fool, the eunuch are all his:
He's the true father of his family,
In all, save me; but he has giv'n 'em nothing.

CORVINO
That's well, that's well. Art sure he does not hear us?   50

MOSCA
Sure, sir? Why look you, credit your own sense.
[*Aloud to* VOLPONE] The pox approach, and add to your
  diseases,
If it would send you hence the sooner, sir.
For, your incontinence, it hath deserved it
Throughly, and throughly, and the plague to boot.   55
[*To* CORVINO] You may come near, sir. [*Aloud to* VOLPONE]
                                 Would you would once close
Those filthy eyes of yours, that flow with slime,
Like two frog-pits; and those same hanging cheeks,
Covered with hide, instead of skin. [*To* CORVINO] Nay, help, sir,
[*Aloud to* VOLPONE] That look like frozen dish-clouts, set on
  end.   60

CORVINO
Or, like an old smoked wall, on which the rain
Ran down in streaks.

MOSCA   Excellent, sir, speak out;
You may be louder yet: a culverin,
Dischargèd in his ear would hardly bore it.

CORVINO
His nose is like a common sewer, still running.   65

46   *'Tis the common fable* This is widely known. Again the play stresses the perversion
      of Volpone's reproductive powers.
51   *credit* believe
52   *pox* either smallpox or (as line 54 hints) syphilis. The series of insults that follow
      offers several layers of irony, as Corvino thinks they are making fun of Volpone,
      Volpone thinks they are actually making fun of that delusion of Corvino's, and
      Mosca may actually be taking advantage of the situation to insult Volpone after all.
53   *send you hence* kill you off
54   *your incontinence . . . deserved it* your sexual promiscuity and other indulgences
      should have earned you the pox
58   *frog-pits* stagnant puddles, or possibly 'frogspit', the froth around insect larvae
60   *clouts* rags
63–4 *culverin, / Dischargèd* handgun fired

MOSCA

'Tis good! And, what his mouth?

CORVINO   A very draught.

MOSCA

[*Taking up a pillow to smother* VOLPONE]

O stop it up –

CORVINO   By no means.

MOSCA   'Pray you let me.

Faith, I could stifle him, rarely, with a pillow,

As well as any woman that should keep him.

CORVINO

Do as you will, but I'll be gone.

MOSCA   Be so: 70

It is your presence makes him last so long.

CORVINO

I pray you, use no violence.

MOSCA   No, sir? Why?

Why should you be thus scrupulous? 'Pray you, sir.

CORVINO

Nay, at your discretion.

MOSCA   Well, good sir, be gone.

CORVINO

I will not trouble him now, to take my pearl?   75

MOSCA

Puh, nor your diamond. [*Taking the jewels*] What a needless

     care

Is this afflicts you? Is not all, here, yours?

Am not I here? whom you have made? your creature?

That owe my being to you?

CORVINO   Grateful Mosca!

Thou art my friend, my fellow, my companion,   80

My partner, and shalt share in all my fortunes.

MOSCA

Excepting one.

CORVINO   What is that?

---

66   *draught* sewer drain, or possibly, chimney flue
68   *Faith* a common condensation of the oath, '[I swear by my] faith'
       rarely skilfully
69   *that should keep him* who would be his caretaker
73   *'Pray you* I ask you, pray tell me
74   *Nay . . . discretion* Well, I'll leave it up to you

MOSCA   Your gallant wife, sir.

                         [*Exit* CORVINO *hurriedly*]

Now is he gone: we had no other means,
To shoot him hence, but this.

VOLPONE   My divine Mosca!
Thou hast today outgone thyself.

                         Another knocks

                  Who's there?   85
I will be troubled with no more. Prepare
Me music, dances, banquets, all delights:
The Turk is not more sensual, in his pleasures,
Than will Volpone.

                        [*Exit* MOSCA]

        Let me see, a pearl?
A diamond? Plate? Chequins? Good morning's purchase!   90
Why this is better than rob churches, yet;
Or fat, by eating, once a month, a man.

               [*Enter* MOSCA]

Who is't?
MOSCA   The beauteous Lady Would-Be, sir,
Wife to the English knight, Sir Politic Would-Be,
(This is the style, sir, is directed me),   95
Hath sent to know, how you have slept tonight,
And if you would be visited.

VOLPONE   Not now.
Some three hours hence –
MOSCA   I told the squire so much.

VOLPONE
When I am high with mirth, and wine: then, then.
'Fore heaven, I wonder at the desperate valour   100
Of the bold English, that they dare let loose

83–4   *we had . . . but this* the only way to get him to leave was to remind him that he has
       left his wife alone
85   *outgone* outdone
88   *The Turk* Either Turks in general, or Mahomet III, Sultan of the Ottoman empire;
       in either case, a person devoted to sensual pleasures.
90   *Good morning's purchase!* A profitable morning!
92   *fat* grow fat
95   *This is . . . directed me* That is how she told me to identify her
98   *squire* attendant, but sometimes with a suggestion of 'pimp'
101   *bold English* By Venetian standards, English husbands gave their wives an unusual
       and risky degree of freedom.

Their wives, to all encounters!

MOSCA   Sir, this knight
Had not his name for nothing, he is politic,
And knows, howe'er his wife affect strange airs,
She hath not yet the face to be dishonest.   105
But had she Signior Corvino's wife's face –

VOLPONE
Has she so rare a face?

MOSCA   O, sir, the wonder,
The blazing star of Italy! A wench
O' the first year, a beauty, ripe, as harvest!
Whose skin is whiter then a swan, all over!   110
Than silver, snow, or lilies! A soft lip,
Would tempt you to eternity of kissing!
And flesh, that melteth, in the touch, to blood!
Bright as your gold, and lovely, as your gold!

VOLPONE
Why had not I known this, before?

MOSCA   Alas, sir.   115
Myself but yesterday discovered it.

VOLPONE
How might I see her?

MOSCA   O, not possible:
She's kept as warily as is your gold;
Never does come abroad, never takes air,
But at a window. All her looks are sweet,   120
As the first grapes, or cherries; and are watched
As near as they are.

VOLPONE   I must see her –

---

104 *affect strange airs* probably a pun on 1) visiting foreign countries, 2) putting on
     pretentious behaviour, and possibly 3) producing unusual odours
105 *She hath . . . dishonest* She is no longer pretty enough to commit adultery, and/or,
     She nonetheless lacks the nerve to commit adultery
109 *O' the first year* Of the best vintage, and/or, In the innocent first bloom of
     womanhood
113 *melteth . . . to blood* blushes when touched, or responds with passionate heat to
     touch, or is as yielding to the touch as warm liquid. 'Touch' was also a term for
     testing the quality of gold, and so leads to Mosca's next line, which shows his
     understanding of Volpone's deepest desires.
119 *abroad* outside
122 *near* closely. The fruit comparisons recall Aesop's fable of the fox and the grapes,
     and Volpone's earlier reference to the game of bob-cherry; Volpone again fails to
     notice that Mosca is doing to him what he does to the legacy-hunters.

MOSCA   Sir.
   There is a guard, of ten spies thick, upon her:
   All his whole household, each of which is set
   Upon his fellow, and have all their charge –   125
   When he goes out, when he comes in – examined.

VOLPONE
   I will go see her, though but at her window.

MOSCA
   In some disguise, then?

VOLPONE   That is true, I must
   Maintain mine own shape, still, the same: we'll think.

                                        [Exeunt]

ACT 2, SCENE 1

[*Enter Sir*] POLITIC WOULD-BE, PEREGRINE

SIR POLITIC
   Sir, to a wise man, all the world's his soil.
   It is not Italy, nor France, nor Europe,
   That must bound me, if my fates call me forth.
   Yet, I protest, it is no salt desire
   Of seeing countries, shifting a religion,   5
   Nor any disaffection to the state
   Where I was bred and unto which I owe
   My dearest plots, hath brought me out; much less,
   That idle, antique, stale, grey-headed project
   Of knowing men's minds and manners, with Ulysses;   10

124–6   *each ... examined* each of whom is assigned to spy on the others, and is inter-
        rogated about his responsibilities (or, about Corvino's wife) every time Corvino
        departs or returns home
  129   *Maintain mine own shape* Maintain the appearance that I am confined to my
        death-bed
    4   *salt* intense, with connotations of sexual appetite and a possible pun on the salti-
        ness of sea voyages
    5   *shifting* changing; recusant Englishmen (and Jonson may have been one) sometimes
        fled that Protestant country so that they could practice openly in Catholic Italy.
    8   *plots* plans (of which Sir Pol has many)
  10   *knowing ... Ulysses* The opening lines of Homer's *Odyssey* describe the hero as one
        who 'learned the minds of many distant men' (trans. Robert Fitzgerald).

But, a peculiar humour of my wife's,
Laid for this height of Venice, to observe,
To quote, to learn the language, and so forth –
I hope you travel, sir, with licence?
PEREGRINE   Yes.
SIR POLITIC
I dare the safelier converse – How long, sir,   15
Since you left England?
PEREGRINE   Seven weeks.
SIR POLITIC   So lately!
You ha' not been with my lord ambassador?
PEREGRINE
Not yet, sir.
SIR POLITIC   'Pray you, what news, sir, vents our climate?
I heard, last night, a most strange thing reported
By some of my lord's followers, and I long   20
To hear how 'twill be seconded!
PEREGRINE   What was't, sir?
SIR POLITIC
Marry, sir, of a raven, that should build
In a ship royal of the King's.
PEREGRINE   [*Aside*] This fellow,
Does he gull me, trow? or is gulled? [*To* SIR POLITIC] Your
name, sir?

---

11   *humour* whim or obsession; Jonson wrote two comedies about characters
      controlled by 'humours' – four bodily fluids whose balance was believed to dictate
      psychological tendencies.
12   *Laid for this height* Aimed for this place; 'height' may refer to latitude, it may reflect
      Pol's folly, since Venice is decidedly at sea-level, or it may refer to the famous
      arched bridge of the Rialto (from *rivo alto*) where (as a common meeting-place)
      this scene may be set.
13   *quote* take note of things, whether mentally or in writing
14   *licence* a kind of passport or visa, required by the Privy Council for overseas travel,
      and often excluding Catholic countries as dangerous to the traveller's soul and
      England's safety
17   *my lord ambassador* Sir Pol may be partly a caricature of England's crafty ambas-
      sador to Venice in this period, Sir Henry Wotton, a close friend of John Donne's.
18   *vents our climate* blows in from our home country, or is breathily reported about it
21   *seconded* confirmed by some other source
22   *Marry . . . build* I swear by Mary, news of a raven that was said to build (birds
      building nests were bad omens on a ship, as Shakespeare suggests at 4.12.4 of
      Antony and Cleopatra)
24   *Does . . . gulled?* Is he trying to make a fool of me, I wonder, or is he fooled him-self
      (by this grandiose gossip)?

41

SIR POLITIC
My name is Politic Would-Be.

PEREGRINE   [*Aside*] O, that speaks him.   25
[*To* SIR POLITIC] A knight, sir?

SIR POLITIC   A poor knight, sir.

PEREGRINE   Your lady
Lies here in Venice for intelligence
Of tires, and fashions, and behaviour,
Among the courtesans? The fine Lady Would-Be?

SIR POLITIC
Yes, sir: the spider and the bee, ofttimes,   30
Suck from one flower.

PEREGRINE   Good Sir Politic!
I cry you mercy: I have heard much of you.
'Tis true, sir, of your raven.

SIR POLITIC   On your knowledge?

PEREGRINE
Yes, and your lion's whelping, in the Tower.

SIR POLITIC
Another whelp?

PEREGRINE   Another, sir.

SIR POLITIC   Now heaven!   35
What prodigies be these? The fires at Berwick!
And the new star! These things concurring, strange!
And full of omen! Saw you those meteors?

PEREGRINE
I did, sir.

25   *speaks* defines
27   *Lies* Stays (but with possible sexual connotations)
      for intelligence to gather information
28   *Of tires* About attire, clothing
29   *courtesans* high-class prostitutes, for which Venice was famous
30–1 *the spider . . . flower* A common proverb (Tilley, B208); Sir Pol means that, as one
      kind of creature can draw sweetness from the same place another kind draws
      poison, so his wife could use virtuously the Venetian arts the courtesans use
      sinfully.
32   *I cry you mercy* I beg your pardon (for not recognizing you sooner)
33   *your raven* the aforementioned raven; as in the next line, the 'your' is impersonal
34   *lion's whelping* A lioness kept in the Tower of London bore cubs in 1604 and 1605.
36   *fires at Berwick* Armies were reported seen fighting in the sky near Scotland in
      1604, perhaps an effect of the *aurora borealis*.
37   *the new star* a supernova observed by Kepler in 1604
38   *meteors* Meteors were believed ominous, since they evinced disruption in the
      heavens.

SIR POLITIC Fearful! 'Pray you, sir, confirm me:
    Were there three porpoises seen, above the bridge,   40
    As they give out?
PEREGRINE   Six, and a sturgeon, sir.
SIR POLITIC
    I am astonished.
PEREGRINE   Nay, sir, be not so:
    I'll tell you a greater prodigy than these –
SIR POLITIC
    What should these things portend!
PEREGRINE   The very day
    (Let me be sure) that I put forth from London,   45
    There was a whale discovered, in the river,
    As high as Woolwich, that had waited there,
    Few know how many months, for the subversion
    Of the Stode fleet.
SIR POLITIC   Is't possible? Believe it,
    'Twas either sent from Spain, or the Archdukes!   50
    Spinola's whale, upon my life, my credit!
    Will they not leave these projects? Worthy sir,
    Some other news.
PEREGRINE   Faith, Stone, the fool, is dead;
    And they do lack a tavern fool, extremely.
SIR POLITIC
    Is Mas' Stone dead?
PEREGRINE   He's dead sir; why? I hope   55
    You thought him not immortal? [*Aside*] O this knight,

---

40   *porpoises* According to Stow's *Annals*, early in 1606 'a great Porpus was taken alive
       at Westham ... and within a few dayes after, a very great whale came up within 8
       mile of London'; this reference suggests that Jonson did not finish *Volpone* until
       1606.
       the bridge London Bridge
41   *sturgeon* Peregrine is making fun of Sir Pol here, since sturgeon were common in
       the Thames (Parker).
49   *the Stode fleet* the ships of the English Merchant Adventurers, near the mouth of
       the Elbe river
51   *Spinola* a Spanish general feared in England for his ingenious secret weapons,
       including a whale 'hir'd to have drown'd London by snuffling up the Thames and
       spouting it upon the City' (Charles Herle, *Worldly Policy and Moral Prudence*
       [1654])
53   *Stone* a London clown who had been whipped in 1605 for 'a blasphemous speech'
55   *Stone dead* Here, and again at line 60, playing off the sense 'completely dead'; see
       1.4.107.

Were he well known, would be a precious thing
To fit our English stage. He that should write
But such a fellow should be thought to feign
Extremely, if not maliciously.

SIR POLITIC   Stone dead?   60

PEREGRINE
Dead. Lord, how deeply, sir, you apprehend it!
He was no kinsman to you?

SIR POLITIC   That I know of.
Well; that same fellow was an unknown fool.

PEREGRINE
And yet you know him, it seems?

SIR POLITIC   I did so. Sir,
I knew him one of the most dangerous heads   65
Living within the state, and so I held him.

PEREGRINE
Indeed, sir?

SIR POLITIC   While he lived, in action.
He has received weekly intelligence,
Upon my knowledge, out of the Low Countries,
For all parts of the world, in cabbages;   70
And those dispensed again t' ambassadors,
In oranges, musk-melons, apricots,
Lemons, pome-citrons, and such-like; sometimes,
In Colchester oysters, and your Selsey cockles.

PEREGRINE
You make me wonder!

SIR POLITIC   Sir, upon my knowledge.   75
Nay, I have observed him, at your public ordinary,
Take his advertisement from a traveller
(A concealed statesman) in a trencher of meat;
And, instantly, before the meal was done,

62   *That I know of* Not that I know of
63   *that . . . unknown fool* Stone's actual cleverness was successfully concealed; ironi-
      cally, Sir Pol, who is a fool fancying himself a clever spy, believes Stone was a clever
      spy masquerading as a fool.
66   *held* considered
67   *in action* while active, or, in actuality
70   *cabbages* England imported cabbage from Holland; Sir Pol's paranoid fantasies
      echo many that were produced by the failed Gunpowder Plot of 1605.
76   *ordinary* tavern/restaurant
77   *advertisement* information, instructions

Convey an answer in a toothpick.
PEREGRINE   Strange!   80
  How could this be, sir?
SIR POLITIC   Why, the meat was cut
  So like his character, and so laid, as he
  Must easily read the cipher.
PEREGRINE   I have heard,
  He could not read, sir.
SIR POLITIC   So 'twas given out,
  In polity, by those that did employ him;   85
  But he could read, and had your languages,
  And to't, as sound a noddle –
PEREGRINE   I have heard, sir,
  That your baboons were spies; and that they were
  A kind of subtle nation, near to China.
SIR POLITIC
  Ay, ay, your *Mamuluchi*. Faith, they had   90
  Their hand in a French plot, or two; but they
  Were so extremely given to women, as
  They made discovery of all. Yet I
  Had my advices here, on Wednesday last,
  From one of their own coat, they were returned,   95
  Made their relations (as the fashion is)
  And now stand fair, for fresh employment.
PEREGRINE   [*Aside*] 'Heart!
  This Sir Pol will be ignorant of nothing.

---

  82   *character* writing or code; Shakespeare's *Cymbeline* 4.2.49 describes a similarly
       intricate cutting of food.
84–5   *given out, / In polity* deliberately spread as part of his disguise
  87   *And to't, as sound a noddle* And in addition to that ability, he had as healthy a brain
  89   *subtle* crafty
  90   *Mamuluchi* slaves who seized power in Egypt in the thirteenth century; the irrele-
       vance emphasizes Sir Pol's ridiculous efforts to sound knowledgeable.
  91   *hand in a French plot* role in a French conspiracy, but probably with an unwitting
       sexual implication
  92   *given* susceptible (Topsell claimed baboons were so 'lustful' that they tried 'to defile
       all sorts of women' [Parker]).
  93   *made discovery of all* disclosed all their secrets
  94   *advices* news dispatches
  95   *coat* faction
  96   *relations* reports
  97   *stand . . . employment* are ready to resume their spying
       '*Heart!* I swear by God's heart

[*To* SIR POLITIC] It seems, sir, you know all?

SIR POLITIC   Not all, sir. But,
    I have some general notions; I do love   100
    To note, and to observe; though I live out,
    Free from the active torrent, yet I'd mark
    The currents, and the passages of things,
    For mine own private use; and know the ebbs,
    And flows of state.

PEREGRINE   Believe it, sir, I hold   105
    Myself, in no small tie, unto my fortunes,
    For casting me thus luckily, upon you;
    Whose knowledge, if your bounty equal it,
    May do me great assistance, in instruction
    For my behaviour, and my bearing, which   110
    Is yet so rude, and raw –

SIR POLITIC   Why, came you forth
    Empty of rules for travel?

PEREGRINE   Faith, I had
    Some common ones, from out that vulgar grammar,
    Which he that cried Italian to me taught me.

SIR POLITIC
    Why, this it is that spoils all our brave bloods,   115
    Trusting our hopeful gentry unto pedants,
    Fellows of outside, and mere bark. You seem
    To be a gentleman, of ingenuous race –
    I not profess it, but my fate hath been
    To be where I have been consulted with,   120
    In this high kind, touching some great men's sons,
    Persons of blood, and honour –

PEREGRINE   Who be these, sir?

105–7   *I hold . . . upon you* I count myself very lucky to have run into you
  108   *bounty* generosity
  114   *cried* taught
  115   *brave bloods* aristocratic young men
  116   *hopeful* promising
  118   *ingenuous race* noble lineage
  121   *touching* concerning
  122   *blood* noble birth

ACT 2, SCENE 2

[*Enter* MOSCA *and* NANO, *disguised as mountebank's
assistants and carrying the makings of a scaffold stage,
followed by a* CROWD]

MOSCA
Under that window, there't must be. The same.

SIR POLITIC
Fellows to mount a bank! Did your instructor
In the dear tongues never discourse to you
Of the Italian mountebanks?

PEREGRINE   Yes, sir.

SIR POLITIC   Why,
Here shall you see one.

PEREGRINE   They are quacksalvers,   5
Fellows that live by venting oils, and drugs?

SIR POLITIC
Was that the character he gave you of them?

PEREGRINE
As I remember.

SIR POLITIC   Pity his ignorance.
They are the only knowing men of Europe!
Great, general scholars, excellent physicians,   10
Most admired statesmen, professed favourites,
And cabinet counsellors, to the greatest princes!
The only languaged men of all the world!

PEREGRINE
And, I have heard, they are most lewd impostors;

---

2   *mount a bank* 'An itinerant quack who from an elevated platform appealed to his
     audience by means of stories, tricks, juggling, and the like' (OED). Such figures
     were common in Venice, and had probably appeared in London as well. The travel-
     ling show dispensing patent medicines in rural America was a more recent equiva-
     lent. This set-up also strongly resembles the travelling scaffold stage on which
     most English drama had been performed in Jonson's youth (Kernan).

3   *dear* valuable

6   *venting* advertising and selling (vending)

7   *Was that . . . them?* Was that how your instructor characterized mountebanks?

9   *knowing* truly knowledgeable

12 *cabinet* private

Made all of terms, and shreds; no less beliers   15
Of great men's favours, than their own vile med'cines;
Which they will utter upon monstrous oaths,
Selling that drug for two pence, ere they part,
Which they have valued at twelve crowns, before.

SIR POLITIC
Sir, calumnies are answered best with silence: 20
Yourself shall judge. [*To* MOSCA *and* NANO] Who is it mounts,
my friends?

MOSCA
Scoto of Mantua, sir.

SIR POLITIC   Is't he? Nay, then
I'll proudly promise, sir, you shall behold
Another man than has been fant'sied to you.
I wonder, yet, that he should mount his bank   25
Here, in this nook, that has been wont t' appear
In face of the Piazza! Here, he comes.

[*Enter* VOLPONE, *disguised as a mountebank*]

VOLPONE
[*To* NANO] Mount, zany.

CROWD   Follow, follow, follow, follow, follow.

SIR POLITIC
See how the people follow him! He's a man
May write ten thousand crowns, in bank, here.

[VOLPONE *climbs onto the platform*]

                        Note,   30
Mark but his gesture; I do use to observe
The state he keeps, in getting up!

---

15   *terms, and shreds* impressive jargon, and bits of undigested learning
15–16 *no less . . . med'cines* as dishonest in claiming great patrons as in claiming that their
       disgusting potions are healthy (or, possibly, as treacherous to their great patrons as
       the supposed medicines are)
17   *utter* offer for sale
19   *crowns* silver coins stamped with a crown (Parker)
22   *Scoto of Mantua* A famous Italian juggler and sleight-of-hand performer who
       visited Elizabethan England, and whose name became a by-word for a skilful
       deceiver.
26   *wont* accustomed. Sir Pol believes Scoto normally rates a grander setting.
28   *zany* the clownish assistant of a performer
31–2 *I do use . . . getting up* I always admire the dignity Scoto maintains in climbing onto
       the stage

PEREGRINE   'Tis worth it, sir.

VOLPONE

Most noble gentlemen and my worthy patrons, it may seem
strange, that I, your Scoto Mantuano, who was ever wont to fix
my bank in face of the public Piazza, near the shelter of the   35
portico to the *Procuratía*, should, now, after eight months
absence from this illustrious city of Venice, humbly retire myself
into an obscure nook of the Piazza.

SIR POLITIC

Did not I, now, object the same?

PEREGRINE   Peace, sir.

VOLPONE

Let me tell you: I am not (as your Lombard proverb saith) cold   40
on my feet, or content to part with my commodities at a cheaper
rate than I accustomed: look not for it. Nor, that the calum-
nious reports of that impudent detractor, and shame to our
profession (Alessandro Buttone, I mean) who gave out, in
public, I was condemned *a sforzato* to the galleys, for poisoning   45
the Cardinal Bembo's – cook, hath at all attached, much less
dejected me. No, no, worthy gentlemen, to tell you true, I cannot
endure to see the rabble of these ground *ciarlitani*, that spread
their cloaks on the pavement, as if they meant to do feats of

---

33–248   Throughout this scene, Jonson not only builds on standard episodes from the
         beast-fable and *commedia dell'arte* traditions, but also builds an extended meta-
         phor that makes Volpone/Scoto a playful parody of Jonson himself (as Kernan has
         shown): a proud intellectual selling his goods now at a lower price to a public audi-
         ence (at the Globe) instead of his usual aristocratic private one (at Blackfriars),
         after being jailed for offending a powerful man (Jonson angered King James, a
         Scot, by satirizing Scots in *Eastward Ho!*). Scoto and Jonson alike scorn their less
         scholarly competitors (whom they dismiss as poor imitators of their work, and
         purveyors of stale material), while trying to argue that their products have the
         power to cure his audience (notice the ways Jonson's boastful Prologue and Epistle
         resemble Scoto's sales-pitch). Many of the Londoners from whom Jonson was now
         trying to coax the occasional sixpence (the likely cost of admission to *Volpone*)
         would surely have appreciated the in-joke.

   36   *portico to the Procuratía* arcade of the residence of senior Venetian officials on the
         Piazza di San Marco

40–41   *cold on my feet* stage-frightened, or, desperate to sell

   45   *a sforzato* by force (into enslavement)

   46   *Cardinal Bembo's – cook* Bembo was a great Venetian Renaissance humanist; the
         dash suggests a hesitation about naming a more scandalous relationship (perhaps,
         'mistress').

   48   *ground ciarlitani* lowly charlatans who lack a bank or bench to mount

49–50   *feats of activity* gymnastics

activity, and then come in, lamely, with their mouldy tales out 50
of Boccaccio, like stale Tabarin, the fabulist; some of them
discoursing their travels, and of their tedious captivity in the
Turk's galleys, when indeed, were the truth known, they were
the Christian's galleys, where very temperately they ate bread,
and drunk water, as a wholesome penance, enjoined them by 55
their confessors, for base pilferies.

SIR POLITIC
Note but his bearing, and contempt of these.

VOLPONE
These turdy-facey-nasty-patey-lousy-fartical rogues, with one
poor groatsworth of unprepared antimony, finely wrapped up
in several *scartoccios*, are able, very well, to kill their twenty a 60
week, and play; yet these meagre starved spirits, who have half
stopped the organs of their minds with earthy oppilations, want
not their favourers among your shrivelled, salad-eating artisans,
who are overjoyed that they may have their half-pe'rth of physic,
though it purge them into another world, makes no matter. 65

SIR POLITIC
Excellent! Ha' you heard better language, sir?

VOLPONE
Well, let 'em go. And gentlemen, honourable gentlemen, know,
that for this time, our bank, being thus removed from the clam-
ours of the *canaglia*, shall be the scene of pleasure, and delight;
for I have nothing to sell, little or nothing to sell. 70

SIR POLITIC
I told you, sir, his end.

PEREGRINE   You did so, sir.

---

51   *Boccaccio* fourteenth-century author whose *Decameron* provided plots for many
     later writers, including Shakespeare
     Tabarin, the fabulist a travelling Venetian zany, contemporary with Scoto, here
     identified as a story-teller as well as comic performer; also a stock minor character
     in the *commedia*
55   *enjoined them* prescribed for them
59   *groatsworth of unprepared antimony* fourpence worth of native trisulphide (known
     as monksbane)
60   *several scartoccios* separate paper bins
61   *play* keep their show running
62   *earthy oppilations* mundane thoughts, which function like constipating foods
64   *half-pe'rth of physic* half-penny worth of medicine
69   *canaglia* rabble

VOLPONE

I protest, I and my six servants are not able to make of this
precious liquor so fast as it is fetched away from my lodging, by
gentlemen of your city; strangers of the *terra-firma*; worshipful
merchants; ay, and senators too – who, ever since my arrival,   75
have detained me to their uses, by their splendidous liberalities.
And worthily. For what avails your rich man to have his
magazines stuffed with *moscadelli*, or the purest grape, when
his physicians prescribe him (on pain of death) to drink nothing
but water, cocted with anise-seeds? O health! health! the blessing   80
of the rich, the riches of the poor! Who can buy thee at too dear
a rate, since there is no enjoying this world, without thee? Be
not then so sparing of your purses, honourable gentlemen, as to
abridge the natural course of life –

PEREGRINE

You see his end?

SIR POLITIC   Ay, is't not good?   85

VOLPONE

For, when a humid flux, or catarrh, by the mutability of air, falls
from your head, into an arm or shoulder, or any other part, take
you a ducat, or your chequin of gold, and apply to the place
affected: see what good effect it can work. No, no, 'tis this
blessed *unguento*, this rare extraction, that hath only power to   90
disperse all malignant humours, that proceed, either of hot,
cold, moist or windy causes –

PEREGRINE

I would he had put in dry too.

SIR POLITIC   'Pray you, observe.

VOLPONE

To fortify the most indigest, and crude stomach – ay, were it of
one that, through extreme weakness, vomited blood – applying   95
only a warm napkin to the place, after the unction, and fricace;

---

74   *terra-firma* mainland, especially the parts owned by Venice
78   *magazines* storehouses
     moscadelli muscatel wines
80   *cocted* boiled
86   *humid flux* Scoto/Volpone here uses the Renaissance theory of 'humours', which
     linked bodily and spiritual conditions to the balance of four fluids, to warn that
     inclement weather could send dampness from the head down into the body.
90   *unguento* ointment
96   *fricace* massage

for the *vertigine* in the head, putting but a drop into your
nostrils, likewise, behind the ears; a most sovereign and
approved remedy: the *mal caduco*, cramps, convulsions, para-
lyses, epilepsies, *tremor cordia*, retired nerves, ill vapours of the   100
spleen, stoppings of the liver, the stone, the strangury, *hernia
ventosa, iliaca passio*; stops a dysenteria, immediately; easeth the
torsion of the small guts; and cures *melancholia hypocondriaca*,
being taken and applied, according to my printed receipt.
(*Pointing to his bill and his glass.*) For, this is the physician, this   105
the medicine; this counsels, this cures; this gives the direction,
this works the effect; and, in sum, both together may be termed
an abstract of the theoric and practic in the Aesculapian art.
'Twill cost you eight crowns. [*Aloud to* NANO] And, Zan Fritada,
'pray thee sing a verse, extempore, in honour of it.   110

SIR POLITIC
How do you like him, sir?
PEREGRINE   Most strangely, I!
SIR POLITIC
Is not his language rare?
PEREGRINE   But alchemy,
I never heard the like; or Broughton's books.

Song [*by* VOLPONE'S SERVANTS]

    Had old Hippocrates, or Galen,
    That to their books put med'cines all in,   115
    But known this secret, they had never

97–102   Scoto/Volpone claims to cure a variety of common medical problems: *vertigine*:
          vertigo, dizziness; *mal caduco*: epilepsy; *tremor cordia*: heart palpitations; *retired
          nerves*: shrunken sinews; *stone*: kidney stone; *strangury*: difficult urination; *iliaca
          passio*: intestinal cramps.
104   *receipt* recipe, prescription
105   *his bill and his glass* Volpone points alternately to his prescription list and his
          beaker of medicinal oil.
108   *the Aesculapian art* medicine, of which Aesculapius was the classical god
109   *Zan Fritada* Volpone calls on Nano by the name of a well-known zany.
111   *strangely* exceptionally, but not necessarily in a positive sense
113   *Broughton* Hugh Broughton, a scholarly Puritan minister whose eccentric works
          Jonson mocks in *The Alchemist* (2.3.237, 4.5.1–32)
113   s.d. *Song* This song, and the one at line 181, are sung by some combination of
          Nano, as the zany, and perhaps Mosca (since Volpone refers to their 'voices'); it is
          also possible that Castrone appears and sings, since a primary purpose of castra-
          tion was to preserve a pure soprano singing-voice.
114   *Hippocrates, or Galen* revered masters of ancient medicine, and inventor and
          propagator respectively, of the theory of humours

(Of which they will be guilty ever)
Been murderers of so much paper,
Or wasted many a hurtless taper;
No Indian drug had e'er been famèd,   120
Tobacco, sassafras not namèd;
Ne yet, of guacum one small stick, sir,
Nor Raymond Lully's great elixir;
Ne had been known the Danish Gonswart,
Or Paracelsus, with his long-sword.   125

PEREGRINE

All this, yet, will not do: eight crowns is high.

VOLPONE

No more. Gentlemen, if I had but time to discourse to you the
miraculous effects of this my oil, surnamed *Oglio del Scoto*, with
the countless catalogue of those I have cured of th' aforesaid,
and many more diseases, the patents and privileges of all the   130
princes and commonwealths of Christendom; or but the depo-
sitions of those that appeared on my part, before the signiory of
the *Sanità*, and most learned college of physicians, where I was
authorized, upon notice taken of the admirable virtues of my
medicaments, and mine own excellency in matter of rare and   135
unknown secrets, not only to disperse them publicly in this
famous city, but in all the territories that happily joy under the
government of the most pious and magnificent states of Italy.
But may some other gallant fellow say, 'O, there be divers, that
make profession to have as good, and as experimented receipts,   140
as yours.' Indeed, very many have assayed, like apes, in imitation
of that which is really and essentially in me, to make of this oil;
bestowed great cost in furnaces, stills, alembics, continual fires,
and preparation of the ingredients, (as indeed there goes to it
six hundred several simples, beside some quantity of human fat,   145

119   *hurtless taper* innocent candle
122   *guacum* The wood and resin of the West Indian guaiacum tree were used
      medically.
123   *Lully* a Medieval astrologer later rumoured to have discovered the alchemical elixir
      of life
125   *Paracelsus* a revolutionary Renaissance theorist of the body-chemistry of health,
      said to keep his medicines inside a sword handle
128   *Oglio del Scoto* Scoto's Oil
132–3 *signiory of the Sanità* Venetian medical board
139   *divers* many other people
145   *several simples* separate herbs

53

for the conglutination, which we buy of the anatomists); but,
when these practitioners come to the last decoction, blow, blow,
puff, puff, and all flies *in fumo*: ha, ha, ha! Poor wretches! I
rather pity their folly, and indiscretion, than their loss of time,
and money; for those may be recovered by industry, but to be a   150
fool born is a disease incurable. For myself, I always from my
youth have endeavoured to get the rarest secrets, and book
them, either in exchange or for money; I spared nor cost,
nor labour, where anything was worthy to be learned. And
gentlemen, honourable gentlemen, I will undertake, by virtue   155
of chemical art, out of the honourable hat that covers your
head, to extract the four elements; that is to say, the fire, air,
water, and earth, and return you your felt without burn or stain.
For, whilst others have been at the *balloo*, I have been at my
book; and am now past the craggy paths of study, and come to   160
the flowery plains of honour, and reputation.

SIR POLITIC
I do assure you, sir, that is his aim.

VOLPONE
But, to our price.

PEREGRINE   And that withal, Sir Pol.

VOLPONE
You all know, honourable gentlemen, I never valued this
ampulla, or vial, at less than eight crowns, but for this time, I am   165
content to be deprived of it for six: six crowns is the price, and
less in courtesy I know you cannot offer me; take it, or leave it,
howsoever, both it, and I am at your service. I ask you not as the
value of the thing, for then I should demand of you a thousand
crowns: so the Cardinals Montalto, Fernese, the great Duke of   170
Tuscany, my gossip, with divers other princes have given me;
but I despise money. Only to show my affection to you, honour-

---

146   *conglutination* gluing together
147   *decoction* boiling down
147–8   *blow, blow, puff, puff* Volpone imitates alchemists trying to increase the heat of
        their fires with breath or bellows.
148   *in fumo* up in smoke; a similar catastrophe is reported in *The Alchemist*.
159   *balloo* a Venetian ball-game
163   *that withal* Peregrine points out that Scoto is also aiming at money.
170   *Montalto, Fernese* sixteenth-century popes; but Jonson may also be alluding to the
        contrast between the inexpensive tickets to *Volpone* and his well-paid work writing
        single-performance masques for powerful Jacobean courtiers.
171   *gossip* godfather or close friend

able gentlemen, and your illustrious state here, I have neglected
the messages of these princes, mine own offices, framed my
journey hither, only to present you with the fruits of my travels. 175
Tune your voices once more, to the touch of your instruments,
and give the honourable assembly some delightful recreation.

PEREGRINE

What monstrous, and most painful circumstance
Is here, to get some three or four gazets?
Some threepence, i' th' whole; for that 'twill come to. 180

Song [by VOLPONE'S SERVANTS, *during which* CELIA
appears at a window above]

You that would last long, list to my song,
Make no more coil, but buy of this oil.
Would you be ever fair? and young?
Stout of teeth? and strong of tongue?
Tart of palate? quick of ear? 185
Sharp of sight? of nostril clear?
Moist of hand? and light of foot?
Or – I will come nearer to't –
Would you live free from all diseases?
Do the act your mistress pleases; 190
Yet fright all aches from your bones?
Here's a med'cine, for the nones.

VOLPONE

Well, I am in a humour, at this time, to make a present of the
small quantity my coffer contains: to the rich, in courtesy, and
to the poor, for God's sake. Wherefore, now mark: I asked you 195
six crowns, and six crowns, at other times, you have paid me.
You shall not give me six crowns; nor five, nor four, nor three,
nor two, nor one; nor half a ducat; no, nor a *moccenigo*. Six
pence it will cost you, or six hundred pound – expect no lower

---

174   *offices* duties
178   *painful circumstance* careful and elaborate set-up
179   *gazets* Venetian pennies
182   *coil* fuss
185   *Tart* Keen
191   *aches from your bones* possibly arthritis, but more likely venereal disease; 'aches' is
        two syllables, probably pronounced 'aitches'.
192   *nones* nonce, occasion
198   *moccenigo* small Venetian coin

price, for by the banner of my front, I will not bate a *bagatine,*   200
that I will have, only, a pledge of your loves, to carry something
from amongst you, to show I am not contemned by you.
Therefore, now, toss your handkerchiefs, cheerfully, cheerfully;
and be advertised, that the first heroic spirit, that deigns to
grace me with a handkerchief, I will give it a little remembrance   205
of something, beside, shall please it better than if I had presented
it with a double pistolet.

PEREGRINE
Will you be that heroic spark, Sir Pol?

CELIA *at the window throws down her handkerchief*

O, see! The window has prevented you.

VOLPONE
Lady, I kiss your bounty; and, for this timely grace you have done   210
your poor Scoto of Mantua, I will return you, over and above my
oil, a secret of that high and inestimable nature, shall make you
for ever enamoured on that minute wherein your eye first
descended on so mean (yet not altogether to be despised) an
object. Here is a powder, concealed in this paper, of which, if I   215
should speak to the worth, nine thousand volumes were but as
one page, that page as a line, that line as a word; so short is this
pilgrimage of man (which some call life) to the expressing of it.
Would I reflect on the price? Why, the whole world were but as an
empire, that empire as a province, that province as a bank, that   220
bank as a private purse, to the purchase of it. I will only tell you:
it is the powder that made Venus a goddess, given her by Apollo,
that kept her perpetually young, cleared her wrinkles, firmed her
gums, filled her skin, coloured her hair; from her, derived to
Helen, and at the sack of Troy, unfortunately, lost; till now, in this   225

200   *banner of my front* a sheet advertising the mountebank's cures
       bate a bagatine drop the price by even the tiniest amount
202   *contemned* scorned
203   *handkerchiefs* Payments were often tossed to mountebanks, and the purchase
       tossed back, in tied handkerchiefs. But – as Shakespeare's *Othello* demonstrates –
       handkerchiefs could also serve as symbols of erotic interest.
207   *pistolet* valuable Spanish coin
208   *spark* gallant
209   *The window has prevented you* Someone above has beaten you to it; the Jacobean
       stage set had an upper level where (at some unspecified point) Celia appears at a
       window.
222–4   *made Venus ... colour their hair* The decreasing dignity of the powder's roles
       parallels the history of Pythagoras's soul in 1.2.

our age, it was as happily recovered, by a studious antiquary, out
of some ruins of Asia, who sent a moiety of it to the Court of
France (but much sophisticated) wherewith the ladies there now
colour their hair. The rest, at this present, remains with me,
extracted, to a quintessence; so that, wherever it but touches, in   230
youth it perpetually preserves, in age restores the complexion;
seats your teeth, did they dance like virginal jacks, firm as a wall;
makes them white, as ivory, that were black, as –

ACT 2, SCENE 3

[Enter] CORVINO *[shouting up to* CELIA*]*

CORVINO

Blood of the devil, and my shame! Come down, here;
Come down! No house but mine to make your scene?
Signior Flaminio, will you down, sir? down?

He beats away the mountebank, etc.

What, is my wife your Franciscina? sir?
No windows on the whole Piazza, here,   5
To make your properties, but mine? but mine?
Heart! ere tomorrow, I shall be new christened,
And called the *Pantalone di Besogniosi*,
About the town.   *[Exit]*

PEREGRINE   What should this mean, Sir Pol?

SIR POLITIC

Some trick of state, believe it. I will home.   10

PEREGRINE

It may be some design on you.

226   *antiquary* scholar who studies the ancient world
227   *moiety* portion
228   *sophisticated* adulterated
232   *did they dance like virginal jacks* even if they danced like little piano keys
  1   Corvino's line plausibly completes Scoto/Volpone's phrase, 'black as'; F reads,
      'Spite of the devil', meaning the seducible woman, the devil's spite against man.
3–8   *Flaminio . . . Besogniosi* Among the play's many references to the *commedia dell'*
      arte tradition, these names of actors and stock characters reflect Corvino's fear that
      he has been put in the role of laughable old cuckold.
  6   *properties* stage props, but punning on the way Scoto has impinged on Corvino's
      property – his house, and perhaps also his wife
 11   *design on* plot against

SIR POLITIC   I know not.
  I'll stand upon my guard.
PEREGRINE   'Tis your best, sir.
SIR POLITIC
  This three weeks, all my advices, all my letters,
  They have been intercepted.
PEREGRINE   Indeed, sir?
  Best have a care.
SIR POLITIC   Nay, so I will.   [*Exit*]
PEREGRINE   This knight,   15
  I may not lose him, for my mirth, till night.   [*Exit*]

ACT 2, SCENE 4

[*Enter*] VOLPONE, MOSCA

VOLPONE
  O, I am wounded.
MOSCA   Where, sir?
VOLPONE   Not without:
  Those blows were nothing; I could bear them ever.
  But angry Cupid, bolting from her eyes,
  Hath shot himself into me, like a flame;
  Where, now, he flings about his burning heat,   5
  As in a furnace, some ambitious fire,
  Whose vent is stopped. The fight is all within me.
  I cannot live, except thou help me, Mosca:
  My liver melts, and I, without the hope
  Of some soft air, from her refreshing breath,   10
  Am but a heap of cinders.
MOSCA   'Las, good sir,
  Would you had never seen her.
VOLPONE   Nay, would thou
  Hadst never told me of her.
MOSCA   Sir, 'tis true:
  I do confess, I was unfortunate,
  And you unhappy; but I am bound in conscience,   15

  1   *without* on the outside
  3   *bolting* shooting like an arrow, often called a 'bolt'; cf. Anacreon's Odes 14 and 16.
  9   *liver* believed to be the location of violent emotions

No less than duty, to effect my best
To your release of torment, and I will, sir.

VOLPONE
Dear Mosca, shall I hope?

MOSCA   Sir, more than dear,
I will not bid you to despair of aught,
Within a human compass.

VOLPONE   O, there spoke   20
My better angel. Mosca, take my keys,
Gold, plate, and jewels, all's at thy devotion;
Employ them, how thou wilt; nay, coin me, too;
So thou, in this, but crown my longings. Mosca?

MOSCA
Use but your patience.

VOLPONE   So I have.

MOSCA   I doubt not   25
To bring success to your desires.

VOLPONE   Nay, then,
I not repent me of my late disguise.

MOSCA
If you can horn him, sir, you need not.

VOLPONE   True;
Besides, I never meant him for my heir.
Is not the colour of my beard, and eyebrows,   30
To make me known?

MOSCA   No jot.

VOLPONE   I did it well.

MOSCA
So well, would I could follow you in mine,
With half the happiness; and, yet, I would
Escape your epilogue.

VOLPONE   But, were they gulled

19–20   *aught, / Within a human compass* anything within human reach (or imagination)
24   *So . . . longings* If you can fulfil my desires in this regard
28   *horn* cuckold (betrayed husbands were said to grow horns)
29–31   *Besides . . . known* Perhaps reminded by his use of the word 'heir', Volpone worries that his (fox-red?) hair ruined his disguise.
31   *No jot* Not in the slightest
32   *mine* my role in this trickery
33–4   *I would / Escape your epilogue* I would like to avoid the beating you took from Corvino. The line is also another oblique signal that Mosca intends to come out better than Volpone when their show ends.

With a belief, that I was Scoto?

MOSCA   Sir,   35
    Scoto himself could hardly have distinguished!
    I have not time to flatter you, we'll part;
    And, as I prosper, so applaud my art.

                                        [*Exeunt*]

ACT 2, SCENE 5

[*Enter*] CORVINO, CELIA

CORVINO
    Death of mine honour, with the city's fool?
    A juggling, tooth-drawing, prating mountebank?
    And, at a public window? where whilst he,
    With his strained action, and his dole of faces,
    To his drug-lecture draws your itching ears,   5
    A crew of old, unmarried, noted lechers,
    Stood leering up, like satyrs; and you smile,
    Most graciously! and fan your favours forth,
    To give your hot spectators satisfaction!
    What, was your mountebank their call? their whistle?   10
    Or were you enamoured on his copper rings?
    His saffron jewel, with the toad-stone in't?
    Or his embroidered suit, with the cope-stitch,
    Made of a hearse-cloth? or his old tilt-feather?
    Or his starched beard? Well! you shall have him, yes.   15
    He shall come home, and minister unto you
    The fricace, for the mother. Or, let me see,

---

2   *tooth-drawing* Mountebanks sometimes performed dental extractions.
4   *his strained action . . . faces* his exaggerated gestures, and his poor repertoire of
      masks or facial expressions
10   *their call? their whistle?* Apparently a reference to bird-calls, with hints of prostitu-
      tion, and resonance in the extended bird-metaphors of the play as a whole.
11–12 *copper rings . . . saffron jewel* cheap simulations of the colour of gold
      toad-stone a jewel with magical curative properties believed hidden between the
      eyes of toads
14–15 *hearse-cloth . . . starched beard* The Scoto costume was evidently garish, with fancy
      draperies used in funerals, a large feather from a jousting helmet, and a fashionably
      shaped and waxed beard.
17   *fricace, for the mother* massage for hysteria, believed to arise from the womb; hence,
      a thinly disguised metaphor for sexual ministrations

I think, you'd rather mount? would you not mount?
Why, if you'll mount, you may; yes truly, you may;
And so, you may be seen, down to th' foot.   20
Get you a cittern, Lady Vanity,
And be a dealer with the virtuous man:
Make one; I'll but protest myself a cuckold,
And save your dowry. I am a Dutchman, I!
For, if you thought me an Italian,   25
You would be damned ere you did this, you whore:
Thou'dst tremble to imagine that the murder
Of father, mother, brother, all thy race,
Should follow, as the subject of my justice.

CELIA

Good sir, have patience.

CORVINO [*Drawing a weapon*] What couldst thou propose   30
Less to thyself, than, in this heat of wrath,
And stung with my dishonour, I should strike
This steel into thee, with as many stabs
As thou wert gazed upon with goatish eyes?

CELIA

Alas sir, be appeased: I could not think   35
My being at the window should more, now,
Move your impatience, than at other times.

CORVINO

No? Not to seek and entertain a parley
With a known knave? before a multitude?
You were an actor, with your handkerchief;   40
Which he, most sweetly, kissed in the receipt,
And might, no doubt, return it, with a letter,
And 'point the place where you might meet: your sister's,

---

19   *mount* perform as a mountebank, but also implying sexual mounting with the mountebank
21   *cittern* zither, sometimes played by mountebanks' assistants or prostitutes
        Lady Vanity a stock sinister character in English morality plays
22   *be a dealer* transact business, presumably prostitution
23   *Make one* Make a deal, join a company, or perform a sexual act
24   *save your dowry* An unfaithful wife legally forfeited her dowry.
        Dutchman Englishmen considered Dutchmen oddly sluggish, apathetic, and tolerant.
34   *goatish* lustful
38   *parley* conversation or negotiation
40   *actor* an active participant, and perhaps a deceptive one
43   *'point* appoint, designate

Your mother's, or your aunt's might serve the turn.

CELIA

    Why, dear sir, when do I make these excuses? 45

    Or ever stir abroad but to the church?

    And that, so seldom –

CORVINO   Well, it shall be less;

    And thy restraint, before, was liberty,

    To what I now decree; and therefore, mark me.

    First, I will have this bawdy light dammed up; 50

    And, till't be done, some two, or three yards off,

    I'll chalk a line; o'er which, if thou but chance

    To set thy desp'rate foot, more hell, more horror,

    More wild, remorseless rage shall seize on thee,

    Than on a conjurer, that had heedless left 55

    His circle's safety, ere his devil was laid.

    Then [*Showing a chastity belt*], here's a lock, which I will hang

      upon thee;

    And, now I think on't, I will keep thee backwards:

    Thy lodging shall be backwards, thy walks backwards,

    Thy prospect – all be backwards; and no pleasure 60

    That thou shalt know, but backwards. Nay, since you force

    My honest nature, know, it is your own

    Being too open, makes me use you thus.

    Since you will not contain your subtle nostrils

    In a sweet room, but, they must snuff the air 65

    Of rank and sweaty passengers –

                        Knock within

               One knocks.

    Away, and be not seen, pain of thy life;

---

44   *turn* purpose

49   *To* Compared to

       mark me listen carefully, mark my words

50   *light* window

55–6 *conjurer . . . laid* It was believed that, if a necromancer stepped outside his protec-
       tive chalk-circle before sending the demons he was commanding back to hell, they
       would tear him to pieces.

60   *prospect* future, or, view

61   *backwards* Corvino vows to keep Celia away from the public edges of his house, but
       by this fifth use, the word has taken on sexual implications, probably related to
       some stage business with the chastity belt.

64   *subtle* crafty (for sniffing out sexual interest), or (sarcastically) delicate

67   *pain* on pain

Not look toward the window: if thou dost –

                        [CELIA *begins to exit*]

Nay, stay, hear this – let me not prosper, whore,
But I will make thee an anatomy,   70
Dissect thee mine own self, and read a lecture
Upon thee, to the city, and in public.
Away.

                      [*Exit* CELIA]

Who is there?

          [*Enter* SERVANT]

SERVANT   'Tis Signior Mosca, sir.

ACT 2, SCENE 6

CORVINO
Let him come in, his master's dead. There's yet
Some good, to help the bad.

                    [*Exit* SERVANT]

         [*Enter* MOSCA]

               My Mosca, welcome;
I guess your news.
MOSCA   I fear you cannot, sir.
CORVINO
Is't not his death?
MOSCA   Rather the contrary.
CORVINO
Not his recovery?
MOSCA   Yes, sir.
CORVINO   I am cursed,   5
I am bewitched, my crosses meet to vex me.
How? how? how? how?
MOSCA   Why, sir, with Scoto's oil!
Corbaccio and Voltore brought of it,
Whilst I was busy in an inner room –

---

70   *anatomy* Autopsies became popular public events in this period.
6   *crosses* afflictions

CORVINO

Death! that damned mountebank! but for the law,   10
Now, I could kill the rascal; 't cannot be
His oil should have that virtue. Ha' not I
Known him a common rogue, come fiddling in
To th' *osterìa*, with a tumbling whore,
And, when he has done all his forced tricks, been glad   15
Of a poor spoonful of dead wine, with flies in't?
It cannot be. All his ingredients
Are a sheep's gall, a roasted bitch's marrow,
Some few sod earwigs, pounded caterpillars,
A little capon's grease, and fasting spittle: 20
I know 'em, to a dram.

MOSCA   I know not, sir;
But some on't, there, they poured into his ears,
Some in his nostrils, and recovered him,
Applying but the fricace.

CORVINO   Pox o' that fricace.

MOSCA

And since, to seem the more officious,   25
And flatt'ring of his health, there, they have had,
At extreme fees, the college of physicians
Consulting on him how they might restore him;
Where, one would have a cataplasm of spices,
Another a flayed ape clapped to his breast,   30
A third would ha' it a dog, a fourth an oil
With wild cats' skins. At last, they all resolved
That, to preserve him, was no other means,
But some young woman must be straight sought out –
Lusty, and full of juice – to sleep by him;   35
And, to this service (most unhappily,
And most unwillingly) am I now employed,
Which, here, I thought to pre-acquaint you with,

14   *osterìa* inn
16   *dead* stale
19   *sod* boiled
20   *fasting spittle* the saliva of a starving man – probably Scoto himself
21   *to a dram* down to the most miniscule portion
22   *on't* of it
29   *cataplasm* poultice
34–5 *some young woman . . . sleep by him* King David is similarly cured in I Kings 1.
      straight immediately

For your advice, since it concerns you most,
Because I would not do that thing might cross   40
Your ends, on whom I have my whole dependence, sir.
Yet if I do it not, they may delate
My slackness to my patron, work me out
Of his opinion; and there, all your hopes,
Ventures, or whatsoever, are all frustrate.   45
I do but tell you, sir. Besides, they are all
Now striving, who shall first present him. Therefore –
I could entreat you, briefly, conclude somewhat:
Prevent 'em if you can.
CORVINO   Death to my hopes!
This is my villainous fortune! Best to hire   50
Some common courtesan?
MOSCA   Ay, I thought on that, sir.
But they are all so subtle, full of art,
And age again doting, and flexible,
So as – I cannot tell – we may perchance
Light on a quean may cheat us all.
CORVINO   'Tis true.   55
MOSCA
No, no; it must be one that has no tricks, sir,
Some simple thing, a creature made unto it;
Some wench you may command. Ha' you no kinswoman?
Godso – Think, think, think, think, think, think, think, sir.
One o' the doctors offered, there, his daughter.   60
CORVINO
How!
MOSCA Yes, Signior Lupo, the physician.
CORVINO
His daughter?
MOSCA   And a virgin, sir. Why? Alas,
He knows the state of's body, what it is:

40–1   *cross / Your ends* interfere with your goals
  42   *delate* report
  44   *opinion* favour
  48   *I could . . . somewhat* I beg you to make a quick decision
  53   *age . . . flexible* old men, moreover, tend to become infatuated and thereby manipulated
  55   *quean* whore
  59   *Godso* An exclamatory oath, probably short for 'By God's soul'.
  61   *Lupo* Italian for a wolf

That nought can warm his blood, sir, but a fever;
Nor any incantation raise his spirit: 65
A long forgetfulness hath seized that part.
Besides, sir, who shall know it? Some one, or two –

CORVINO
I pray thee give me leave. [*Moves away, talking to himself*]
                    If any man
But I had had this luck – The thing in't self,
I know, is nothing – Wherefore should not I   70
As well command my blood, and my affections,
As this dull doctor? In the point of honour,
The cases are all one, of wife and daughter.

MOSCA
[*Aside*] I hear him coming.

CORVINO   She shall do't. 'Tis done.
'Slight, if this doctor, who is not engaged,   75
Unless 't be for his counsel (which is nothing)
Offer his daughter, what should I, that am
So deeply in? I will prevent him: wretch!
Covetous wretch! [*To* MOSCA] Mosca, I have determined.

MOSCA
How, sir?

CORVINO   We'll make all sure. The party you wot of,   80
Shall be mine own wife, Mosca.

MOSCA   Sir. The thing –
But that I would not seem to counsel you –
I should have motioned to you at the first;
And, make your count, you have cut all their throats.
Why, 'tis directly taking a possession!   85
And, in his next fit, we may let him go.
'Tis but to pull the pillow from his head,
And he is throttled: 't had been done before,
But for your scrupulous doubts.

CORVINO   Ay, a plague on't,

---

73   *all one* equal
74   *coming* coming around, deciding to cooperate
75   *'Slight* an exclamatory oath, short for 'I swear by God's light'
       not engaged does not have a monetary investment at stake
80   *party you wot of* person you were seeking
83   *motioned* suggested
84   *make your ... throats* count on it, begin inventory of your grand inheritance, because you have thus defeated your rivals for it

My conscience fools my wit. Well, I'll be brief,   90
And so be thou, lest they should be before us:
Go home, prepare him, tell him, with what zeal,
And willingness, I do it; swear it was
On the first hearing (as thou mayst do, truly),
Mine own free motion.
MOSCA   Sir, I warrant you,   95
I'll so possess him with it, that the rest
Of his starved clients shall be banished, all;
And only you received. But come not, sir,
Until I send, for I have something else
To ripen, for your good – you must not know't.   100
CORVINO
But do not you forget to send, now.
MOSCA   Fear not.   [*Exit* MOSCA]

ACT 2, SCENE 7

CORVINO
Where are you, wife? my Celia? wife?

[*Enter* CELIA, *weeping*]

                              What, blubbering?
Come, dry those tears. I think, thou thought'st me in earnest?
Ha? By this light, I talked so but to try thee.
Methinks the lightness of the occasion
Should ha' confirmed thee. Come, I am not jealous.   5
CELIA
No?
CORVINO Faith, I am not, I, nor never was:
It is a poor, unprofitable humour.
Do not I know, if women have a will,

---

90   *fools my wit* has caused my intelligence to fail
99–100 *something else / To ripen* a plot to bring to fruition – tricking Corbaccio into
       making Volpone, rather than his own son Bonario, his heir
3   *try* test
4–5   *the lightness ... confirmed thee* the triviality of the cause of my outburst should
       have assured you I wasn't serious
6   *Faith* In faith
7   *humour* emotion

They'll do 'gainst all the watches o' the world?
And that the fiercest spies are tamed with gold?   10
Tut, I am confident in thee, thou shalt see't;
And see, I'll give thee cause too, to believe it.
Come, kiss me. Go, and make thee ready straight,
In all thy best attire, thy choicest jewels,
Put 'em all on, and, with 'em, thy best looks: 15
We are invited to a solemn feast,
At old Volpone's, where it shall appear
How far I am free from jealousy or fear.

                                                    [*Exeunt*]

ACT 3, SCENE 1

[*Enter*] MOSCA

MOSCA

I fear I shall begin to grow in love
With my dear self, and my most prosp'rous parts,
They do so spring, and burgeon; I can feel
A whimsy i' my blood. I know not how,
Success hath made me wanton. I could skip   5
Out of my skin, now, like a subtle snake,
I am so limber. O! your parasite
Is a most precious thing, dropped from above,
Not bred 'mongst clods and clodpolls here on earth.
I muse the mystery was not made a science,   10
It is so liberally professed! Almost
All the wise world is little else, in nature,
But parasites, or sub-parasites. And yet,

9 *do 'gainst* cheat despite
11 *Tut* Nonsense, don't be silly
2 *parts* qualities – but also body-parts and stage-parts
4 *whimsy* giddiness, or, whirling
5 *wanton* wild, playful, sensual
9 *clods and clodpolls* dull, stupid persons
10 *mystery* craft
   science field of knowledge in higher education

I mean not those, that have your bare town-art,
To know who's fit to feed 'em; have no house,   15
No family, no care, and therefore mould
Tales for men's ears, to bait that sense; or get
Kitchen-invention, and some stale receipts
To please the belly, and the groin; nor those,
With their court-dog-tricks, that can fawn and fleer,   20
Make their revenue out of legs and faces,
Echo my lord, and lick away a moth.
But your fine, elegant rascal, that can rise
And stoop, almost together, like an arrow;
Shoot through the air, as nimbly as a star;   25
Turn short, as doth a swallow; and be here,
And there, and here, and yonder, all at once;
Present to any humour, all occasion;
And change a visor swifter than a thought!
This is the creature had the art born with him;   30
Toils not to learn it, but doth practise it
Out of most excellent nature; and such sparks
Are the true parasites, others but their zanies.

ACT 3, SCENE 2

[*Enter*] BONARIO

MOSCA
Who's this? Bonario? Old Corbaccio's son?

14   *bare town-art* crude skills of street-hustlers; here and in line 19, the commas after
      'those' are dropped by most modern editors, but they may mark opportunities for
      Mosca to point to members of the audience.
20   *court-dog-tricks* obsequious service, begging favours (as opposed to the more prac-
      tical offerings of town-parasites)
21   *legs and faces* either elaborate bows and smiles, or (as under King James) physical
      attractiveness
22   *moth* any small vermin; minute grooming was a common servile behaviour at
      court, and licking would presumably be an even more dog-like form of that
      service.
24   *together* simultaneously
28   *Present . . . occasion* Ready to respond pleasingly to any mood or event, or, Ready to
      offer justification for any mood, or, Ready to satisfy any whim
29   *visor* mask, facial expression, personality

The person I was bound to seek. Fair sir,
You are happ'ly met.

BONARIO   That cannot be, by thee.

MOSCA
Why sir?

BONARIO Nay, 'pray thee, know thy way, and leave me:
I would be loath to interchange discourse   5
With such a mate as thou art.

MOSCA   Courteous sir,
Scorn not my poverty.

BONARIO   Not I, by heaven;
But thou shalt give me leave to hate thy baseness.

MOSCA
Baseness?

BONARIO   Ay, answer me, is not thy sloth
Sufficient argument? Thy flattery?   10
Thy means of feeding?

MOSCA   Heaven, be good to me.
These imputations are too common, sir,
And eas'ly stuck on virtue, when she's poor.
You are unequal to me, and howe'er
Your sentence may be righteous, yet you are not,   15
That ere you know me, thus, proceed in censure;
St Mark bear witness 'gainst you, 'tis inhuman.

BONARIO
[*Aside*] What? Does he weep? The sign is soft, and good;
I do repent me, that I was so harsh.

MOSCA
'Tis true that, swayed by strong necessity,   20
I am enforced to eat my careful bread
With too much obsequy; 'tis true, beside,
That I am fain to spin mine own poor raiment
Out of my mere observance, being not born
To a free fortune; but that I have done   25

    2   *bound* on my way
    6   *mate* lowly companion
  10   *argument* evidence
  14   *unequal* unfair, perhaps because of higher social status
           howe'er however much
  21   *careful* full of cares
23–4   *fain . . . observance* obliged to earn the clothes on my back by nothing more heroic
           than dutiful service

Base offices, in rending friends asunder,
Dividing families, betraying counsels,
Whispering false lies, or mining men with praises,
Trained their credulity with perjuries,
Corrupted chastity, or am in love   30
With mine own tender ease, but would not rather
Prove the most rugged and laborious course
That might redeem my present estimation,
Let me here perish, in all hope of goodness.

BONARIO
This cannot be a personated passion.   35
I was to blame, so to mistake thy nature;
'Pray thee forgive me, and speak out thy business.

MOSCA
Sir, it concerns you; and though I may seem,
At first, to make a main offence in manners,
And in my gratitude unto my master,   40
Yet, for the pure love which I bear all right,
And hatred of the wrong, I must reveal it.
This very hour, your father is in purpose
To disinherit you –

BONARIO   How!

MOSCA   And thrust you forth,
As a mere stranger to his blood; 'tis true, sir,   45
The work no way engageth me, but as
I claim an interest in the general state
Of goodness, and true virtue, which I hear
T' abound in you; and, for which mere respect,
Without a second aim, sir, I have done it.   50

BONARIO
This tale hath lost thee much of the late trust
Thou hadst with me: it is impossible.
I know not how to lend it any thought,
My father should be so unnatural.

29   *Trained* Led on
32   *Prove* Attempt, Endure
33   *estimation* reputation
35   *personated* impersonated, feigned
41   *bear all right* feel toward the good and just
46   *engageth* holds advantage for
49   *for which mere respect* for this reason only
51   *late* recent
53   *lend it any thought* even imagine the possibility that

MOSCA

 It is a confidence that well becomes   55
 Your piety; and formed, no doubt, it is
 From your own simple innocence; which makes
 Your wrong more monstrous, and abhorred. But, sir,
 I now will tell you more. This very minute,
 It is, or will be doing; and, if you   60
 Shall be but pleased to go with me, I'll bring you –
 I dare not say where you shall see, but – where
 Your ear shall be a witness of the deed:
 Hear yourself written bastard, and professed
 The common issue of the earth.

BONARIO   I'm mazed.   65

MOSCA

 Sir, if I do it not, draw your just sword,
 And score your vengeance, on my front, and face:
 Mark me your villain. You have too much wrong,
 And I do suffer for you, sir. My heart
 Weeps blood, in anguish –

BONARIO   Lead. I follow thee. 70

              [Exeunt]

ACT 3, SCENE 3

   [Enter] VOLPONE, NANO, ANDROGYNO, CASTRONE

VOLPONE

 Mosca stays long, methinks. Bring forth your sports
 And help to make the wretched time more sweet.

NANO

 Dwarf, fool, and eunuch, well met here we be.
  A question it were now, whether of us three –
 Being, all, the known delicates of a rich man –   5
  In pleasing him, claim the precedency can?

---

56 *piety* filial love (the Latin *pietas*)
58 *Your wrong* The way you are being wronged
65 *common issue of the earth* child with no acknowledged parent (the Latin *terrae filius*)
4 *whether* which
5 *delicates* favourites; this competition for Volpone's favour parallels that among the
  legacy-hunters.

CASTRONE
    I claim for myself.
ANDROGYNO   And so doth the fool.
NANO
    'Tis foolish indeed: let me set you both to school.
    First, for your dwarf, he's little and witty,
        And everything, as it is little, is pretty;   10
    Else, why do men say to a creature of my shape
        So soon as they see him, 'It's a pretty little ape'?
    And, why a pretty ape, but for pleasing imitation
        Of greater men's action, in a ridiculous fashion?
    Beside, this feat body of mine doth not crave   15
        Half the meat, drink, and cloth, one of your bulks will have.
    Admit, your fool's face be the mother of laughter,
        Yet, for his brain, it must always come after;
    And, though that do feed him, it's a pitiful case,
        His body is beholding to such a bad face.   20
                                        One knocks

VOLPONE
    Who's there? My couch, away, look, Nano, see:
    Give me my caps, first – go, inquire.

        [*Exeunt* NANO, ANDROGYNO, *and* CASTRONE]

                                Now, Cupid
    Send it be Mosca, and with fair return.

        [VOLPONE *lies on his bed;* NANO *enters*]

NANO
    It is the beauteous madam –
VOLPONE   Would-Be – is it?
NANO
    The same.
VOLPONE   Now, torment on me! Squire her in;   25
    For she will enter, or dwell here forever.

    8   *set you both to school* instruct you both
    15   *feat* dainty
    19   *that* his face
    22   s.d. *Exeunt* NANO No re-entry is marked for Nano before his next line; perhaps he
         speaks through the doorway.
    22–3 *Cupid . . . return* may Cupid grant my wish that it is Mosca knocking, and bringing
         good news

73

Nay, quickly, that my fit were past.

[Exit NANO]

I fear

A second hell too, that my loathing this
Will quite expel my appetite to the other:
Would she were taking, now, her tedious leave.   30
Lord, how it threats me, what I am to suffer!

ACT 3, SCENE 4

[Enter NANO, bringing] LADY WOULD-BE

LADY WOULD-BE
[To NANO] I thank you, good sir. 'Pray you signify
Unto your patron, I am here. This band
Shows not my neck enough – I trouble you, sir,
Let me request you, bid one of my women
Come hither to me –

[Exit NANO]

In good faith, I, am dressed   5

Most favourably, today, it is no matter,
'Tis well enough.

[Enter NANO with first SERVING-WOMAN]

Look, see, these petulant things,

How they have done this!
VOLPONE   [Aside] I do feel the fever
Ent'ring, in at mine ears: O, for a charm
To fright it hence.
LADY WOULD-BE   Come nearer: is this curl   10
In his right place? or this? Why is this higher
Than all the rest? You ha' not washed your eyes, yet?

---

27   *that my fit were past* so that I can get it over with
29   *the other* the other woman, Celia
2   *band* ruff or collar; this line may refer to what the English considered shockingly
     low necklines on Italian dresses (Coryat I, 399–400, cited by Parker); it may also
     refer to the band around the neck of a parrot, a bird the English commonly called
     'Pol' or 'Polly', thus extending the avian metaphor to this fourth legacy-hunter.
5–6 *in good . . . today* Lady Would-Be is speaking sarcastically.
9   *charm* magic spell

Or do they not stand even in your head?
Where is your fellow? Call her.

> [*Exit first* SERVING-WOMAN]

NANO   [*Aside*] Now, St Mark
  Deliver us: anon, she'll beat her women,   15
  Because her nose is red.

> [*Enter first* SERVING-WOMAN *with another*]

LADY WOULD-BE   I pray you, view
  This tire, forsooth; are all things apt, or no?
1st WOMAN
  One hair a little, here, sticks out, forsooth.
LADY WOULD-BE
  Does't so, forsooth? And where was your dear sight
  When it did so, forsooth? What now? Bird-eyed?   20
  And you too? 'Pray you both approach, and mend it.
  Now, by that light, I muse you are not ashamed!
  I, that have preached these things so oft unto you,
  Read you the principles, argued all the grounds,
  Disputed every fitness, every grace,   25
  Called you to counsel of so frequent dressings –
NANO
  [*Aside*] More carefully, than of your fame, or honour.
LADY WOULD-BE
  Made you acquainted what an ample dowry
  The knowledge of these things would be unto you,
  Able, alone, to get you noble husbands   30
  At your return; and you, thus, to neglect it?
  Besides, you seeing what a curious nation
  Th' Italians are, what will they say of me?
  'The English lady cannot dress herself':
  Here's a fine imputation, to our country.   35

---

13   *do they . . . head?* can't you see straight?
15   *anon* in a moment
17   *tire* head-dress
22   *I muse* I am amazed
23–6   *preached . . . counsel* Lady Would-Be invokes the high language of theological, logical, rhetorical, aesthetic, and legal education.
27   *fame* reputation
31   *return* return to England
32   *curious* attentive to details

Well, go your ways, and stay i' the next room.
This fucus was too coarse too, it's no matter.
Good sir, you'll give 'em entertainment?

[*Exit*] NANO *with serving-women*]

VOLPONE
[*Aside*] The storm comes toward me.

LADY WOULD-BE   How does my Volp?

VOLPONE
Troubled with noise, I cannot sleep: I dreamt   40
That a strange fury entered, now, my house,
And, with the dreadful tempest of her breath,
Did cleave my roof asunder.

LADY WOULD-BE   Believe me, and I
Had the most fearful dream, could I remember't –

VOLPONE
[*Aside*] Out on my fate! I ha' giv'n her the occasion   45
How to torment me: she will tell me hers.

LADY WOULD-BE
Methought, the golden mediocrity,
Polite and delicate –

VOLPONE   O, if you do love me,
No more: I sweat, and suffer, at the mention
Of any dream; feel, how I tremble yet.   50

LADY WOULD-BE
Alas, good soul, the passion of the heart!
Seed-pearl were good now, boiled with syrup of apples,
Tincture of gold, and coral, citron-pills,
Your elecampane root, myrobalanes –

---

37   *fucus* a paste or paint used as a cosmetic base
45   *Out* Curses
     occasion opportunity
47   *golden mediocrity* Lady Would-Be's characteristically protracted and mannered
     term (out of Theophrastus) for the Horatian 'golden mean', and also a reminder
     that gold is what diverts all the play's characters from safe moderation. Unlike
     modern editors, neither Q nor F (both usually generous with commas) places a
     comma at the end of this line; so if Lady Would-Be's dream was indeed 'fearful', she
     may be preparing (after a 'but') to describe the shocking transformation of this
     supposedly decorous 'mediocrity' into something monstrous.
52–4 *Seed-pearl . . . myrobalanes* A medley of popular remedies, mostly stimulants and
     cures for melancholy.

VOLPONE
    [*Aside*] Ay me, I have ta'en a grasshopper by the wing.   55
LADY WOULD-BE
    Burnt silk, and amber, you have muscadel
    Good i' the house –
VOLPONE   You will not drink, and part?
LADY WOULD-BE
    No, fear not that. I doubt, we shall not get
    Some English saffron – half a dram would serve –
    Your sixteen cloves, a little musk, dried mints,   60
    Bugloss, and barley-meal –
VOLPONE   [*Aside*] She's in again;
    Before I feigned diseases, now I have one.
LADY WOULD-BE
    And these applied with a right scarlet cloth –
VOLPONE
    [*Aside*] Another flood of words! A very torrent!
LADY WOULD-BE
    Shall I, sir, make you a poultice?
VOLPONE   No, no, no: 65
    I'm very well; you need prescribe no more.
LADY WOULD-BE
    I have, a little, studied physic; but, now,
    I'm all for music – save, i' the forenoons,
    An hour, or two, for painting. I would have
    A lady, indeed, to have all, letters and arts,   70
    Be able to discourse, to write, to paint,
    But principal (as Plato holds) your music
    (And, so does wise Pythagoras, I take it)

---

55   *ta'en a grasshopper by the wing* Volpone here complains about the constant whining noise of Lady Would-Be's voice, but may also have in mind a Renaissance locution: 'someone *seizes the grasshopper by the wing* when he incites and prompts someone else to do something, which the latter is prepared to do even more promptly and readily on his own initiative' (Parker, citing Stephanus's gloss to Erasmus's *Adagia*).

56   *Burnt silk* a treatment for smallpox

58   *doubt* fear

61   *Bugloss* recommended (as are many of Lady Would-Be's remedies) in Burton's *Anatomy of Melancholy*, this one as a heart stimulant

63   *scarlet cloth* Smallpox patients were sometimes wrapped in scarlet cloth.

70, 75   *indeed* Apparently a familiar pretentious verbal tic in Jacobean society; overuse of 'indeed' is mocked in Marston's *What You Will*, 3.3.136 (Parker).

Is your true rapture: when there is concent
In face, in voice, and clothes; and is, indeed,   75
Our sex's chiefest ornament.
VOLPONE   The poet,
    As old in time as Plato, and as knowing,
    Says that your highest female grace is silence.
LADY WOULD-BE
    Which o' your poets? Petrarch? or Tasso? or Dante?
    Guarini? Ariosto? Aretine?   80
    Cieco di Hadria? I have read them all.
VOLPONE
    [*Aside*] Is every thing a cause, to my destruction?
LADY WOULD-BE
    I think I ha' two or three of 'em about me.
VOLPONE
    [*Aside*] The sun, the sea will sooner, both, stand still,
    Then her eternal tongue: nothing can scape it.   85
LADY WOULD-BE
    [*Holding up a book*] Here is *Pastor Fido* –
VOLPONE   [*Aside*] Profess obstinate silence,
    That's, now, my safest.
LADY WOULD-BE   All our English writers,
    I mean such as are happy in th' Italian,
    Will deign to steal out of this author, mainly –
    Almost as much, as from Montagni –   90
    He has so modern, and facile a vein,
    Fitting the time, and catching the court-ear.
    Your Petrarch is more passionate, yet he,

---

74   *concent* harmony
76   *The poet* Sophocles (*Ajax*, line 293, Loeb edition), or possibly Euripides (*Children of Hercules*, lines 476–7, Loeb edition).
79–81 *Petrarch . . . Hadria* Yet another degrading downward succession, since Aretine was a notorious (if skilful) pornographer, and Cieco di Hadria far below the others in literary merit.
82   *cause* Again the comma allows a first meaning – *causa*, the classical term for a topic for debate – to emerge before being subsumed in the more conventional modern notion of cause and (destructive) effect, implying a sequence of thought and verbal association in the speaker.
86   Guarini's 1590 play appeared in English as *The Faithful Shepherd* in 1602, and though widely popular, was condemned by Jonson in the *Conversations with Drummond* (H&S I, 134).
90   *Montagni* Lady Pol mistakes the French philosopher Montaigne for an Italian.

In days of sonneting, trusted 'em with much;
Dante is hard, and few can understand him.   95
But, for a desperate wit, there's Aretine;
Only, his pictures are a little obscene –
You mark me not?
VOLPONE   Alas, my mind's perturbed.
LADY WOULD-BE
Why, in such cases we must cure ourselves,
Make use of our philosophy –
VOLPONE   [*Aside*] O'ay me!   100
LADY WOULD-BE
And, as we find our passions do rebel,
Encounter them with reason; or divert them,
By giving scope unto some other humour
Of lesser danger; as, in politic bodies,
There's nothing more doth overwhelm the judgement,   105
And clouds the understanding, than too much
Settling, and fixing, and (as 'twere) subsiding
Upon one object. For the incorporating
Of these same outward things, into that part
Which we call mental, leaves some certain faeces,   110
That stop the organs, and as Plato says,
Assassinates our knowledge.
VOLPONE   [*Aside*] Now, the spirit
Of patience help me.
LADY WOULD-BE   Come, in faith, I must
Visit you more, a-days; and make you well:

---

94   *sonneting* Jonson also criticizes Petrarch's sonnets in the *Conversations* (H&S, I,
      133–4).
      trusted 'em with much entrusted his successors (Wyatt, Surrey, Sidney, and Spenser)
      with a legacy worth imitating
96   *desperate* outrageous
98   *You mark me not?* Are you listening to me? (though Jonson sometimes used the
      question mark in place of an exclamation mark, so this could be a more direct
      accusation)
100   *O'ay me* A cry of anguish, like 'Alas'; perhaps a version of the Italian *Ohimé*, which
      Parker substitutes here; compare 'O me!' or 'Ay me!' several times later in this play
      (and in Milton's 'Lycidas', lines 56 and 154).
104   *politic bodies* Lady Would-Be seems to mean wise persons, though the term would
      normally refer to kingdoms.
107   *Settling . . . subsiding* terms from alchemy – aptly, since all the characters here are
      diseased by their obsession with acquiring gold

Laugh, and be lusty.

VOLPONE   [*Aside*] My good angel save me.   115

LADY WOULD-BE

There was but one sole man, in all the world,
With whom I e'er could sympathize; and he
Would lie you often three, four hours together,
To hear me speak: and be, sometime, so rapt,
As he would answer me quite from the purpose,   120
Like you, and you are like him, just. I'll discourse
(And't be but only, sir, to bring you asleep)
How we did spend our time, and loves, together,
For some six years.

VOLPONE   Oh, oh, oh, oh, oh, oh.

LADY WOULD-BE

For we were *coaetanei*, and brought up –   125

VOLPONE

[*Aside*] Some power, some fate, some fortune rescue me.

ACT 3, SCENE 5

[*Enter*] MOSCA

MOSCA

God save you, madam.

LADY WOULD-BE   Good sir.

VOLPONE   Mosca? Welcome,

Welcome to my redemption.

MOSCA   Why, sir?

VOLPONE   O,

Rid me of this my torture, quickly, there:
My madam, with the everlasting voice.
The bells, in time of pestilence, ne'er made   5

---

115   *lusty* merry, but the modern sexual sense begins to impinge
118   *lie you* lie
119   *rapt* enraptured, or lost in thought
120   *quite from the purpose* entirely off the topic; her supposed paramour does not seem
       to have been listening.
125   *coaetanei* of the same age
5–6   *The bells . . . noise* The church-bells, even when the plague had them ringing death-
       knells constantly, never made so much noise

Like noise, or were in that perpetual motion;
The cock-pit comes not near it. All my house,
But now, steamed like a bath, with her thick breath.
A lawyer could not have been heard; nor scarce
Another woman, such a hail of words   10
She has let fall. For hell's sake, rid her hence.

MOSCA
Has she presented?

VOLPONE   O, I do not care,
I'll take her absence, upon any price,
With any loss.

MOSCA   Madam.

LADY WOULD-BE   I ha' brought your patron
A toy, a cap here, of mine own work –

MOSCA   'Tis well;   15
I had forgot to tell you, I saw your knight,
Where you'd little think it –

LADY WOULD-BE   Where?

MOSCA   Marry,
Where yet, if you make haste, you may apprehend him,
Rowing upon the water in a gondole,
With the most cunning courtesan of Venice.   20

LADY WOULD-BE
Is't true?

MOSCA Pursue 'em, and believe your eyes;
Leave me to make your gift.

                              [*Exit* LADY WOULD-BE]
                    I knew't would take.
For lightly they, that use themselves most license,
Are still most jealous.

VOLPONE   Mosca, hearty thanks,
For thy quick fiction, and delivery of me.   25
Now, to my hopes, what sayst thou?

---

7   *cock-pit* Cock fights were fashionable in this period – King James liked them – and
     were always raucous.
8   *But now* Just a moment ago
12   *presented* given a present; Volpone's reply puns on 'presents' and 'presence'.
15   *toy* silly trifle
23   *lightly* usually
24   *still* always

[LADY WOULD-BE *enters*]

LADY WOULD-BE   But do you hear, sir?
VOLPONE
  Again! I fear a paroxysm.
LADY WOULD-BE   Which way
  Rowed they together?
MOSCA   Toward the Rialto.
LADY WOULD-BE
  I pray you, lend me your dwarf.
MOSCA   I pray you, take him –
                                  [*Exit* LADY WOULD-BE]
  Your hopes, sir, are like happy blossoms, fair,   30
  And promise timely fruit, if you will stay
  But the maturing: keep you at your couch,
  Corbaccio will arrive straight, with the will;
  When he is gone, I'll tell you more.   [*Exit*]
VOLPONE   My blood,
  My spirits are returned: I am alive;   35
  And like your wanton gamester, at primero,
  Whose thought had whispered to him not go less,
  Methinks I lie, and draw – for an encounter.

ACT 3, SCENE 6

[MOSCA *brings in* BONARIO *and hides him*]

MOSCA
  Sir, here concealed, you may hear all. But 'pray you
                                          One knocks
  Have patience, sir; the same's your father, knocks:
  I am compelled to leave you.
BONARIO   Do so. Yet,
  Cannot my thought imagine this a truth.

36   *wanton gamester, at primero* reckless gambler playing a popular card-game;
     Volpone uses technical terms of the game – go less, lie, draw, encounter – as meta-
     phors for his anticipated seduction of Celia.
4   *Cannot . . . truth* I cannot believe my father would really disinherit me as Mosca
     claims

ACT 3, SCENE 7

[MOSCA *opens the door, enter*] CORVINO, CELIA

MOSCA
Death on me! You are come too soon, what meant you?
Did not I say, I would send?
CORVINO   Yes, but I feared
You might forget it, and then they prevent us.
MOSCA
[*Aside*] Prevent? Did e'er man haste so, for his horns?
A courtier would not ply it so, for a place.   5
[To CORVINO] Well, now there is no helping it, stay here;
I'll presently return.   [MOSCA *goes to* BONARIO]
CORVINO   Where are you, Celia?
You know not wherefore I have brought you hither?
CELIA
Not well, except you told me.
CORVINO   Now, I will:
Hark hither.
MOSCA (*To* BONARIO) Sir, your father hath sent word,   10
It will be half an hour, ere he come;
And therefore, if you please to walk, the while,
Into that gallery – at the upper end,
There are some books, to entertain the time;
And I'll take care, no man shall come unto you, sir.   15
BONARIO
Yes, I will stay there. [*Aside*] I do doubt this fellow.   [*Exit*]
MOSCA
There, he is far enough: he can hear nothing;
And, for his father, I can keep him off. [*goes to* VOLPONE]
CORVINO
Nay, now, there is no starting back; and therefore,

---

1   *Death on me!* Apparently an exclamatory curse, like 'Damn it!', but oddly parallel
     to Corvino's 'Death of mine honour' at the beginning of 2.5.
4   *horns* marks of the cuckold
5   *ply it so, for a place* strive so diligently for appointment to a higher office
9   *except you told me* unless you tell me, or possibly, except what little you have told
     me
10   *Hark hither* Listen here
19   *no starting back* no turning back, or possibly, no use drawing back startled

Resolve upon it: I have so decreed. 20
It must be done. Nor would I move't afore,
Because I would avoid all shifts and tricks
That might deny me.

CELIA   Sir, let me beseech you,
Affect not these strange trials. If you doubt
My chastity, why, lock me up, for ever; 25
Make me the heir of darkness. Let me live,
Where I may please your fears, if not your trust.

CORVINO
Believe it, I have no such humour, I.
All that I speak, I mean; yet I am not mad –
Not horn-mad, see you? Go to, show yourself 30
Obedient, and a wife.

CELIA   O heaven!

CORVINO   I say it,
Do so.

CELIA   Was this the train?

CORVINO   I've told you reasons:
What the physicians have set down; how much
It may concern me; what my engagements are;
My means; and the necessity of those means, 35
For my recovery. Wherefore, if you be
Loyal, and mine, be won, respect my venture.

CELIA
Before your honour?

CORVINO   Honour? tut, a breath;
There's no such thing, in nature: a mere term

21 *Nor would I move't afore* Nor was I willing to suggest this plan earlier
22 *shifts* evasions
24 *Affect not* Do not attempt, or pretend to attempt
27 *please your fears, if not your trust* allay your jealous fears, if not earn your actual trust
30 *horn-mad* sexually jealous, or (almost the opposite), eager to be cuckolded
32 *train* plan, trap
33 *set down* recorded as their prognosis (for Volpone's sexual impotence and imminent death)
34 *engagements* investments (in courting Volpone), perhaps also consequent debts to others
35 *means* method, means to the end, which is winning Volpone's inheritance
37 *venture* risky commercial undertaking
38 *tut, a breath* nonsense, an empty word

Invented to awe fools. What is my gold   40
The worse, for touching? clothes, for being looked on?
Why, this 's no more. An old, decrepit wretch,
That has no sense, no sinew; takes his meat
With others' fingers; only knows to gape,
When you do scald his gums; a voice; a shadow;   45
And what can this man hurt you?

CELIA   Lord! what spirit
Is this hath entered him?

CORVINO   And for your fame,
That's such a jig; as if I would go tell it,
Cry it, on the Piazza! Who shall know it?
But he, that cannot speak it; and this fellow,   50
Whose lips are i' my pocket; save yourself –
If you'll proclaim't, you may – I know no other
Should come to know it.

CELIA   Are heaven and saints then nothing?
Will they be blind, or stupid?

CORVINO   How?

CELIA   Good sir,
Be jealous still, emulate them; and think   55
What hate they burn with, toward every sin.

CORVINO
I grant you; if I thought it were a sin,
I would not urge you. Should I offer this
To some young Frenchman, or hot Tuscan blood,
That had read Aretine, conned all his prints,   60
Knew every quirk within lust's labyrinth,
And were professed critic in lechery,
And I would look upon him, and applaud him,
This were a sin; but here, 'tis contrary,
A pious work, mere charity, for physic,   65
And honest polity, to assure mine own.

---

43   *no sense, no sinew* no sensory awareness, no physical strength
48   *jig* farcical diversion, silly excuse
51   *Whose lips are i' my pocket* Whose silence I have purchased
      save except
60   *conned all his prints* studied all Aretine's pornographic illustrations
62   *professed critic* expert scholar
63   *And* If
66   *polity, to assure mine own* stratagem to secure the fortune that is rightfully mine

CELIA

O heaven! canst thou suffer such a change?

VOLPONE

[*Aside to* MOSCA] Thou art mine honour, Mosca, and my pride,
My joy, my tickling, my delight! Go, bring 'em.

MOSCA

Please you draw near, sir.

CORVINO   Come on, what –   70

[CELIA *resists as he drags her toward the bed*]

You will not be rebellious? By that light –

MOSCA

Sir, Signior Corvino, here, is come to see you.

VOLPONE

Oh.

MOSCA   And, hearing of the consultation had,
So lately, for your health, is come to offer,
Or rather, sir, to prostitute –

CORVINO   Thanks, sweet Mosca.   75

MOSCA

Freely, unasked, or unentreated –

CORVINO   Well.

MOSCA

As the true, fervent instance of his love,
His own most fair and proper wife: the beauty,
Only of price, in Venice –

CORVINO   'Tis well urged.

MOSCA

To be your comfortress, and to preserve you.   80

VOLPONE

Alas, I'm past already. 'Pray you, thank him,
For his good care, and promptness. But for that,
'Tis a vain labour, e'en to fight, 'gainst heaven:

---

71   *You will not be rebellious?* Are you really going to disobey me? or, Didn't you
      promise to be an obedient wife?

78   *proper* Three meanings simultaneously: respectable, attractive, and privately
      owned

78–9   *the beauty, / Only of price* the most prized and precious beauty (but with a reminder
       that even she can be bought)

81–9   *Alas . . . to't* The heavy punctuation in this speech (both in Q and in F) suggests
       Volpone struggling for breath as he speaks.

Applying fire to a stone – uh, uh, uh, uh –
Making a dead leaf grow again. I take   85
His wishes gently, though; and, you may tell him,
What I've done for him. Marry, my state is hopeless.
Will him to pray for me; and t' use his fortune,
With reverence, when he comes to't.

MOSCA   Do you hear, sir?
Go to him, with your wife.

CORVINO   Heart of my father!   90
Wilt thou persist thus? Come, I pray thee, come.
Thou seest 'tis nothing, Celia. By this hand,
I shall grow violent. Come, do't, I say.

CELIA
Sir, kill me, rather: I will take down poison,
Eat burning coals, do anything –

CORVINO   Be damned!   95
Heart, I will drag thee hence, home, by the hair;
Cry thee a strumpet through the streets; rip up
Thy mouth, unto thine ears; and slit thy nose,
Like a raw rotchet – do not tempt me, come;
Yield, I am loath – Death, I will buy some slave,   100
Whom I will kill, and bind thee to him, alive;
And, at my window, hang you forth; devising
Some monstrous crime, which I, in capital letters,
Will eat into thy flesh, with *aquafortis*,
And burning cor'sives, on this stubborn breast.   105
Now, by the blood thou hast incensed, I'll do't.

CELIA
Sir, what you please, you may: I am your martyr.

CORVINO
Be not thus obstinate, I ha' not deserved it.

---

84   *Applying fire to a stone* A proverb for futility (Tilley S892), but Volpone is also
     playing slyly on 'stone' as Renaissance slang for 'testicle'.
92   *By this hand* A familiar oath, short for 'I swear by this hand', but also suggesting
     that Corvino raises his hand threateningly here.
95   *Eat burning coals* Portia, wife of Brutus and legendary for her virtue and loyalty,
     chose this method of suicide.
97   *Cry* Proclaim
99   *rotchet* a reddish fish; Jonson had been threatened with judicial nose-slitting for
     mocking Scots in *Eastward Ho!*
104 *aquafortis* nitric acid, used for etching; Corvino threatens to engrave his false accu-
     sation against Celia in her flesh with corrosives.

Think who it is entreats you. 'Pray thee, sweet:
Good faith, thou shalt have jewels, gowns, attires,   110
What thou wilt think, and ask – do but go kiss him.
Or touch him, but. For my sake. At my suit.
This once. No? Not? I shall remember this.
Will you disgrace me, thus? Do you thirst my undoing?

MOSCA
Nay, gentle lady, be advised.

CORVINO   No, no.   115
She has watched her time. God's precious, this is scurvy;
'Tis very scurvy; and you are –

MOSCA   Nay, good, sir.

CORVINO
An errant locust, by heaven, a locust. Whore,
Crocodile, that hast thy tears prepared,
Expecting how thou'lt bid 'em flow.

MOSCA   Nay, 'pray you, sir,   120
She will consider.

CELIA   Would my life would serve
To satisfy –

CORVINO   'Sdeath, if she would but speak to him,
And save my reputation, 'twere somewhat;
But, spitefully to affect my utter ruin –

MOSCA
Ay, now you've put your fortune in her hands.   125
Why, i' faith, it is her modesty, I must 'quit her:

---

111   *What thou wilt think, and ask* Anything you can imagine and ask for, or, Think of
      anything you wish for, and ask me for it
      but merely
112   *At my suit* Because I am begging you
115   *be advised* take your husband's advice, believe his warning
116   *watched her time* waited for the opportunity to do me the most damage
      God's precious I swear by God's precious blood
118   *errant* arrant, notorious; or possibly, erring, devious
      locust a Biblical plague, a pest that swallows up the harvest
119–20 *Crocodile . . . flow* Crocodiles were believed to lure their victims with false tears.
120   *Expecting* Anticipating, Plotting
121–2 *Would my life . . . satisfy* I would be happy to be killed if only that would solve the
      problem
123   *'twere somewhat* that would count for something
124   *affect* attempt
126   *'quit* acquit, excuse; or possibly, leave her in privacy

If you were absent, she would be more coming;
I know it, and dare undertake for her.
What woman can, before her husband? 'Pray you,
Let us depart, and leave her here.

CORVINO   Sweet Celia,   130
Thou mayst redeem all, yet; I'll say no more:
If not, esteem yourself as lost –

> [CELIA *tries to exit*]

Nay, stay there.

> [*Exeunt* CORVINO *and* MOSCA]

CELIA
O God, and his good angels! Whither, whither.
Is shame fled human breasts? that, with such ease,
Men dare put off your honours, and their own?   135
Is that, which ever was a cause of life,
Now placed beneath the basest circumstance?
And modesty an exile made, for money?

> *He* [VOLPONE] *leaps off from his couch*

VOLPONE
Ay, in Corvino, and such earth-fed minds,
That never tasted the true heav'n of love.   140
Assure thee, Celia, he that would sell thee,
Only for hope of gain, and that uncertain,
He would have sold his part of Paradise
For ready money, had he met a cope-man.
Why art thou mazed, to see me thus revived?   145
Rather, applaud thy beauty's miracle:
'Tis thy great work, that hath, not now alone,
But sundry times, raised me, in several shapes,
And, but this morning, like a mountebank,
To see thee at thy window. Ay, before   150

127   *coming* forthcoming, agreeable, perhaps with sexual connotations
129   *can, before* can (commit adultery) in sight of
135   *put off your honours* ignore or betray the divine principles of honour, or, dishonour
         the divine by doing so
136–7 *Is that . . . circumstance?* Is honour, which has always been considered a cause
         worth dying for, now valued less than the lowliest and most trivial advantage?
142   *and that uncertain* when the gain is not even guaranteed
144   *cope-man* suitable merchant
145   *mazed* amazed, bewildered

89

I would have left my practice for thy love,
In varying figures, I would have contended
With the blue Proteus, or the hornèd flood.
Now, art thou welcome.

CELIA   Sir!

VOLPONE   Nay, fly me not;
Nor let thy false imagination   155
That I was bed-rid, make thee think, I am so:
Thou shalt not find it. I am, now, as fresh,
As hot, as high, and in as jovial plight,
As when (in that so celebrated scene,
At recitation of our comedy,   160
For entertainment of the great Valois)
I acted young Antinous; and attracted
The eyes and ears of all the ladies present,
To admire each graceful gesture, note, and footing.

Song

Come, my Celia, let us prove,   165
While we can, the sports of love:
Time will not be ours forever,
He, at length, our good will sever;
Spend not then his gifts, in vain.
Suns that set may rise again;   170

151   *practice for* scheming to win
152   *figures* disguises, shapes
153   *blue Proteus, or the hornèd flood* Proteus was a sea-god who could change shape at
       will; the hornèd flood is the river-god Achelous who turned himself into various
       animals while battling Hercules for a woman's love.
158   *jovial plight* thriving condition, with some reference to Jove's persistent courting of
       beautiful mortal women
161   *Valois* Henry Valois, later King Henry III of France, was lavishly entertained in
       Venice in 1574.
162   *Antinous* either the manly chief suitor to Odysseus's chaste wife Penelope, or the
       boy beloved by the Emperor Hadrian; considering how often Jonson traps this
       play's characters into self-aggrandizing masculine poses that can be ironically
       reinterpreted as signs of sterility and perversion (which was evidently his view of
       homosexuality), the ambiguity may be deliberate.
164   *footing* dance step
164   s.d. *Song* Jonson based this *carpe diem* song on Catullus's Ode V, had his friend
       Antonio Ferrabosco set it to music, and later reprinted it in his poetry collection
       The Forest.
165   *prove* experience, try out
168   *our good will sever* will cut off our good times

But if, once, we lose this light,
'Tis with us perpetual night.
Why should we defer our joys?
Fame and rumour are but toys.
Cannot we delude the eyes   175
Of a few poor household-spies?
Or his easier ears beguile,
Thus removèd by our wile?
'Tis no sin, love's fruits to steal,
But the sweet thefts to reveal;   180
To be taken, to be seen,
These have crimes accounted been.

CELIA

Some serene blast me, or dire lightning strike
This my offending face.
VOLPONE   Why droops my Celia?
Thou hast, in place of a base husband, found   185
A worthy lover: use thy fortune well,
With secrecy, and pleasure. See, behold, [*Shows the treasure*]
What thou art queen of; not in expectation,
As I feed others, but possessed, and crowned.
See, here, a rope of pearl; and each more orient   190
Than that the brave Egyptian queen caroused:
Dissolve, and drink 'em. See, a carbuncle,
May put out both the eyes of our St Mark;

174   *toys* silly trifles
177   *his* Corvino's
178   *Thus removèd by our wile* Since we have cleverly got him out of the room
181   *taken* caught
183   *Some serene blast me* I wish some poisonous mist would destroy me
184   *offending* Her beauty has committed an offence, she feels, in provoking this sinful
       proposal.
190   *orient* rare, fine, precious; see the note at 1.5.9.
191   *the brave Egyptian queen caroused* The glamorous Cleopatra, according to Pliny,
       was challenged by her lover Antony to spend a fortune on a meal, which she did by
       dissolving a pearl in vinegar and drinking it.
192   *carbuncle* a round red gem
193   *put out both the eyes of our St Mark* Perhaps Venice, known to possess some
       precious rubies, had a statue of its patron saint with carbuncles for the eyes.
       Volpone (possibly echoing Pietro Aretino) offers a jewel that will either put to
       shame, or bribe into looking the other way, the grand patron saint of the city. In
       any case – as when Volpone's worship of gold 'darkens' the sun in the opening
       scene – Jonson suggests monetary values eclipsing religious ones (Kernan).

A diamond, would have bought Lollia Paulina,
When she came in, like starlight, hid with jewels,   195
That were the spoils of provinces. Take these,
And wear, and lose 'em; yet remains an earring
To purchase them again, and this whole state.
A gem but worth a private patrimony
Is nothing: we will eat such at a meal.   200
The heads of parrots, tongues of nightingales,
The brains of peacocks, and of ostriches
Shall be our food; and, could we get the phoenix,
Though nature lost her kind, she were our dish.

CELIA

Good sir, these things might move a mind affected   205
With such delights; but I, whose innocence
Is all I can think wealthy, or worth th' enjoying,
And which, once lost, I have nought to lose beyond it,
Cannot be taken with these sensual baits.
If you have conscience –
VOLPONE   'Tis the beggar's virtue;   210
If thou hast wisdom, hear me, Celia.
Thy baths shall be the juice of July-flowers,
Spirit of roses, and of violets,
The milk of unicorns, and panthers' breath
Gathered in bags, and mixed with Cretan wines.   215
Our drink shall be preparèd gold, and amber;
Which we will take, until my roof whirl round
With the vertigo; and my dwarf shall dance,
My eunuch sing, my fool make up the antic.

194   *Lollia Paulina* consort of the Emperor Caligula; Pliny describes her as covered with
       jewels. Volpone neglects to mention that her opulent story, like that of Cleopatra,
       ends in suicide.
196   *spoils of provinces* greatest treasures stolen from conquered territories
197–8 *yet remains . . . whole state* there would still be left an earring that would purchase
       all the aforementioned jewellry, and all of Venice too
199   *but worth a private patrimony* worth only as much as a single person's estate
203   *phoenix* a mythical bird, supposedly reborn from its own ashes every five hundred
       years; Volpone is willing to render the species ('kind') extinct by eating it.
210   *'Tis the beggar's virtue* Conscience is good only for those so poor they can't afford
       great pleasures anyway
212   *July-flowers* gillyflowers, or clove-scented pinks, which Perdita in Shakespeare's
       Winter's Tale (4.4) mistrusts as an exotic graft
214   *panthers' breath* Panthers were supposed to lure their prey with sweet breath (as
       Volpone is luring Celia with sweet words).
219   *antic* strange dance

Whilst, we, in changèd shapes, act Ovid's tales,   220
Thou, like Europa now, and I like Jove,
Then I like Mars, and thou like Erycine,
So, of the rest, till we have quite run through
And wearied all the fables of the gods.
Then will I have thee, in more modern forms,   225
Attirèd like some sprightly dame of France,
Brave Tuscan lady, or proud Spanish beauty;
Sometimes, unto the Persian Sophy's wife;
Or the Grand Signior's Mistress; and, for change,
To one of our most artful courtesans,   230
Or some quick Negro, or cold Russian;
And I will meet thee, in as many shapes,
Where we may, so, transfuse our wand'ring souls,
Out at our lips, and score up sums of pleasures,

[*Sings*] That the curious shall not know,   235
      How to tell them, as they flow;
      And the envious, when they find
      What their number is, be pined.

CELIA

If you have ears, that will be pierced – or eyes,

---

220   *Ovid's tales* Ovid's *Metamorphoses* recounts many transformations and seductions, such as Zeus disguising himself as a bull to capture Europa; Jonson mocks the male appetite for such pornographic role-playing in several of his works.

222   *Erycine* Venus

228   *Persian Sophy* Shah of Iran

229   *Grand Signior* Sultan of Turkey

231   *quick* lively, hot-blooded

233   *transfuse* cause to flow from one to another (OED); this exotic but finally pathetic wandering through many identities recalls the degrading transmigration of Pythagoras's soul in 1.2.1–62.

236   *tell* count

238   *pined* pained, caused to pine away with envy

239–59 Q's punctuation of Celia's speech with dashes suggests breathless panic, or struggles to escape Volpone's embraces or his bedchamber; F provides grammatically and logically accurate punctuation instead. This edition, trusting the theatrical wisdom of Jonson in 1606 and recognizing that the 1616 version may reflect Jonson's effort to impose a consistent form on the page rather than a rethinking of Celia's demeanour on the stage here, preserves Q's dashes. Still, it is worth acknowledging a feminist argument for the F version, which would create a much stronger Celia – less a wide-eyed damsel in distress than a well-spoken, cool-headed defender of her chastity, appealing eloquently to what little is left of Volpone's reason and (though this immediately backfires) to his manly pride.

That can be opened – a heart, may be touched –   240
Or any part, that yet sounds man, about you –
If you have touch of holy saints – or Heaven –
Do me the grace, to let me 'scape – if not,
Be bountiful, and kill me – you do know,
I am a creature, hither ill betrayed,   245
By one whose shame I would forget it were –
If you will deign me neither of these graces,
Yet feed your wrath, sir, rather than your lust –
It is a vice, comes nearer manliness –
And punish that unhappy crime of nature,   250
Which you miscall my beauty – flay my face,
Or poison it, with ointments, for seducing
Your blood to this rebellion – rub these hands,
With what may cause an eating leprosy,
E'en to my bones and marrow – anything,   255
That may disfavour me, save in my honour –
And I will kneel to you, pray for you, pay down
A thousand hourly vows, sir, for your health –
Report, and think you virtuous –

VOLPONE   Think me cold,
Frozen, and impotent, and so report me?   260
That I had Nestor's hernia, thou wouldst think.
I do degenerate, and abuse my nation,
To play with opportunity thus long:
I should have done the act, and then have parleyed.
Yield, or I'll force thee.

CELIA   O, just God!

VOLPONE   In vain –   265

> He [BONARIO] *leaps out from where Mosca had*
> *placed him*

BONARIO

Forbear, foul ravisher, libidinous swine!
Free the forced lady, or thou diest, impostor.
But that I am loath to snatch thy punishment

---

241   *yet sounds man* still retains some echo of manly honour or humane mercy
256   *disfavour* disfigure, destroy whatever makes me sexually appealing
261   *Nestor's hernia* impotence; Nestor was the aged Greek commander in Homer's *Iliad* (cf. Juvenal's *Satires* VI, 326).
262   *abuse my nation* dishonour the reputation of Italians for ferocious virility

Out of the hand of justice, thou shouldst yet
Be made the timely sacrifice of vengeance,   270
Before this altar, and this dross [*Gesturing toward the gold*,] thy
    idol.
Lady, let's quit the place: it is the den
Of villainy. Fear nought, you have a guard;
And he, ere long, shall meet his just reward.

VOLPONE

Fall on me, roof, and bury me in ruin,   275
Become my grave, that wert my shelter. O!
I am unmasked, unspirited, undone,
Betrayed to beggary, to infamy –

ACT 3, SCENE 8

[*Enter*] MOSCA, [*bleeding*]

MOSCA

Where shall I run, most wretched shame of men,
To beat out my unlucky brains?

VOLPONE   Here, here.
What! dost thou bleed?

MOSCA   O, that his well-driven sword
Had been so courteous to have cleft me down
Unto the navel, ere I lived to see   5
My life, my hopes, my spirits, my patron, all
Thus desperately engagèd, by my error.

VOLPONE

Woe on thy fortune.

MOSCA   And my follies, sir.

VOLPONE

Th' hast made me miserable.

MOSCA   And myself, sir.
Who would have thought he would have hearkened so?   10

---

271   *dross* a dismissive term for Volpone's gold
274   *he* presumably Volpone; but the situation conventionally suggests (though this
      play stubbornly refuses to fulfil the expectation) that Bonario should be rewarded
      with the hand of the young woman he has saved.
7   *engagèd* entrapped, entangled, or thrown into debt
10   *he would have hearkened* Bonario would have eavesdropped

VOLPONE
What shall we do?

MOSCA   I know not; if my heart
Could expiate the mischance, I'd pluck it out.
Will you be pleased to hang me? Or cut my throat?
And I'll requite you, sir. Let's die like Romans,
Since we have lived like Grecians.

They knock without

VOLPONE   Hark, who's there?   15
I hear some footing: officers, the *Saffi*,
Come to apprehend us! I do feel the brand
Hissing, already, at my forehead; now,
Mine ears are boring.

MOSCA   To your couch, sir; you
Make that place good, however, [VOLPONE] *gets into bed*
                    Guilty men   20
Suspect what they deserve still. [*Opens the door*] Signior Corbaccio!

ACT 3, SCENE 9

[*Enter*] CORBACCIO; VOLTORE [*enters unnoticed
behind him*]

CORBACCIO
Why, how now, Mosca?

MOSCA   O, undone, amazed, sir.
Your son (I know not by what accident)
Acquainted with your purpose to my patron,

---

14   *requite you* repay you in kind
      Romans Ancient Rome had a Stoic tradition of answering adversity and preserving
      honour by suicide.
15   *like Grecians* craftily, and (above all) for high pleasures
16   *Saffi* bailiffs assigned to make arrests
17–19 *brand ... boring* permanently disfiguring punishments with hot or sharp metal;
      Jonson himself had been branded on the thumb for killing a fellow-actor.
20   *Make that place good, however* Try to resume playing the dying man convincingly,
      in whatever way you can, or whatever happens
21   *Suspect what they deserve still* Always expect, with dread, their due punishment
1   *undone, amazed* ruined, bewildered
3–4   *your purpose ... will* your intention toward Volpone, regarding your last will and
      testament

Touching your will, and making him your heir,
Entered our house with violence, his sword drawn,   5
Sought for you, called you wretch, unnatural,
Vowed he would kill you.
CORBACCIO   Me?
MOSCA   Yes, and my patron.
CORBACCIO
This act shall disinherit him indeed:
Here is the will.
MOSCA   'Tis well, sir.
CORBACCIO   Right, and well.
Be you as careful, now, for me.
MOSCA   My life, sir,   10
Is not more tendered; I am only yours.
CORBACCIO
How does he? Will he die shortly, think'st thou?
MOSCA   I fear
He'll outlast May.
CORBACCIO   Today?
MOSCA   No, last out May, sir.
CORBACCIO
Couldst thou not gi' him a dram?
MOSCA   O, by no means, sir.
CORBACCIO
Nay, I'll not bid you.
VOLTORE   This is a knave, I see.   15
MOSCA
[*Aside*] How, Signior Voltore! Did he hear me?
VOLTORE   Parasite!
MOSCA
Who's that? O, sir, most timely welcome –
VOLTORE   Scarce,
To the discovery of your tricks, I fear.
You are his, only? and mine, also? are you not?
MOSCA
Who? I, sir?
VOLTORE   You, sir. What device is this   20

11   *tendered* tenderly cared for
14   *dram* drug, presumably a fatal overdose or poison
15   *This* Mosca
17   *Scarce* Hardly welcome, or, Just in time

97

About a will?

MOSCA   A plot for you, sir.

VOLTORE   Come,
  Put not your foists upon me, I shall scent 'em.

MOSCA
  Did you not hear it?

VOLTORE   Yes, I hear, Corbaccio
  Hath made your patron, there, his heir.

MOSCA   'Tis true;
  By my device, drawn to it by my plot,   25
  With hope –

VOLTORE   Your patron should reciprocate?
  And you have promised?

MOSCA   For your good, I did, sir.
  Nay, more, I told his son, brought, hid him here,
  Where he might hear his father pass the deed;
  Being persuaded to it by this thought, sir: 30
  That the unnaturalness, first, of the act,
  And then, his father's oft disclaiming in him,
  Which I did mean t' help on, would sure enrage him
  To do some violence upon his parent,
  On which the law should take sufficient hold,   35
  And you be stated in a double hope.
  Truth be my comfort, and my conscience,
  My only aim was, to dig you a fortune
  Out of these two, old, rotten sepulchres –

VOLTORE
  I cry thee mercy, Mosca.

MOSCA   Worth your patience,   40
  And your great merit, sir. And, see the change!

VOLTORE
  Why? what success?

MOSCA   Most hapless! You must help, sir.

---

22   *foists* tricks, but with a secondary meaning of 'odours of decay', which a vulture
     would be attuned to notice
32   *oft disclaiming in him* repeatedly disowning him
35   *sufficient hold* severe enough penalty to make Bonario ineligible for Corbaccio's
     inheritance
36   *stated in a double hope* instated with both inheritances
40   *cry thee mercy* beg your pardon
42   *what success?* how successful was this?
     hapless unlucky

Whilst we expected th' old raven, in comes
Corvino's wife, sent hither by her husband –

VOLTORE
What, with a present?

MOSCA   No, sir, on visitation   45
(I'll tell you how, anon); and, staying long,
The youth, he grows impatient, rushes forth,
Seizeth the lady, wounds me, makes her swear –
Or he would murder her, that was his vow –
T' affirm my patron would have done her rape –   50
Which how unlike it is, you see! – and, hence,
With that pretext, he's gone t' accuse his father;
Defame my patron; defeat you –

VOLTORE   Where's her husband?
Let him be sent for, straight.

MOSCA   Sir, I'll go fetch him.

VOLTORE
Bring him to the *Scrutineo*.

MOSCA   Sir, I will.   55

VOLTORE
This must be stopped.

MOSCA   O, you do nobly, sir.
Alas, 'twas laboured all, sir, for your good;
Nor was there want of counsel in the plot;
But fortune can, at any time, o'erthrow
The projects of a hundred learned clerks, sir.   60

CORBACCIO
What's that?

VOLTORE   Will't please you, sir, to go along?
                    [*Exeunt* VOLTORE *and* CORBACCIO]

MOSCA
Patron, go in, and pray for our success.

VOLPONE
Need makes devotion: heaven your labour bless.

                                        [*Exeunt*]

---

55 *Scrutineo* The law court in the Venetian Senate House
58 *want of counsel* lack of deliberation
60 *clerks* learnèd men

ACT 4, SCENE 1

[*Enter*] POLITIC, PEREGRINE

SIR POLITIC

I told you, sir, it was a plot: you see
What observation is. You mentioned me
For some instructions: I will tell you, sir,
Since we are met, here, in this height of Venice,
Some few particulars I have set down   5
Only for this meridian, fit to be known
Of your crude traveller; and they are these.
I will not touch, sir, at your phrase, or clothes,
For they are old.

PEREGRINE   Sir, I have better.

SIR POLITIC   Pardon,
I meant, as they are themes.

PEREGRINE   O, sir, proceed: 10
I'll slander you no more of wit, good sir.

SIR POLITIC

First, for your garb, it must be grave, and serious;
Very reserved, and locked; not tell a secret,
On any terms, not to your father; scarce
A fable, but with caution; make sure choice   15
Both of your company, and discourse; beware
You never speak a truth –

PEREGRINE   How!

SIR POLITIC   Not to strangers,

1–2   *I told you . . . what observation is* You see how observant I was to suspect (at
      2.3.10–12) that the mountebank scene was all a plot to entrap me

2   *mentioned* asked

4   *height of Venice* Cf. 2.1.12 and the explanatory note there.

7   *crude* raw (implying inexperience and also, perhaps, vulgarity)

8   *touch, sir, at your phrase* make mention, sir, of your style of speech; but Peregrine
      mischievously pretends to mistake the sense of 'touch' as well as the referent of 'old'
      here.

11   *slander you no more of wit* never again mistakenly think you capable of a witty
      insult

12   *garb* bearing, demeanour; like Polonius's advice to Laertes in *Hamlet*, Sir Pol's
      advice emphasizes shallow social tactics rather than deep moral sense.

14   *not* not even

14–15 *scarce . . . caution* hardly even risk telling a fictional story without caution

For those be they you must converse with most;
Others I would not know, sir, but, at distance,
So as I still might be a saver in 'em: 20
You shall have tricks, else, passed upon you, hourly.
And then, for your religion, profess none;
But wonder, at the diversity of all;
And, for your part, protest, were there no other
But simply the laws o' th' land, you could content you: 25
Nick Machiavel and Monsieur Bodin, both,
Were of this mind. Then, must you learn the use,
And handling of your silver fork, at meals;
The metal of your glass – these are main matters,
With your Italian – and to know the hour,   30
When you must eat your melons, and your figs.

PEREGRINE
   Is that a point of state, too?

SIR POLITIC   Here it is.
   For your Venetian, if he see a man
Preposterous in the least, he has him straight;
He has: he strips him. I'll acquaint you, sir,   35
I now have lived here, 'tis some fourteen months;
Within the first week of my landing here,
All took me for a citizen of Venice;
I knew the forms so well –

PEREGRINE   [*Aside*] And nothing else.

SIR POLITIC
   I had read Contarine, took me a house,   40

---

19   *Others* presumably, other travellers from your own country
20   *be a saver in 'em* be safer around them (by being an acquaintance) or save time and
     money (by not becoming close enough to be asked for favours or loans)
26   *Nick Machiavel and Monsieur Bodin* Sir Pol has a characteristically fashionable
     misunderstanding of Niccolo Machiavelli (whose book arguably advocated
     putting political considerations ahead of religious ones) and Jean Bodin (who
     argued for religious toleration, a cause that might have appealed to Jonson, himself
     a convert to the banned Catholicism).
28   *fork* Forks were still uncommon silverware in Jacobean England.
29   *metal* material
34   *Preposterous* Not doing things in the proper order (literally, putting afterwards
     what should come before)
     has him straight instantly sees through his pretences and takes advantage of him
35   *strips him* exposes him to ridicule
40   *Contarine* Cardinal Gasparo Contarini's book on Venice was translated into
     English in 1599.

Dealt with my Jews, to furnish it with movables –
Well, if I could but find one man – one man,
To mine own heart, whom I durst trust – I would –

PEREGRINE

What? What, sir?

SIR POLITIC   Make him rich; make him a fortune:
He should not think again. I would command it.   45

PEREGRINE

As how?

SIR POLITIC   With certain projects, that I have;
Which, I may not discover.

PEREGRINE   [*Aside*] If I had
But one to wager with, I would lay odds, now,
He tells me, instantly.

SIR POLITIC   One is – and that
I care not greatly who knows – to serve the state   50
Of Venice with red herrings, for three years,
And at a certain rate, from Rotterdam,
Where I have correspondence. There's a letter,
Sent me from one o' th' States, and to that purpose;

                        [*Shows a letter*]

He cannot write his name, but that's his mark.   55

PEREGRINE

He is a chandler?

SIR POLITIC   No, a cheesemonger.
There are some other too, with whom I treat

---

41   *Jews* Venice supported a Jewish community to handle the money-lending business which was forbidden to Christians but necessary for their capitalist economy; cf. Shakespeare's misrepresentation of this relationship in *The Merchant of Venice*. *movables* furniture other than fixtures

46   *projects* In this period, the word connotes highly speculative schemes; Jonson mocks such ingenious 'projectors' again in *The Devil is an Ass*.

47   *may not discover* must not reveal

51   *red herrings* a basic cheap food in England, but considered a dainty in Venice; the modern meaning of strategic diversion or delusion was not yet common, but seems relevant, especially in parallel with the same three-year period Volpone has been misleading the legacy-hunters (Parker).

54   *th' States* Holland

56   *chandler* candle-maker or retailer of provisions; Peregrine may be joking about the messiness of the paper or the size of the wax seal
cheesemonger Sir Pol has settled on an illiterate cheese-seller as his source for correspondence and herrings; a further joke lies in the standard English mockery of the Dutch fondness for butter and cheese.

About the same negotiation;
And I will undertake it. For, 'tis thus,
I'll do't with ease, I've cast it all: your hoy   60
Carries but three men in her, and a boy;
And she shall make me three returns, a year;
So, if there come but one of three, I save,
If two, I can defalk. But this is now
If my main project fail.
PEREGRINE   Then, you have others?   65
SIR POLITIC
I should be loath to draw the subtle air
Of such a place without my thousand aims.
I'll not dissemble, sir: where'er I come,
I love to be considerative; and, 'tis true,
I have, at my free hours, thought upon   70
Some certain goods unto the state of Venice,
Which I do call my cautions; and, sir, which
I mean (in hope of pension) to propound
To the Great Council, then unto the Forty,
So to the Ten. My means are made already –   75
PEREGRINE
By whom?
SIR POLITIC   Sir, one, that though his place be obscure,
Yet, he can sway, and they will hear him. He's
A *commandatore*.
PEREGRINE   What, a common sergeant?
SIR POLITIC
Sir, such as they are, put it in their mouths,

60   *cast* calculated
       hoy small boat for coastal transportation; probably not adequate for safe voyaging
       between Venice and Rotterdam
63–4   *if there come ... defalk* The sense of this seems to be that Sir Pol can afford to have
       only one of his three shiploads arrive safely, and that if two arrive he can reduce his
       debt, or maybe his price; but Jonson may not intend Sir Pol's plans to make perfect
       sense.
64   *now* only
66   *draw the subtle air* breathe the atmosphere of intrigue
71   *goods* benefits; Sir Pol intends to offer such valuable precautionary schemes to the
       three highest levels of the Venetian government that they will pay him a pension.
78   *commandatore* officer charged with bringing offenders to court – the disguise
       Volpone will later assume
79–80 *such as ... greater* lowly officials such as sergeants, as well as more exalted ones,
       sometimes advise these authorities what to say

What they should say, sometimes, as well as greater.   80
  I think I have my notes, to show you –
PEREGRINE   Good, sir.
SIR POLITIC
  But, you shall swear unto me, on your gentry,
  Not to anticipate –
PEREGRINE   I, sir?
SIR POLITIC   Nor reveal
  A circumstance – My paper is not with me.
PEREGRINE
  O, but, you can remember, sir.
SIR POLITIC   My first is   85
  Concerning tinderboxes. You must know,
  No family is, here, without its box.
  Now sir, it being so portable a thing,
  Put case, that you or I were ill affected
  Unto the state: sir, with it in our pockets,   90
  Might not I go into the Arsenale?
  Or you? Come out again? And none the wiser?
PEREGRINE
  Except yourself, sir.
SIR POLITIC   Go to, then. I, therefore,
  Advertise to the state how fit it were
  That none, but such as were known patriots,   95
  Sound lovers of their country, should be suffered
  T' enjoy them in their houses; and even those,
  Sealed, at some office, and at such a bigness,
  As might not lurk in pockets.
PEREGRINE   Admirable!
SIR POLITIC
  My next is, how t' enquire, and be resolved   100

82–3   *swear unto . . . anticipate* swear, on your good name, not to use my ideas before I do
89   *Put case, that* What if, suppose hypothetically
91   *Arsenale* the place Venice kept its ships and weapons, where a spark from a tinderbox could have devastating effects; it had exploded and burnt in 1568–9, and a Jacobean audience might again have been reminded of the 1605 Gunpowder Plot. Jonson was dangerously close to being implicated in that notorious Catholic attempt to kill King James and Parliament in a massive explosion.
93   *Go to* standard Jacobean equivalent of the colloquial modern 'All right'
96   *suffered* allowed; Sir Pol's scheme would make it impossible for most Venetians to maintain the fires they need for cooking and heating.
98   *Sealed* Licensed, perhaps sealed shut

By present demonstration, whether a ship,
Newly arrived from *Sorìa*, or from
Any suspected part of all the Levant,
Be guilty of the plague: and, where they use
To lie out forty, fifty days, sometimes,   105
About the Lazaretto, for their trial,
I'll save that charge and loss unto the merchant,
And, in an hour, clear the doubt.
PEREGRINE   Indeed, sir?
SIR POLITIC
Or – I will lose my labour.
PEREGRINE   My faith, that's much.
SIR POLITIC
Nay, sir, conceive me. 'Twill cost me, in onions,   110
Some thirty *livres* –
PEREGRINE   Which is one pound sterling.
SIR POLITIC
Beside my waterworks. For this I do, sir:
First, I bring in your ship, 'twixt two brick walls
(But those the state shall venture); on the one
I strain me a fair tarpaulin; and, in that,   115
I stick my onions, cut in halves; the other
Is full of loopholes, out at which, I thrust
The noses of my bellows; and those bellows
I keep, with waterworks, in perpetual motion
(Which is the easiest matter of a hundred).   120
Now, sir, your onion, which doth naturally
Attract th' infection, and your bellows, blowing
The air upon him, will show, instantly,
By his changed colour, if there be contagion;

---

101   *present* immediate
102   *Sorìa* Sir Pol suavely employs the Italian name for Syria.
106   *About the Lazaretto* Near Venice's quarantine areas for those suspected of bubonic
        plague or leprosy; as a world port, Venice had various schemes to prevent importa-
        tion of disease, including lengthy quarantines and purifying incoming goods with
        vinegar.
109   *that's much* Peregrine is unimpressed, to the point of sarcasm, with the 'labour'
        that much have gone into Pol's scheme.
111   *livres* French coins
114   *venture* invest in
115   *strain* stretch

Or else, remain as fair as at the first. 125
Now 'tis known, 'tis nothing.

PEREGRINE   You are right, sir.

SIR POLITIC
I would I had my note.

PEREGRINE   Faith, so would I;
But, you ha' done well, for once, sir.

SIR POLITIC   Were I false,
Or would be made so, I could show you reasons,
How I could sell this state, now, to the Turk; 130
Spite of their galleys, or their –

PEREGRINE   'Pray you, Sir Pol.

SIR POLITIC
I have 'em not, about me.

PEREGRINE   That I feared.
They're there, sir?

SIR POLITIC   No. This is my diary,
Wherein I note my actions of the day.

PEREGRINE
'Pray you, let's see, sir. What is here? 'Notandum, 135
A rat had gnawn my spur leathers; notwithstanding,
I put on new, and did go forth; but, first,
I threw three beans over the threshold. Item,
I went and bought two toothpicks, whereof one
I burst, immediately, in a discourse 140
With a Dutch merchant, 'bout ragion' del stato.
From him, I went and paid a moccenigo,
For piecing my silk stockings; by the way,

125 Now 'tis known ... right, sir With false humility, Pol acknowledges that the idea
      may seem obvious once it has been explained; but Peregrine exploits Pol's wording
      to suggest (with characteristic suave irony) that the idea is worthless rather than
      obvious.
128 false treacherous
131 'Pray you Probably, a version of 'Please', either asking Pol to finish his sentence, or
      asking him to show his papers, or asking him to forget about his papers: throughout
      the scene Jonson suggests stage-business in which Pol fumbles with miscellaneous
      documents.
133 diary Travellers in this period were notorious for keeping diaries filled with self-
      serious trivia.
138 threw three beans a superstition (drawn from Theophrastus)
141 ragion' del stato reasons of state, politics
142 moccenigo small coin
143 piecing mending, piecing together

I cheapened sprats; and at St Mark's, I urined'.
Faith, these are politic notes!

SIR POLITIC   Sir, I do slip   145
No action of my life, thus, but I quote it.

PEREGRINE
Believe me, it is wise!

SIR POLITIC   Nay, sir, read forth.

ACT 4, SCENE 2

[*Enter*] LADY WOULD-BE, NANO, SERVING-WOMEN

LADY WOULD-BE
Where should this loose knight be, trow? Sure he's housed.

NANO
Why, then he's fast.

LADY WOULD-BE   Ay, he plays both with me.
I pray you, stay. This heat will do more harm
To my complexion than his heart is worth.
I do not care to hinder, but to take him.   5
[*Rubbing her cheeks*] How it comes off!

1st WOMAN   My master's yonder.

LADY WOULD-BE   Where?

1st WOMAN
With a young gentleman.

LADY WOULD-BE   That same's the party,
In man's apparel! 'Pray you, sir, jog my knight.
I will be tender to his reputation,

---

144   *cheapened sprats* bargained for herring
145   *slip* allow to pass
  1   *loose* promiscuous, wandering
      trow? do you think?
      housed hidden away, presumably in a house of prostitution, maybe in the prosti-
      tute herself
  2   *fast* caught, with a pun on the game of fast-and-loose, referred to at 1.2.8
  5   *take him* catch him in the act
  6   *How it comes off* Perspiration is making Lady Would-Be's heavy make-up run.
  8   *man's apparel* Lady Would-Be's error here is partly explained by a tradition of
      Venetian courtesans dressing as men.
      jog nudge (to get his attention)

However he demerit.

SIR POLITIC   My lady!

PEREGRINE   Where?   10

SIR POLITIC

'Tis she indeed, sir, you shall know her. She is,
Were she not mine, a lady of that merit,
For fashion, and behaviour; and, for beauty
I durst compare –

PEREGRINE   It seems you are not jealous,
That dare commend her.

SIR POLITIC   Nay, and for discourse –   15

PEREGRINE

Being your wife, she cannot miss that.

SIR POLITIC [*Approaching* LADY WOULD-BE *to introduce*
PEREGRINE] Madam,
Here is a gentleman, 'pray you, use him fairly,
He seems a youth, but he is –

LADY WOULD-BE   None?

SIR POLITIC   Yes, one
Has put his face, as soon, into the world –

LADY WOULD-BE

You mean, as early? But today?

SIR POLITIC   How's this?   20

LADY WOULD-BE

Why, in this habit, sir: you apprehend me.
Well, Master Would-Be, this doth not become you.
I had thought, the odour, sir, of your good name
Had been more precious to you; that you would not
Have done this dire massàcre on your honour –   25
One of your gravity, and rank, besides –
But, knights, I see, care little for the oath
They make to ladies; chiefly their own ladies.

SIR POLITIC

Now, by my spurs, the symbol of my knighthood –

PEREGRINE

[*Aside*] Lord, how his brain is humbled for an oath! 30

---

10   *However he demerit* Even though, or even if, he doesn't deserve it
21   *habit* clothing; Lady Would-Be is sardonically suggesting that Peregrine is new in the
     world because the supposed courtesan had only newly assumed this male 'disguise'
26   *gravity* seriousness
30   *humbled* brought low – down to the level of his spurs, which seem to be an impor-
     tant item to Sir Pol, and probably notable in his costume

SIR POLITIC
    I reach you not.
LADY WOULD-BE   Right, sir, your polity
    May bear it through thus. [*To* PEREGRINE] Sir, a word with you.
    I would be loath, to contest, publicly,
    With any gentlewoman or to seem
    Froward, or violent: as *The Courtier* says,   35
    It comes too near rusticity, in a lady,
    Which I would shun, by all means; and, however
    I may deserve from Master Would-Be, yet,
    To have one fair gentlewoman, thus, be made
    The unkind instrument to wrong another,   40
    And one she knows not; ay, and to persèver;
    In my poor judgement, is not warranted
    From being a solecism in our sex,
    If not in manners.
PEREGRINE   How is this?
SIR POLITIC   Sweet madam,
    Come nearer to your aim.
LADY WOULD-BE   Marry, and will, sir.   45
    Since you provoke me, with your impudence,
    And laughter of your light land-siren, here,
    Your Sporus, your hermaphrodite –
PEREGRINE   What's here?
    Poetic fury, and historic storms?

---

31   *reach* understand
31–2   *your polity / May bear it through* sustaining your clever bluff may spare you having
        to confess your adultery. The *Sir* may be sarcastic.
35   *Froward* Ill-humoured, unreasonable
        The Courtier Castiglione's famous sixteenth-century courtesy manual
36   *rusticity* crude country-bumpkin conduct
41   *persèver* persist (in denying involvement?); accented on second syllable
42   *warranted* exempted
43   *solecism* breach of propriety (usually in grammar)
44   *Come nearer to your aim* Explain more clearly what you mean by all this
47   *light land-siren* immoral temptress
48   *Sporus* a young man whom the emperor Nero, finding him attractive, had
        castrated, and dressed as a woman; this recalls Volpone's attachment to Androgyno
        and Castrone.
49   *Poetic fury* Peregrine plays off Plato's term for poetic inspiration (in the *Ion*
        dialogue).
        historic Now Peregrine balances 'poetic' with the historical Sporus reference, and
        perhaps plays off 'hysterical' and 'histrionic'.

SIR POLITIC
The gentleman, believe it, is of worth,   50
And of our nation.

LADY WOULD-BE   Ay, your Whitefriars nation!
Come, I blush for you, Master Would-Be, I;
And am ashamed you should ha' no more forehead
Than thus to be the patron or St George
To a lewd harlot, a base fricatrice,   55
A female devil, in a male outside.

SIR POLITIC   Nay,
And you be such a one, I must bid adieu
To your delights! The case appears too liquid.   [*Exit*]

LADY WOULD-BE
Ay, you may carry't clear, with your state-face!
But, for your carnival concupiscence,   60
Who here is fled for liberty of conscience,
From furious persecution of the marshal,
Her will I disc'ple.

PEREGRINE   This is fine, i' faith!
And do you use this, often? Is this part

51   *Whitefriars* a section of London (called a 'liberty') which was exempt from the
      City's jurisdiction, and therefore became a haven for criminals and prostitutes;
      Q ends this line with a question mark.
53   *forehead* sense of shame, ability to blush
54   *St George* England's patron saint was also a patron saint of Venice, and was famous
      for rescuing a princess from a dragon.
55   *fricatrice* masseuse, prostitute
57   *You* Probably Peregrine, whom Sir Pol (always looking for tricky plots) now
      suspects may actually be the courtesan his wife claims Peregrine is; some editors
      suggest Sir Pol means the indignant Lady Pol.
58   *liquid* transparent, or perhaps hard to grasp; Sir Pol may also be punning on his
      wife's sweat and tears ('case' often meant 'mask').
59   *state-face* calculated, dignified public demeanour
61   *liberty of conscience* religious freedom, for which Venice was famous, here turned
      into an ironic euphemism for sexual licentiousness (playing on the previous
      reference to the Whitefriars liberty)
63   *disc'ple* discipline; in many productions, Lady Would-Be here attacks Peregrine
      physically.
64   *use this* behave this way
65   *'gainst you have occasion* to keep your wit in practice, so it will be ready when really
      needed; or possibly, whenever you have an opportunity

Of your wit's exercise, 'gainst you have occasion?   65
Madam –

LADY WOULD-BE   Go to, sir.

PEREGRINE   Do you hear me, lady?
Why, if your knight have set you to beg shirts,
Or to invite me home, you might have done it
A nearer way, by far.

LADY WOULD-BE   This cannot work you
Out of my snare.

PEREGRINE   Why, am I in it, then?   70
Indeed, your husband told me you were fair,
And so you are; only, your nose inclines
(That side, that's next the sun) to the queen-apple.

LADY WOULD-BE

This cannot be endured, by any patience.

ACT 4, SCENE 3

[Enter] MOSCA

MOSCA

What's the matter, madam?

LADY WOULD-BE   If the Senate
Right not my quest in this, I will protest 'em,
To all the world, no aristocracy.

MOSCA

What is the injury, lady?

---

67 *beg shirts* Lady Would-Be may be tugging at Peregrine's shirt here (trying to expose
a courtesan's breasts?), or Peregrine may be referring to a common cover story for
sexual solicitation.

69 *nearer* more direct

73 *queen-apple* large red fruit; Peregrine plays off the common idealization of
'fair' (pale) complexion, which Lady Would-Be's heavy make-up has failed to
sustain.

2   *Right not . . . protest 'em* Does not enforce my complaint against this courtesan, I
will proclaim that they are; Machiavelli argued that the leading Venetians were not
truly aristocrats, since they were merchants.

LADY WOULD-BE   Why, the callet
  You told me of, here I have ta'en disguised.   5
MOSCA
  Who? This? What means your ladyship? The creature
  I mentioned to you is apprehended, now,
  Before the Senate, you shall see her –
LADY WOULD-BE   Where?
MOSCA
  I'll bring you to her. This young gentleman,
  I saw him land, this morning, at the port.   10
LADY WOULD-BE
  Is't possible? How has my judgement wandered!
  Sir, I must, blushing, say to you, I have erred;
  And plead your pardon.
PEREGRINE   What, more changes, yet?
LADY WOULD-BE
  I hope y' ha' not the malice to remember
  A gentlewoman's passion. If you stay   15
  In Venice here, please you to use me, sir –
MOSCA
  Will you go, madam?
LADY WOULD-BE   'Pray you, sir, use me. In faith,
  The more you use me the more I shall conceive
  You have forgot our quarrel.
    [*Exeunt* LADY WOULD-BE, SERVING-WOMEN, MOSCA, NANO]
PEREGRINE   This is rare!
  Sir Politic Would-Be? No, Sir Politic Bawd!   20
  To bring me, thus, acquainted with his wife!
  Well, wise Sir Pol: since you have practised, thus,
  Upon my freshmanship, I will try your salt-head,
  What proof it is against a counter-plot.   [*Exit*]

    4   *callet* prostitute
  16 *use me* let me be helpful, find me useful; but the common sense of sexual use
       comes through strongly, especially in conjunction with 'conceive' in the next
       line.
  21 *acquainted* Since Peregrine suspects Sir Pol of being a wittol who abets his wife's
       adulteries, there may be a pun here on 'quaint', Jacobean slang for a woman's
       genitalia.
  22–4 *practised . . . proof it is* plotted thus to take advantage of my inexperience here, I'll
       test how well your more seasoned mind can defend you

ACT 4, SCENE 4

[*Enter*] VOLTORE, CORBACCIO, CORVINO, MOSCA

VOLTORE
   Well, now you know the carriage of the business,
   Your constancy is all that is required
   Unto the safety of it.

MOSCA   Is the lie
   Safely conveyed amongst us? Is that sure?
   Knows every man his burden?

CORVINO   Yes.

MOSCA   Then, shrink not.   5

CORVINO
   [*Taking* MOSCA *aside*] But, knows the advocate the truth?

MOSCA   O, sir,
   By no means. I devised a formal tale,
   That salved your reputation. But, be valiant, sir.

CORVINO
   I fear no one but him: that this his pleading
   Should make him stand for a co-heir –

MOSCA   Co-halter.   10
   Hang him: we will but use his tongue, his noise,
   As we do Croaker's here.

CORVINO   Ay, what shall he do?

MOSCA
   When we have done, you mean?

CORVINO   Yes.

MOSCA   Why, we'll think:
   Sell him for mummia, he's half dust already.
   (*To* VOLTORE) Do not you smile, to see this buffalo,   15
   How he does sport it with his head? [*To himself*] I should

---

1   *the carriage* the management, how to carry it off
5   *burden* the refrain of a song; hence, his part in the group performance
7   *formal tale* elaborate fiction (to conceal Corvino's attempt to prostitute his wife – a thematic connection to the Would-Be scene that just ended)
12   *Croaker* Corbaccio, whose voice may have been crow-like
14   *mummia* a supposedly medicinal substance derived from preserved corpses
15   *buffalo* Mosca is now confiding in Voltore instead, joking about the cuckold's horns Corvino has earned.

If all were well, and past. (*To* CORBACCIO) Sir, only you
Are he that shall enjoy the crop of all,
And these not know for whom they toil.
CORBACCIO   Ay, peace.
MOSCA
(*To* CORVINO) But you shall eat it. [*To himself*] Much! (*To*
VOLTORE) Worshipful sir,   20
Mercury sit upon your thund'ring tongue,
Or the French Hercules, and make your language
As conquering as his club, to beat along,
As with a tempest, flat, our adversaries;
But, much more, yours, sir.
VOLTORE   Here they come, ha' done.   25
MOSCA
I have another witness, if you need, sir,
I can produce.
VOLTORE   Who is it?
MOSCA   Sir, I have her.

ACT 4, SCENE 5

[*Enter*] *four* AVOCATORI, BONARIO, CELIA, NOTARIO,
COMMANDATORI

1st AVOCATORE
The like of this the Senate never heard of.
2nd AVOCATORE
'Twill come most strange to them, when we report it.

---

20   *Much!* Probably an ironic exclamation, like the sarcastic, modern 'Yeah, right, like
      that will ever happen'; Mosca may be speaking to Voltore to assure him that the
      previous assurances to Corvino and Corbaccio were merely ploys. Mosca's
      handling of these three rival suitors in the same room at the same time is a bravura
      juggling act.
21   *Mercury* the god of eloquence, but also associated with thievery
22   *French Hercules* Late in life Hercules was believed to have fathered the Celts in
      Gaul, and to have compensated for his lost physical strength with oratorical
      powers.
25   *yours* your adversaries
      ha' done stop, be quiet
27   *her* Lady Would-Be

4th AVOCATORE
  The gentlewoman has been ever held
  Of unreprovèd name.
3rd AVOCATORE   So has the youth.
4th AVOCATORE
  The more unnatural part that of his father.   5
2nd AVOCATORE
  More of the husband.
1st AVOCATORE   I not know to give
  His act a name, it is so monstrous!
4th AVOCATORE
  But the impostor, he is a thing created
  T' exceed example!
1st AVOCATORE   And all after-times!
2nd AVOCATORE
  I never heard a true voluptuary   10
  Described but him.
3rd AVOCATORE   Appear yet those were cited?
NOTARIO
  All but the old *magnifico*, Volpone.
1st AVOCATORE
  Why is not he here?
MOSCA   Please your fatherhoods,
  Here is his advocate. Himself's so weak,
  So feeble –
4th AVOCATORE What are you?
BONARIO   His parasite,   15
  His knave, his pander! I beseech the court
  He may be forced to come, that your grave eyes
  May bear strong witness of his strange impostures.
VOLTORE
  Upon my faith, and credit with your virtues,
  He is not able to endure the air.   20

---

  3   *the gentlewoman* Celia
  9   *example* precedent
  11 *cited* subpoenaed, summoned
  12 *magnifico* nobleman
  13 *fatherhoods* As Kernan points out, this is not only a technically correct form of
      address, but also a rhetorically advantageous one, since it inclines the judges to side
      with the father Corbaccio.

2nd AVOCATORE
    Bring him, however.
3rd AVOCATORE   We will see him.
4th AVOCATORE   Fetch him.
                            [*Exit* COMMANDATORE]

VOLTORE
    Your fatherhoods' fit pleasures be obeyed,
    But sure, the sight will rather move your pities,
    Than indignation. May it please the court,
    In the meantime, he may be heard in me;   25
    I know this place most void of prejudice,
    And therefore crave it, since we have no reason
    To fear our truth should hurt our cause.
3rd AVOCATORE   Speak free.
VOLTORE
    Then know, most honoured fathers, I must now
    Discover, to your strangely abused ears,   30
    The most prodigious, and most frontless piece
    Of solid impudence, and treachery,
    That ever vicious nature yet brought forth
    To shame the state of Venice. This lewd woman, [*Pointing to*
        CELIA]
    That wants no artificial looks, or tears,   35
    To help the visor, she has now put on,
    Hath long been known a close adulteress,
    To that lascivious youth there [*Pointing to* BONARIO]; not
        suspected,
    I say, but known; and taken, in the act;
    With him; and by this man [*Pointing to* CORVINO], the easy   40
        husband,
    Pardoned; whose timeless bounty makes him, now,
    Stand here, the most unhappy, innocent person
    That ever man's own virtue made accused.

31 *frontless* shameless
35 *wants* lacks
36 *visor* mask; either Celia has now modestly masked herself, or Voltore is implying
    that her appearance of anguished innocence is merely a disguise.
37 *close* secret
40 *easy* lenient, or overtrusting

For these, not knowing how to owe a gift
Of that dear grace but with their shame, being placed   45
So above all powers of their gratitude,
Began to hate the benefit; and, in place
Of thanks, devise t' extirp the memory
Of such an act. Wherein, I pray your fatherhoods,
To observe the malice, yea, the rage of creatures   50
Discovered in their evils; and what heart
Such take, even from their crimes. But that, anon,
Will more appear. This gentleman [*pointing to* CORBACCIO],
   the father,
Hearing of this foul fact, with many others,
Which daily struck at his too tender ears,   55
And, grieved in nothing more than that he could not
Preserve himself a parent (his son's ills
Growing to that strange flood), at last decreed
To disinherit him.

1st AVOCATORE   These be strange turns!

2nd AVOCATORE
   The young man's fame was ever fair and honest.   60

VOLTORE
   So much more full of danger is his vice,
That can beguile so, under shade of virtue.
But as I said, my honoured sires, his father
Having this settled purpose – by what means
To him betrayed, we know not – and this day   65
Appointed for the deed, that parricide
(I cannot style him better), by confederacy
Preparing this his paramour to be there,
Entered Volpone's house – who was the man
Your fatherhoods must understand, designed   70
For the inheritance – there, sought his father.
But, with what purpose sought he him, my sires?
I tremble to pronounce it, that a son
Unto a father, and to such a father,

44–7   *For these . . . benefit* Celia and Bonario do not know how to respond to such gener-
          osity except by feeling shamed, since it goes beyond their sadly limited capacity for
          gratitude, and so they began to resent the gift
48   *extirp* eradicate
51   *heart* audacity, encouragement
65   *To him betrayed* Revealed to Bonario
70   *designed* designated, intended

Should have so foul, felonious intent: 75
It was, to murder him. When, being prevented
By his more happy absence, what then did he?
Not check his wicked thoughts; no, now new deeds –
Mischief doth ever end, where it begins –
An act of horror, fathers! He dragged forth   80
The agèd gentleman, that had there lain, bed-rid,
Three years and more, out off his innocent couch,
Naked upon the floor, there left him; wounded
His servant in the face; and, with this strumpet,
The stale to his forged practice, who was glad   85
To be so active (I shall here desire
Your fatherhoods to note but my collections,
As most remarkable), thought at once to stop
His father's ends; discredit his free choice
In the old gentleman; redeem themselves,   90
By laying infamy upon this man
To whom, with blushing, they should owe their lives.

1st AVOCATORE
What proofs have you of this?

BONARIO   Most honoured fathers,
I humbly crave there be no credit given
To this man's mercenary tongue.

2nd AVOCATORE   Forbear.   95

BONARIO
His soul moves in his fee.

3rd AVOCATORE   O, sir.

BONARIO   This fellow,
For six sols more, would plead against his Maker.

1st AVOCATORE
You do forget yourself.

VOLTORE   Nay, nay, grave fathers,
Let him have scope: can any man imagine
That he will spare 's accuser, that would not   100
Have spared his parent?

---

77   *his more happy* Corbaccio's fortunate
85   *The stale . . . practice* The prostitute used as a lure for his deceptive plot
87   *collections* conclusions, inferences
89   *ends* intentions
90   *the old gentleman* Volpone, whom Corbaccio had chosen as his heir
91   *this man* Corvino
97   *sols* low-value French coins

1st AVOCATORE	Well, produce your proofs.
CELIA	

    I would I could forget I were a creature.

VOLTORE

    Signior Corbaccio.

4th AVOCATORE   What is he?

VOLTORE   The father.

2nd AVOCATORE

    Has he had an oath?

NOTARIO   Yes.

CORBACCIO   What must I do now?

NOTARIO

    Your testimony's craved.

CORBACCIO   Speak to the knave?   105

    I'll ha' my mouth, first, stopped with earth! My heart

    Abhors his knowledge; I disclaim in him.

1st AVOCATORE

    But, for what cause?

CORBACCIO   The mere portent of nature.

    He is an utter stranger to my loins.

BONARIO

    Have they made you to this?

CORBACCIO   I will not hear thee,   110

    Monster of men, swine, goat, wolf, parricide;

    Speak not, thou viper.

BONARIO   Sir, I will sit down,

    And rather wish my innocence should suffer,

    Than I resist the authority of a father.

VOLTORE

    Signior Corvino.

2nd AVOCATORE   This is strange!

1st AVOCATORE   Who's this?   115

NOTARIO

    The husband.

4th AVOCATORE   Is he sworn?

---

102   *I would ... creature* I wish I could forget that I am created by God (so I could choose suicide), or, I wish I could separate myself totally from these beasts

105   *Speak to the knave?* The half-deaf Corbaccio has misheard the Notario's response.

107   *Abhors his knowledge* Hates to acknowledge him, or, Hates even to think about him

108   *The mere portent* An absolute freak; unnatural births were considered portentous, and Corbaccio is distancing himself from his natural fatherhood of Bonario.

110   *made you* forced you, or, put you up

NOTARIO   He is.

3rd AVOCATORE   Speak, then.

CORVINO

This woman, please your fatherhoods, is a whore,
Of most hot exercise, more than a partridge,
Upon recòrd –

1st AVOCATORE No more.

CORVINO   Neighs like a jennet.

NOTARIO

Preserve the honour of the court.

CORVINO   I shall,   120
And modesty of your most reverend ears.
And yet I hope that I may say, these eyes
Have seen her glued unto that piece of cedar,
That fine well-timbered gallant; and that, here, [*Pointing to his
   forehead*]
The letters may be read, thorough the horn,   125
That make the story perfect.

MOSCA   [*Aside to* CORVINO] Excellent, sir!

CORVINO

[*Aside to* MOSCA] There is no shame in this, now, is there?

MOSCA   [*Aside to* CORVINO] None.

CORVINO

Or if I said, I hoped that she were onward
To her damnation, if there be a hell
Greater than whore, and woman: a good Catholic   130
May make the doubt.

---

118   *partridge* nature's most lecherous creature, according to Pliny's *Natural History*

119   *Upon recòrd* A recorded fact
       jennet small, lively Spanish horse

124   *well-timbered gallant* well-built young man (Bonario)

124–6 *here . . . perfect* here on my forehead is legible the letter V that makes the shape of
       cuckold's horns – or maybe the word 'cuckold' that can be read through the trans-
       parent horn that covered the printed sheets on which Elizabethan schoolchildren
       were taught their letters – that completes the story of my betrayal

127   *There is . . . None* Corvino wants reassurance that he has not humiliated himself by
       claiming to have been cuckolded; Mosca's gives the desired answer, but (by
       changing Q's 'harm' to F's 'shame' here) Jonson allows him a sly implication that
       Corvino's performance was shameless.

128   *onward* well on her way

131   *make the doubt* suspect that women and whores are themselves hell; Jonson was
       apparently no longer a Catholic at the time of F, allowing him to replace Q's 'a good
       Christian' with a more pointed implication about Catholicism's powerful ambiva-
       lence toward women.

3rd AVOCATORE	His grief hath made him frantic.
1st AVOCATORE	

    Remove him, hence.

[CELIA] swoons

2nd AVOCATORE   Look to the woman.

CORVINO   Rare!

    Prettily feigned! Again!

4th AVOCATORE   Stand from about her.

1st AVOCATORE

    Give her the air.

3rd AVOCATORE [*To* MOSCA] What can you say?

MOSCA   My wound,

    May it please your wisdoms, speaks for me, received   135
    In aid of my good patron, when he missed
    His sought-for father, when that well-taught dame
    Had her cue given her, to cry out a rape.

BONARIO

    O, most laid impudence! Fathers –

3rd AVOCATORE   Sir, be silent,

    You had your hearing free, so must they theirs.   140

2nd AVOCATORE

    I do begin to doubt th' imposture, here.

4th AVOCATORE

    This woman has too many moods.

VOLTORE   Grave fathers,

    She is a creature of a most professed
    And prostituted lewdness.

CORVINO   Most impetuous!   145

    Unsatisfied, grave fathers!

VOLTORE   May her feignings

    Not take your wisdoms; but this day, she baited
    A stranger, a grave knight, with her loose eyes,
    And more lascivious kisses. This man saw them
    Together, on the water, in a gondola.

MOSCA

    Here is the lady herself, that saw 'em too,   150

---

136   *he* Bonario
139   *most laid* deeply plotted
141   *doubt th' imposture* suspect fraud by Celia and Bonario
146   *take* take in, deceive, charm
       but this day this very day

Without; who then had in the open streets
Pursued them, but for saving her knight's honour.

1st AVOCATORE
Produce that lady.

2nd AVOCATORE   Let her come.

                                        [*Exit* MOSCA]

4th AVOCATORE   These things,
They strike with wonder!

3rd AVOCATORE   I am turned a stone!

ACT 4, SCENE 6

[*Enter*] MOSCA [*with*] LADY WOULD-BE

MOSCA
Be resolute, Madam.

LADY WOULD-BE [*Pointing at* CELIA] Ay, this same is she.
Out, thou chameleon harlot; now thine eyes
Vie tears with the hyena. Dar'st thou look
Upon my wrongèd face? [*To the* AVOCATORI] I cry your pardons.
I fear I have, forgettingly, transgressed   5
Against the dignity of the court –

2nd AVOCATORE   No, madam.

LADY WOULD-BE
And been exorbitant –

2nd AVOCATORE   You have not, lady.

---

151 *Without* Outside

2   *chameleon* creature famous for its changing camouflage; Lady Would-Be now
     assumes that Celia was the woman disguised as a man she heard was accompa-
     nying her husband.

3   *hyena* Lady Would-Be confuses the hyena, which was thought to capture people
     by imitating a human voice, with the crocodile, which was thought to use unfelt
     tears for the same purpose; in fact, in her make-up and shifting stories, her
     destructive voice and eagerness to feed on Volpone's moribund flesh, she herself
     becomes both chameleon and hyena, extending Jonson's fable of human beings
     who degrade themselves into beasts.

7   *exorbitant* excessive or disorderly
     s.p. *2nd* AVOCATORE Both parts of the reply are given to the 4th Avocatore by
     Q and F, but with separate speech headings, so this edition (like others) follows
     F3 (Jonson's 1692 *Works*) in giving the first part to the 2nd Avocatore; in any case,
     the judges (like Volpone earlier) seem desperate throughout the scene to forestall,
     by futile interruptions, any long explanations from Lady Would-Be.

4th AVOCATORE
These proofs are strong.
LADY WOULD-BE   Surely, I had no purpose,
To scandalise your honours, or my sex's.
3rd AVOCATORE
We do believe it.
LADY WOULD-BE   Surely, you may believe it.   10
2nd AVOCATORE
Madam, we do.
LADY WOULD-BE   Indeed, you may: my breeding
Is not so coarse –
4th AVOCATORE   We know it.
LADY WOULD-BE   To offend
With pertinacy –
3rd AVOCATORE   Lady.
LADY WOULD-BE   Such a presence;
No, surely.
1st AVOCATORE   We well think it.
LADY WOULD-BE   You may think it.
1st AVOCATORE
Let her o'ercome. [*To* CELIA *and* BONARIO] What witnesses have
you,   15
To make good your report?
BONARIO   Our consciences.
CELIA
And heaven, that never fails the innocent.
4th AVOCATORE
These are no testimonies.
BONARIO   Not in your courts,
Where multitude and clamour overcomes.
1st AVOCATORE
Nay, then you do wax insolent.

        VOLPONE *is brought in, as impotent*

---

13   *pertinacy* pertinacity, stubbornness; or possibly Lady Would-Be's mistake for
      'impertinence'
15   *o'ercome* conquer – either by believing her testimony against Celia, or by letting her
      characteristic verbal persistence grant her the last word in the exchange of cour-
      teous remarks
19   *multitude and clamour* the larger number of witnesses, and louder ones
20   s.d. *as impotent* seemingly devoid of bodily strength; Volpone is presumably
      carried in draped on a litter or stretcher

| VOLTORE | Here, here, | 20 |

The testimony comes, that will convince,
And put to utter dumbness, their bold tongues.
See here, grave fathers, here is the ravisher,
The rider on men's wives, the great impostor,
The grand voluptuary! Do you not think,   25
These limbs should affect venery? or these eyes
Covet a concubine? 'Pray you, mark these hands:
Are they not fit to stroke a lady's breasts?
Perhaps, he doth dissemble.

| BONARIO | So he does. |

VOLTORE

Would you have him tortured?

| BONARIO | I would have him proved. | 30 |

VOLTORE

Best try him, then, with goads, or burning irons;
Put him to the *strappado*! I have heard,
The rack hath cured the gout: 'faith, give it him,
And help him of a malady, be courteous.
I will undertake, before these honoured fathers,   35
He shall have, yet, as many left diseases,
As she has known adulterers, or thou strumpets.
O, my most equal hearers, if these deeds –
Acts of this bold and most exorbitant strain –
May pass with sufferance, what one citizen   40
But owes the forfeit of his life, yea, fame,
To him that dares traduce him? Which of you
Are safe, my honoured fathers? I would ask,
With leave of your grave fatherhoods, if their plot
Have any face, or colour like to truth?   45

26   *affect venery* pursue sexual pleasure
30   *proved* tested
32   *strappado* hoisting prisoners by a rope tied to their wrists behind their back and then dropping them; all these forms of torture were practised by the Venetian republic.
34   *help* relieve
38   *equal* fair-minded
39   *strain* type
40–2   *May pass . . . traduce him?* May occur and be tolerated, can any citizen defend his life or even his reputation against anyone who has the nerve to slander him?
44   *leave* permission
45   *face, or colour* resemblance; but the irony is that Voltore's own case consists entirely of face (surface and shamelessness) and colour (rhetorical devices)

Or if, unto the dullest nostril here,
It smell not rank, and most abhorrèd slander?
I crave your care of this good gentleman,
Whose life is much endangered by their fable;
And, as for them, I will conclude with this: 50
That vicious persons when they are hot, and fleshed
In impious acts, their constancy abounds:
Damned deeds are done with greatest confidence.

1st AVOCATORE
Take 'em to custody, and sever them.

          [CELIA *and* BONARIO *are led out separately*]

2nd AVOCATORE
'Tis pity two such prodigies should live.   55

1st AVOCATORE
Let the old gentleman be returned, with care;
I'm sorry, our credulity wronged him.

          [VOLPONE *is carried out*]

4th AVOCATORE
These are two creatures!

3rd AVOCATORE   I have an earthquake in me!

2nd AVOCATORE
Their shame, even in their cradles, fled their faces.

4th AVOCATORE
[*To* VOLTORE] You've done a worthy service to the state, sir,   60
In their discovery.

1st AVOCATORE   You shall hear, ere night,
What punishment the court decrees upon 'em.

VOLTORE
We thank your fatherhoods.

        [*Exeunt* AVOCATORI, NOTARIO, *and all other* OFFICIALS]
        How like you it?

MOSCA   Rare.
I'd ha' your tongue, sir, tipped with gold, for this;
I'd ha' you be the heir to the whole city;   65

51 *fleshed* initiated (as in the passion of a hunt)
52 *constancy* resolution
54 *sever them* keep them separate
55 *prodigies* ominous monsters
61 *ere night* before tonight (another signal that Jonson is obeying 'unity of time' by limiting the action to a single day)
63 *Rare* Unusually good; Jonson's tombstone reads simply, 'O Rare Ben Jonson'

The earth I'd have want men, ere you want living!
They're bound to erect your statue, in St Mark's.
Signior Corvino, I would have you go
And show yourself, that you have conquered.

CORVINO   Yes.

MOSCA

It was much better that you should profess   70
Yourself a cuckold, thus, than that the other
Should have been proved.

CORVINO   Nay, I considered that:
Now, it is her fault:

MOSCA   Then, it had been yours.

CORVINO

True. I do doubt this advocate, still.

MOSCA   I' faith,
You need not, I dare ease you of that care.   75

CORVINO

I trust thee, Mosca.

MOSCA   As your own soul, sir.

[*Exit* CORVINO]

CORBACCIO   Mosca.

MOSCA

Now for your business, sir.

CORBACCIO   How? Ha' you business?

MOSCA

Yes, yours, sir.

CORBACCIO   O, none else?

MOSCA   None else, not I.

CORBACCIO

Be careful, then.

MOSCA   Rest you, with both your eyes, sir.

CORBACCIO

Dispatch it.

MOSCA   Instantly.

CORBACCIO   And look that all,   80

---

66   *The earth . . . living* I would rather have the earth lack human beings than have you
      lack a lawyer's livelihood
71   *the other* that Corvino had deliberately prostituted his own wife
74   *I do . . . still* I still don't trust this lawyer Voltore
79   *Rest . . . eyes* Relax completely
80   *Dispatch it* Quickly begin an inventory of Volpone's property

Whatever, be put in: jewels, plate, moneys,
Household stuff, bedding, curtains.

MOSCA   Curtain-rings, sir.
Only, the advocate's fee must be deducted.

CORBACCIO
I'll pay him now: you'll be too prodigal.

MOSCA
Sir, I must tender it.

CORBACCIO   Two chequins is well?   85

MOSCA
No, six, sir.

CORBACCIO   'Tis too much.

MOSCA   He talked a great while;
You must consider that, sir.

CORBACCIO [*Giving* MOSCA *coins*] Well, there's three –

MOSCA
I'll give it him.

CORBACCIO   Do so, and there's for thee.
                          [*Gives* MOSCA *a small tip and exits*]

MOSCA
Bountiful bones! What horrid strange offence
Did he commit 'gainst nature, in his youth,   90
Worthy this age? [*To* VOLTORE] You see, sir, how I work
Unto your ends; take you no notice.

VOLTORE   No,
I'll leave you.

MOSCA   All is yours –

                              [*Exit* VOLTORE]
                     the devil and all,
Good advocate. [*To* LADY WOULD-BE] Madam, I'll bring you
home.

LADY WOULD-BE
No, I'll go see your patron.

85   *tender* give
89   *Bountiful bones* A sarcastic exclamation associating Corbaccio's stinginess with his
      shrunken, skeletal physique; the connection between moral and physical condition
      is important throughout the play.
91   *Worthy this age* To have earned such an ugly old age
92   *take you no notice* don't worry that I seem to be conspiring with your rivals, or,
      don't acknowledge what I am doing for or saying to you (because Lady Would-Be
      is still present)

MOSCA	That you shall not.	95

I'll tell you why. My purpose is, to urge
My patron to reform his will; and, for
The zeal you've shown today, whereas before
You were but third or fourth, you shall be now
Put in the first; which would appear as begged,
If you be present. Therefore –   100

LADY WOULD-BE   You shall sway me.

[*Exeunt*]

ACT 5, SCENE 1

[*Enter*] VOLPONE

VOLPONE
Well, I am here; and all this brunt is past!
I ne'er was in dislike with my disguise,
Till this fled moment: here, 'twas good, in private,
But in your public – *cavè*, whilst I breathe.
'Fore God, my left leg 'gan to have the cramp;   5
And I appre'nded, straight, some power had struck me
With a dead palsy! Well, I must be merry,
And shake it off. A many of these fears
Would put me into some villainous disease,
Should they come thick upon me: I'll prevent 'em.   10
Give me a bowl of lusty wine, to fright
This humour from my heart – hum, hum, hum; (*He drinks*)
'Tis almost gone already: I shall conquer.
Any device, now, of rare, ingenious knavery,
That would possess me with a violent laughter,   15

101   *sway* persuade, perhaps (as often with Lady Would-Be) with a secondary sexual
        meaning
1   *brunt* stress, attack, crisis
3   *fled* past
4   *cavè* beware; Volpone is warning the audience, himself, or an attendant to make
        sure he isn't seen standing up.
6   *appre'nded, straight* thought immediately
7   *dead palsy* total paralysis; Jonson suffered some kind of palsy later in life.

128

Would make me up, again! So, so, so, so. (*Drinks again*)
This heat is life; 'tis blood, by this time! Mosca!

ACT 5, SCENE 2

[*Enter*] MOSCA

MOSCA
How now, sir? Does the day look clear again?
Are we recovered? And wrought out of error,
Into our way? To see our path before us?
Is our trade free once more?
VOLPONE   Exquisite Mosca!
MOSCA
Was it not carried learnèdly?
VOLPONE   And stoutly.   5
Good wits are greatest in extremities.
MOSCA
It were a folly, beyond thought, to trust
Any grand act unto a cowardly spirit.
You are not taken with it enough, methinks?
VOLPONE
O, more than if I had enjoyed the wench!   10
The pleasure of all womankind's not like it.
MOSCA
Why, now you speak, sir. We must here be fixed;
Here, we must rest; this is our masterpiece;
We cannot think to go beyond this.
VOLPONE   True,
Thou hast played thy prize, my precious Mosca.
MOSCA   Nay sir,   15
To gull the court –

16   s.d. *Drinks again* Some productions emphasize Volpone's over-indulgence here to
        explain his rash decision to play dead; Tilley, F651, records 'foxed' as a euphemism
        for 'drunk' (Parker).
 7   *beyond thought* unthinkable
 9   *taken* pleased
15   *prize* masterpiece; but Mosca may have another prize in view.
16   *gull* trick, make fools of (as in 'gullible')

VOLPONE   And quite divert the torrent
Upon the innocent.
MOSCA   Yes, and to make
So rare a music out of discords –
VOLPONE   Right.
That, yet, to me's the strangest! How thou'st borne it!
That these, being so divided 'mongst themselves,   20
Should not scent somewhat, or in me, or thee,
Or doubt their own side.
MOSCA   True. They will not see it:
Too much light blinds them, I think; each of 'em
Is so possessed, and stuffed with his own hopes,
That anything unto the contrary,   25
Never so true, or never so apparent,
Never so palpable, they will resist it –
VOLPONE
Like a temptation of the devil.
MOSCA   Right, sir.
Merchants may talk of trade, and your great signiors
Of land that yields well; but if Italy   30
Have any glebe more fruitful than these fellows,
I am deceived. Did not your advocate rare?
VOLPONE
[*Mimicking* VOLTORE] 'O, my most honoured fathers, my grave
    fathers,
Under correction of your fatherhoods,
What face of truth is, here? If these strange deeds   35
May pass, most honoured fathers' – I had much ado
To forbear laughing.
MOSCA   'T seemed to me, you sweat, sir.
VOLPONE
In troth, I did a little.
MOSCA   But confess, sir,

---

18   *discords* the conflicting testimonies, and/or the feuding rival heirs
19   *borne* managed
23   *light* hope, perhaps with a gesture toward the gleaming treasure, as in the play's
    opening line
24   *possessed* The word (like much about Mosca) hovers between material and
    demonic possessions.
31   *glebe* agricultural field
32   *rare* extremely well

Were you not daunted?

VOLPONE   In good faith, I was
A little in a mist; but not dejected;   40
Never, but still myself.

MOSCA   I think it, sir.
Now (so truth help me) I must needs say this, sir,
And, out of conscience, for your advocate:
He's taken pains, in faith, sir, and deserved,
In my poor judgement (I speak it, under favour,   45
Not to contrary you, sir), very richly –
Well – to be cozened.

VOLPONE   Troth, and I think so too,
By that I heard him in the latter end.

MOSCA
O, but before, sir; had you heard him, first,
Draw it to certain heads, then aggravate,   50
Then use his vehement figures – I looked still,
When he would shift a shirt; and, doing this
Out of pure love, no hope of gain –

VOLPONE   'Tis right.
I cannot answer him, Mosca, as I would,
Not yet; but, for thy sake, at thy entreaty,   55
I will begin, even now, to vex 'em all;
This very instant.

MOSCA   Good, sir.

VOLPONE   Call the dwarf
And eunuch forth.

MOSCA   Castrone, Nano.

[*Enter* CASTRONE, NANO]

NANO   Here.

---

45   *under favour* with your permission; Mosca may be parodying the lawyer Voltore's
      obsequious grandiloquence here.
47   *cozened* cheated
48   *By that I heard him* Judging by what I heard him say
50   *Draw . . . aggravate* Gather his arguments into specific topics, then emphasize
51   *figures* rhetorical tropes (figures of speech), or gestures
51–2 *I looked . . . shirt* I kept expecting him to change his clothing (because his extreme
      efforts must have made him sweat)
54   *answer* repay

VOLPONE
    Shall we have a jig now?
MOSCA   What you please, sir.
VOLPONE   Go,
    Straight, give out, about the streets, you two,   60
    That I am dead; do it, with constancy,
    Sadly, do you hear? Impute it to the grief
    Of this late slander.
                      [*Exeunt* CASTRONE, NANO]
MOSCA   What do you mean, sir?
VOLPONE   O,
    I shall have, instantly, my vulture, crow,
    Raven, come flying hither, on the news,   65
    To peck for carrion; my she-wolf, and all,
    Greedy, and full of expectation –
MOSCA
    And then, to have it ravished from their mouths?
VOLPONE
    'Tis true, I will ha' thee put on a gown,
    And take upon thee as thou wert mine heir;   70
    Show 'em a will. Open that chest, and reach
    Forth one of those, that has the blanks. I'll straight
    Put in thy name.
MOSCA   It will be rare, sir.
VOLPONE   Aye,
    When they e'en gape, and find themselves deluded –
MOSCA
    Yes.
VOLPONE And thou use them scurvily. Dispatch,   75
    Get on thy gown.
MOSCA   But, what, sir, if they ask
    After the body?
VOLPONE   Say, it was corrupted.

---

59   *jig* a lively dance, often performed at the end of an Elizabethan play; but Volpone
        seems to be using it as a metaphor for the final satiric dance of death he intends to
        choreograph for the legacy-hunters.
60   *Straight . . . about* Immediately report throughout
61   *with constancy* with conviction and straight faces
63   *mean* intend
70   *take upon thee as* act as if

MOSCA

    I'll say it stunk, sir; and was fain t' have it
    Coffined up instantly, and sent away.

VOLPONE

    Anything, what thou wilt. Hold, here's my will.   80
    Get thee a cap, a count-book, pen and ink,
    Papers afore thee; sit, as thou wert taking
    An inventory of parcels. I'll get up,
    Behind the curtain, on a stool, and hearken;
    Sometime, peep over; see, how they do look;   85
    With what degrees, their blood doth leave their faces!
    O, 'twill afford me a rare meal of laughter.

MOSCA

    Your advocate will turn stark dull upon it.

VOLPONE

    It will take off his oratory's edge.

MOSCA

    But your *clarissimo*, old round-back, he   90
    Will crump you, like a hog-louse, with the touch.

VOLPONE

    And what Corvino?

MOSCA   O, sir, look for him,
    Tomorrow morning, with a rope, and a dagger,
    To visit all the streets: he must run mad.
    My lady too, that came into the court,   95
    To bear false witness for your worship.

VOLPONE   Yes,
    And kissed me 'fore the fathers; when my face
    Flowed all with oils.

MOSCA   And sweat – sir. Why, your gold

---

78   *fain* eager, compelled
81   *count-book* account-book, financial ledger
88   *turn stark dull* be struck dumb; Volpone's reply puns on another meaning of 'dull'.
90   *clarissimo* high-ranking Venetian
90–1   *old round-back . . . touch* Corbaccio, who evidently stoops with age, will curl (or crumple) up like a wood-louse (pill-bug) from the impact of this development
93   *rope, dagger* These were standard symbols of suicidal madness, ones Jonson would have used as props when he played the grieving Hieronimo in Kyd's *Spanish Tragedy*.
98   *And sweat – sir* Mosca needles Volpone with a reminder that he was panicked, not just performing, at the trial; the dash may suggest a pause before reverting to deference with 'sir'.

Is such another med'cine, it dries up
All those offensive savours! It transforms   100
The most deformèd, and restores 'em lovely,
As 'twere the strange poetical girdle. Jove
Could not invent, t' himself, a shroud more subtle,
To pass Acrisius' guards. It is the thing
Makes all the world her grace, her youth, her beauty.   105

VOLPONE
I think she loves me.

MOSCA   Who? The lady, sir?
She is jealous of you.

VOLPONE   Dost thou say so?

                                        [*A knock at the door*]

MOSCA   Hark,
There's some already.

VOLPONE   Look.

MOSCA   It is the vulture:
He has the quickest scent.

VOLPONE   I'll to my place,
Thou, to thy posture.

MOSCA   I'm set.

VOLPONE   But, Mosca,   110
Play the artificer now, torture 'em, rarely.

99   *such another* so great a
102   *girdle* F inserts '*Cestus*' in the margin at the end of this line, probably to clarify the
      reference to Venus's girdle of that name, which is capable (according to Homer's
      Iliad, XIV) of transforming ugliness to beauty and reviving passion in the aged.
104   *Acrisius* the father of Danae, who locked her in a brazen tower to forestall a
      prophecy that her son would kill him; but Jove descended on her in a shower of
      gold and impregnated her with Perseus
106   *The lady* Perhaps Lady Would-Be, and some commentators suggest Celia, but the
      previous lines feminize the gold itself, which is the thing Volpone seeks love from,
      and which proves to be his jealous god.
110   *posture* pose, imposture
111   *Play the artificer* Perform craftily and elaborately

ACT 5, SCENE 3

[*Enter* VOLTORE]

VOLTORE
How now, my Mosca?

MOSCA   Turkey carpets, nine –

VOLTORE
Taking an inventory? That is well.

MOSCA
Two suits of bedding, tissue –

VOLTORE   Where's the will?
Let me read that, the while.

[CORBACCIO *is carried in*]

CORBACCIO   So, set me down;
And get you home.

                              [*Exeunt Chair-Bearers*]

VOLTORE   Is he come, now, to trouble us?   5

MOSCA
Of cloth of gold, two more –

CORBACCIO   Is it done, Mosca?

MOSCA
Of several vellets, eight –

VOLTORE   I like his care.

CORBACCIO
Dost thou not hear?

[*Enter* CORVINO]

CORVINO   Ha? Is the hour come, Mosca?

VOLPONE *peeps from behind a traverse*

VOLPONE
Ay, now they muster.

CORVINO   What does the advocate here?

---

1   *Turkey carpets* imported through Italy, and used as table covers or wall hangings
3   *suits of bedding* sets of bed covers in expensive fabrics
      tissue cloth with silver or gold
4   *the while* while you are completing the inventory
7   *several vellets* separate velvet hangings

Or this Corbaccio?

CORBACCIO   What do these here?

[*Enter* LADY WOULD-BE]

LADY WOULD-BE   Mosca?   10
Is his thread spun?

MOSCA   Eight chests of linen –

VOLPONE   O,
My fine Dame Would-Be, too!

CORVINO   Mosca, the will,
That I may show it these, and rid 'em hence.

MOSCA
Six chests of diaper, four of damask – There. [*Points to papers on
a table*]

CORBACCIO
Is that the will?

MOSCA   Down-beds, and bolsters –

VOLPONE   Rare!   15
Be busy still. Now they begin to flutter;
They never think of me. Look, see, see, see!
How their swift eyes run over the long deed,
Unto the name, and to the legacies,
What is bequeathed them there –

MOSCA   Ten suits of hangings –   20

VOLPONE
Ay, i' their garters, Mosca. Now their hopes
Are at the gasp.

VOLTORE   Mosca the heir!

CORBACCIO   What's that?

VOLPONE
My advocate is dumb. Look to my merchant,
He has heard of some strange storm, a ship is lost:

---

11   *Is his thread spun* Lady Would-Be alludes to the myth of the Three Fates to ask, in
      characteristically pompous fashion, whether Volpone is dead; she may also
      subconsciously be responding to the sight of all these expensive fabrics.

14   *diaper* linen woven into a diamond pattern
      damask intricately woven table-linen

20   *suits of hangings* sets of draperies for poster-beds

21   *i' their garters* Volpone puns on a jeering Elizabethan invitation to suicide, 'Hang
      yourself in your own garters' (Tilley G42).

22   *gasp* last gasp

He faints. My lady will swoon. Old glazen-eyes,   25
He hath not reached his despair, yet.

CORBACCIO   All these
Are out of hope, I'm sure the man.

CORVINO   But, Mosca –

MOSCA

Two cabinets.

CORVINO   Is this in earnest?

MOSCA   One
Of ebony –

CORVINO   Or, do you but delude me?

MOSCA

The other, mother of pearl – I am very busy.   30
Good faith, it is a fortune thrown upon me –
Item, one salt of agate – not my seeking.

LADY WOULD-BE

Do you hear, sir?

MOSCA   A perfumed box – 'pray you forbear,
You see I'm troubled – made of an onyx –

LADY WOULD-BE   How!

MOSCA

Tomorrow, or next day, I shall be at leisure   35
To talk with you all.

CORVINO   Is this my large hope's issue?

LADY WOULD-BE

Sir, I must have a fairer answer.

MOSCA   Madam!
Marry, and shall: 'pray you, fairly quit my house.
Nay, raise no tempest with your looks; but, hark you:
Remember what your ladyship offered me,   40
To put you in, an heir; go to, think on't.
And what you said e'en your best madams did
For maintenance, and why not you? Enough.
Go home, and use the poor Sir Pol, your knight, well,

---

25   *glazen-eyes* Corbaccio needs eyeglasses; line 63 will refer to Corbaccio's 'four
     eyes'

32   *salt* salt-cellar

38   *fairly* simply, completely; but with a sense of poetic justice, a play off her preceding
     line, and another dig at her compromised cosmetic 'fairness' (cf. 4.2.73).

40   *what . . . me* Lady Would-Be has offered herself sexually to Mosca, either by her
     salacious double-entendres, as at 4.6.101, or by a more explicit offer we are now
     invited to imagine.

For fear I tell some riddles: go, be melancholic.   45

                [*Exit* LADY WOULD-BE]

VOLPONE

O, my fine devil!

CORVINO   Mosca, 'pray you a word.

MOSCA

Lord! Will not you take your dispatch hence, yet?
Methinks, of all, you should have been th' example.
Why should you stay here? With what thought? What promise?
Hear you: do not you know, I know you an ass?   50
And that you would, most fain, have been a wittol,
If fortune would have let you? That you are
A declared cuckold, on good terms? This pearl,
You'll say, was yours? Right. This diamond?
I will not deny't, but thank you. Much here else?   55
It may be so. Why, think that these good works
May help to hide your bad; I'll not betray you;
Although you be but extraordinary,
And have it only in title, it sufficeth.
Go home; be melancholic too, or mad.   60

                    [*Exit* CORVINO]

VOLPONE

Rare, Mosca! How his villainy becomes him!

VOLTORE

Certain, he doth delude all these for me.

CORBACCIO

Mosca the heir?

VOLPONE   O, his four eyes have found it.

CORBACCIO

I'm cozened, cheated, by a parasite slave;
Harlot, th'ast gulled me.

MOSCA   Yes, sir. Stop your mouth,   65
Or I shall draw the only tooth is left.
Are not you he – that filthy covetous wretch,

---

47   *dispatch* sending off
51   *fain . . . wittol* eagerly have been a pimp to your own wife
56–7   *think that . . . bad* think of these unrewarded gifts of yours as charity to expiate
       your evil deeds
58–9   *Although . . . sufficeth* Although you are unusual in being a cuckold in public name
       rather than physical fact, that is bad enough
65   *Harlot* Rogue, low-born man; not yet exclusively a synonym for female prostitute

With the three legs – that, here, in hope of prey,
Have, any time this three year, snuffed about,
With your most grov'ling nose; and would have hired   70
Me to the pois'ning of my patron? Sir?
Are not you he, that have, today, in court,
Professed the disinheriting of your son?
Perjured yourself? Go home, and die, and stink;
If you but croak a syllable, all comes out: 75
Away, and call your porters, go, go stink.

                    [*Exit* CORBACCIO]

VOLPONE
  Excellent varlet!
VOLTORE   Now, my faithful Mosca,
  I find thy constancy.
MOSCA   Sir?
VOLTORE   Sincere.
MOSCA   A table
  Of porphyry – I mar'l you'll be thus troublesome.
VOLTORE
  Nay, leave off now, they are gone.
MOSCA   Why, who are you?   80
  What? Who did send for you? O, cry you mercy,
  Reverend sir! Good faith, I am grieved for you,
  That any chance of mine should thus defeat
  Your (I must needs say) most deserving travails;
  But, I protest, sir, it was cast upon me,   85
  And I could, almost, wish to be without it,
  But that the will o' th' dead must be observed.
  Marry, my joy is, that you need it not,
  You have a gift, sir, (thank your education)
  Will never let you want, while there are men,   90
  And malice to breed causes. Would I had
  But half the like, for all my fortune, sir.
  If I have any suits – as I do hope,
  Things being so easy and direct, I shall not –

---

68   *three legs* Corbaccio walks with a cane.
69   *any time this three year* constantly during the past three years
79   *mar'l* marvel, am astonished
81   *cry you mercy* I beg your pardon
83   *chance* luck
91   *causes* lawsuits

I will make bold with your obstreperous aid –   95
Conceive me, for your fee, sir. In meantime,
You, that have so much law, I know ha' the conscience
Not to be covetous of what is mine.
Good sir, I thank you, for my plate: 'twill help
To set up a young man. Good faith, you look   100
As you were costive: best go home, and purge, sir.
                                        [*Exit* VOLTORE]

VOLPONE
Bid him eat lettuce well! My witty mischief,
Let me embrace thee. O, that I could now
Transform thee to a Venus – Mosca, go,
Straight, take my habit of *clarissimo*,   105
And walk the streets; be seen, torment 'em more:
We must pursue, as well as plot. Who would
Have lost this feast?
MOSCA   I doubt it will lose them.
VOLPONE
O, my recovery shall recover all.
That I could now but think on some disguise,   110
To meet 'em in; and ask 'em questions.
How I would vex 'em still, at every turn!
MOSCA
Sir, I can fit you.
VOLPONE   Canst thou?
MOSCA   Yes. I know

95–6   *I will . . . fee* I will not hesitate to enlist your strong voice (in any litigation over Volpone's will) – and, please understand, I will pay your usual fee
99   *my plate* the valuable piece Voltore gave Volpone at 1.3.10
101   *costive* constipated
102   *lettuce* considered a good laxative
104   *Venus* Flies were believed to be bisexual (Parker). This wish renews the Venus allegory and the hermaphroditic theme that have surfaced several times in the play.
105   *habit of clarissimo* The strict Venetian dress code dictated that such gentlemen should wear black gowns edged with black taffeta, and a brimless black felt cap (Parker).
107–8 *Who would . . . feast?* Would anyone willingly miss out on this delicious opportunity to gloat and taunt?
108   *I doubt it will lose them* either (as Volpone understands it), I'm afraid it will make it impossible to exploit these gulls any further; or possibly, I'm afraid it won't get rid of them
110   *That* I wish that
113   *fit you* fit you out for that, provide what you asked for

One o' th' *commandatori*, sir, so like you;
Him will I straight make drunk, and bring you his habit.   115

VOLPONE

A rare disguise, and answering thy brain!
O, I will be a sharp disease unto 'em.

MOSCA

Sir, you must look for curses –

VOLPONE   Till they burst;
The fox fares ever best when he is cursed.

                                                  [*Exeunt*]

ACT 5, SCENE 4

[*Enter*] PEREGRINE [*in disguise, and three* MERCHANTS]

PEREGRINE

Am I enough disguised?

1st MERCHANT   I warrant you.

PEREGRINE

All my ambition is to fright him, only.

2nd MERCHANT

If you could ship him away, 'twere excellent.

3rd MERCHANT

To Zant, or to Aleppo?

PEREGRINE   Yes, and ha' his
Adventures put i' th' *Book of Voyages*,   5
And his gulled story registered for truth?

---

114   *commandatori* officers charged with bringing offenders to court (cf. 4.1.78)
116   *answering* worthy of
118   *look for* expect
119   *The fox . . . cursed* This proverb (Tilley F632) probably meant that hunters curse
         the fox when they cannot catch him.
  1   *warrant* assure
  4   *Zant* an Ionian island, controlled at that time by Venice
  5   *Book of Voyages* probably one of the travel books (such as Hakluyt's) popular in
         this period
  6   *gulled story* Previous editors have assumed this means, the story of Pol's humili-
         ating gulling; but Peregrine may be warning that Sir Pol's grandiose version of his
         downfall might end up recorded as heroic historical truth. Jonson may thus be
         scoffing at the other grandiose tales so recorded.

Well, gentlemen, when I am in a while,
And that you think us warm in our discourse,
Know your approaches.

1st MERCHANT   Trust it to our care.

                              [*Exeunt* MERCHANTS]

            [*Enter* WOMAN]

PEREGRINE
'Save you, fair lady. Is Sir Pol within?   10

WOMAN
I do not know, sir.

PEREGRINE   'Pray you, say unto him,
Here is a merchant, upon earnest business,
Desires to speak with him.

WOMAN   I will see, sir.   [*Exit* WOMAN]

PEREGRINE   'Pray you.
I see, the family is all female, here.

            [*Enter* WOMAN]

WOMAN
He says, sir, he has weighty affairs of state,   15
That now require him whole; some other time,
You may possess him.

PEREGRINE   'Pray you say again,
If those require him whole, these will exact him,
Whereof I bring him tidings.

                              [*Exit* WOMAN]

                    What might be
His grave affair of state, now? How to make   20
Bolognian sausages, here, in Venice, sparing
One o' th' ingredients?

            [*Enter* WOMAN]

WOMAN   Sir, he says he knows
By your word 'tidings' that you are no statesman,

9   *Know your approaches* Remember exactly how and when to enter
16   *require him whole* demand his complete attention
18–19 *these ... tidings* the state affairs of which I bring him news will draw him out;
       Peregrine here mocks Pol's pretentious phrasing.

And therefore, wills you stay.

PEREGRINE   Sweet, 'pray you return him,

I have not read so many proclamations,   25

And studied them, for words, as he has done,

But – here he deigns to come.

               [*Enter* SIR POLITIC]

                            [*Exit* WOMAN]

SIR POLITIC   Sir, I must crave

Your courteous pardon. There hath chanced, today,

Unkind disaster 'twixt my Lady and me;

And I was penning my apology   30

To give her satisfaction, as you came, now.

PEREGRINE

Sir, I am grieved, I bring you worse disaster:

The gentleman you met at th' port, today,

That told you he was newly arrived –

SIR POLITIC   Ay, was

A fugitive punk?

PEREGRINE   No, sir, a spy, set on you,   35

And he has made relation to the Senate,

That you professed to him to have a plot

To sell the state of Venice to the Turk.

SIR POLITIC

O me!

PEREGRINE   For which, warrants are signed by this time,

To apprehend you, and to search your study,   40

For papers –

SIR POLITIC   Alas, sir. I have none, but notes,

Drawn out of play-books –

PEREGRINE   All the better, sir.

SIR POLITIC

And some essays. What shall I do?

---

24   *wills you stay* says – because you said 'tidings' instead of the sophisticated spy-jargon, 'intelligences' – you are not dangerous and may stay, or (almost the opposite), are not important and must wait
        return him say to him in response

35   *punk* prostitute

36   *made relation to* told (Peregrine again adopts Pol's overblown lingo, cf. 2.1.96)

42   *Drawn . . . better, sir* As in the Epistle accompanying this play (lines 64–74), Jonson often complained that he was persecuted by the government because people insisted on reading sinister political implications into his plays.

PEREGRINE   Sir, best
Convey yourself into a sugar-chest,
Or, if you could lie round, a frail were rare;   45
And I could send you aboard.
SIR POLITIC   Sir, I but talked so,
For discourse sake, merely.
PEREGRINE   Hark, they are there.

                                         They knock without

SIR POLITIC
I am a wretch, a wretch.
PEREGRINE   What will you do, sir?
Ha' you ne'er a currant-butt to leap into?
They'll put you to the rack, you must be sudden.   50
SIR POLITIC
Sir, I have an engine –
3rd MERCHANT [*From off-stage*] Sir Politic Would-Be?
2nd MERCHANT
[*From off-stage*] Where is he?
SIR POLITIC   – that I have thought upon beforetime.
PEREGRINE
What is it?
SIR POLITIC [*Aside*] I shall ne'er endure the torture.
[*To* PEREGRINE] Marry, it is, sir, of a tortoise-shell,
Fitted for these extremities; 'pray you sir, help me. [*Climbs into
    the tortoise shell*]   55
Here, I've a place, sir, to put back my legs;
Please you to lay it on, sir. With this cap,
And my black gloves, I'll lie, sir, like a tortoise,
Till they are gone.
PEREGRINE   And call you this an engine?
SIR POLITIC
Mine own device – Good sir, bid my wife's women   60
To burn my papers.

                                         [*Exit* PEREGRINE]

---

45   *lie round . . . rare* curl up, a basket of rushes (such as figs were packed in) would be
      ideal
49   *currant-butt* cask or small barrel used to hold currants or currant-wine
50   *sudden* quick
55   *Fitted for these extremities* Prepared (Q 'apted') for emergencies like this, but
      perhaps also, Made to fit my limbs; tortoises were sold in the Venetian markets, and
      (as Peregrine's remark at line 80 suggests) were a symbol of wise policy.
59   *engine* piece of engineering

[*The* MERCHANTS] *rush in*

1st MERCHANT   Where's he hid?
3rd MERCHANT   We must,
    And will, sure, find him.
2nd MERCHANT   Which is his study?

[*Enter* PEREGRINE]

1st MERCHANT   What
    Are you, sir?
PEREGRINE   I'm a merchant, that came here
    To look upon this tortoise.
3rd MERCHANT   How?
1st MERCHANT   St Mark!
    What beast is this?
PEREGRINE   It is a fish.
2nd MERCHANT   Come out here.   65
PEREGRINE
    Nay, you may strike him, sir, and tread upon him:
    He'll bear a cart.
1st MERCHANT   What, to run over him?
PEREGRINE   Yes.
3rd MERCHANT
    Let's jump upon him.
2nd MERCHANT   Can he not go?
PEREGRINE   He creeps, sir.
1st MERCHANT
    [*Prodding* SIR POLITIC *through the openings in the shell*]
    Let's see him creep.
PEREGRINE   No, good sir, you will hurt him.
2nd MERCHANT
    'Heart, I'll see him creep; or prick his guts.   70
3rd MERCHANT
    Come out here.
PEREGRINE   'Pray you, sir. [*Aside to* SIR POLITIC]
    Creep a little.
1st MERCHANT Forth.
2nd MERCHANT
    Yet further.
PEREGRINE   Good sir. [*Aside to* SIR POLITIC] Creep.

68   *go* move

145

2nd MERCHANT We'll see his legs.
3rd MERCHANT
  Godso, he has garters!

  They pull off the shell and discover him.

1st MERCHANT Ay, and gloves!
2nd MERCHANT Is this
  Your fearful tortoise?
PEREGRINE [*Taking off his own disguise*] Now, Sir Pol, we are even;
  For your next project, I shall be prepared! 75
  I am sorry for the funeral of your notes, sir.
1st MERCHANT
  'Twere a rare motion, to be seen in Fleet Street!
2nd MERCHANT
  Ay, i' the term.
1st MERCHANT Or Smithfield, in the fair.
3rd MERCHANT
  Methinks, 'tis but a melancholic sight!
PEREGRINE
  Farewell, most politic tortoise.

  [*Exeunt* PEREGRINE *and* MERCHANTS]

  [*Enter* WOMAN]

SIR POLITIC Where's my lady? 80
  Knows she of this?
WOMAN I know not, sir.
SIR POLITIC Inquire.

  [*Exit* WOMAN]

  O, I shall be the fable of all feasts;
  The freight of the *gazetti*, ship-boys' tale;

---

74 *even* Peregrine still seems to believe that Pol's pretensions were partly some kind of
    plot against him, deserving vengeance.
76 *funeral* burning, as on a pyre; smoke was sometimes released from trap doors on
    the Jacobean stage.
77 *motion* puppet-show
78 *i' the term* when law courts were in session, which drew crowds to Fleet Street,
    where puppet-shows were often performed
    Smithfield Jonson's play *Bartholomew Fair*, set in Smithfield, culminates with a
    puppet-show.
80 s.d. *Enter* WOMAN Alternatively, the waiting woman could have remained on stage
    instead of exiting at line 27 above; her ongoing reactions to Sir Pol's humiliation
    would present interesting theatrical opportunities.
83 *freight of the gazetti* material for the newspapers

And, which is worst, even talk for ordinaries.

[*Enter* WOMAN]

WOMAN

My lady's come most melancholic home,   85
And says, sir, she will straight to sea, for physic.

SIR POLITIC

And I, to shun this place and clime forever;
Creeping, with house on back; and think it well
To shrink my poor head, in my politic shell.

[*Exeunt*]

ACT 5, SCENE 5

[*Enter*] VOLPONE, MOSCA; *the first, in the habit of a*
commandatore; the other, of a clarissimo

VOLPONE

Am I then like him?

MOSCA   O, sir, you are he:
No man can sever you.

VOLPONE   Good.

MOSCA   But, what am I?

VOLPONE

'Fore heav'n, a brave *clarissimo*; thou becom'st it!
Pity, thou wert not born one.

MOSCA   If I hold
My made one, 'twill be well.

VOLPONE   I will go, and see   5
What news, first, at the court.

MOSCA   Do so.

[*Exit* VOLPONE]

84   *ordinaries* taverns
86   *physic* health, medical purposes
 1   *him* the *commandatore*
 2   *sever* distinguish
 3   *becom'st it* fill the role handsomely
4–5   *If . . . one* If I can maintain my assumed role; what sounds like Mosca's modesty
       actually reveals his intentions.

My fox
Is out on his hole, and, ere he shall re-enter,
I will make him languish, in his borrowed case,
Except he come to composition with me.
Androgyno, Castrone, Nano!

[*Enter* ANDROGYNO, CASTRONE, NANO]

ALL   Here.   10

MOSCA

Go, recreate yourselves, abroad; go, sport!

[*Exeunt* ANDROGYNO, CASTRONE, NANO]

So, now I have the keys, and am possessed.
Since he will needs be dead, afore his time,
I'll bury him, or gain by him. I'm his heir;
And so will keep me, till he share at least.   15
To cozen him of all, were but a cheat
Well placed; no man would construe it a sin.
Let his sport pay for't; this is called the fox-trap.   [*Exit*]

ACT 5, SCENE 6

[*Enter*] CORBACCIO, CORVINO

CORBACCIO

They say the court is set.

CORVINO   We must maintain
Our first tale good, for both our reputations.

6–7   *My fox . . . hole* Volpone has made himself vulnerable (by playing dead and then
       leaving his house); 'Fox in the Hole' was a game in which the players hop and strike
       each other with gloves and a piece of leather.
8   *case* disguise
9   *Except he come to composition* Unless he negotiates a wealth-sharing agreement
12   *possessed* in possession of the riches; but Jonson again (as at 5.2.24 and many other
       places in the play) uses the word to remind us that gold is a demonic possessor, a
       notion which will become explicit in 5.12.
13   *will needs be* insists on being
15   *keep me* remain
16–17 *were but . . . placed* would only be poetic justice
18   *Let his sport pay for't* Let his amusement at this latest trick compensate him for
       what it will cost him
1–2   *maintain . . . good* stick to the story we told the court the first time

CORBACCIO

Why, mine's no tale: my son would, there, have killed me.

CORVINO

That's true, I had forgot; mine is, I am sure.

But, for your will, sir.

CORBACCIO   Ay, I'll come upon him   5

For that, hereafter, now his patron's dead.

[*Enter* VOLPONE, *disguised as a commandatore*]

VOLPONE

Signor Corvino! And Corbaccio! Sir,

Much joy unto you.

CORVINO   Of what?

VOLPONE   The sudden good,

Dropped down upon you –

CORBACCIO   Where?

VOLPONE   – and none knows how –

From old Volpone, sir.

CORBACCIO   Out, errant knave.   10

VOLPONE

Let not your too much wealth, sir, make you furious.

CORBACCIO

Away, thou varlet.

VOLPONE   Why, sir?

CORBACCIO   Dost thou mock me?

VOLPONE

You mock the world, sir: did you not change wills?

CORBACCIO

Out, harlot.

VOLPONE   O! Belike you are the man,

Signor Corvino? 'Faith, you carry it well: 15

You grow not mad withal; I love your spirit.

You are not over-leavened with your fortune.

---

5   *come upon him* make a demand to Mosca
10   *errant* As at 3.7.118, possibly Jonson's version of 'arrant', meaning 'notorious', but
        more likely 'erring', combining the accusation that he is mistaken with a dismissive
        view of the *commandatore*'s itinerant occupation.
13   *You mock the world* You are trying to conceal the truth from everyone, or perhaps,
        You can laugh at everyone
        change exchange (by naming each other as heirs)
14   *Belike* Perhaps
17   *over-leavened* puffed up

You should ha' some would swell, now, like a wine-vat,
With such an autumn – Did he gi' you all, sir?

CORVINO

Avoid, you rascal.

VOLPONE   Troth, your wife has shown   20
Herself a very woman; but, you are well,
You need not care, you have a good estate,
To bear it out sir, better by this chance.
Except Corbaccio have a share?

CORVINO   Hence, varlet.

VOLPONE

You will not be a'known, sir. Why, 'tis wise,   25
Thus do all gamesters, at all games, dissemble:
No man will seem to win.

                    [*Exeunt* CORVINO *and* CORBACCIO]
                              Here comes my vulture,
Heaving his beak up i' the air, and snuffing.

ACT 5, SCENE 7

[*Enter*] VOLTORE

VOLTORE

Out-stripped thus, by a parasite? a slave?
Would run on errands? and make legs, for crumbs?
Well, what I'll do –

VOLPONE   The court stays for your worship.
I e'en rejoice, sir, at your worship's happiness,
And that it fell into so learnèd hands,   5

18   *You should ha' some* There would be some people who
19   *autumn* large harvest
21   *very* true
24   *Except* Unless
25   *a'known* acknowledged (as heir)
26   *gamesters* gamblers
27   *seem to win* acknowledge he is winning
 2   *make legs* bow
 3   *stays* waits
 5   *it* the inheritance

That understand the fingering.

VOLTORE   What do you mean?

VOLPONE

I mean to be a suitor to your worship,
For the small tenement, out of reparations:
That, at the end of your long row of houses,
By the *Piscaria*. It was, in Volpone's time,   10
Your predecessor, ere he grew diseased,
A handsome, pretty, customed bawdy-house
As any was in Venice – none dispraised –
But fell with him; his body and that house
Decayed together.

VOLTORE   Come, sir, leave your prating.   15

VOLPONE

Why, if your worship give me but your hand,
That I may ha' the refusal, I have done.
'Tis a mere toy, to you, sir: candle-rents;
As your learned worship knows –

VOLTORE   What do I know?

VOLPONE

Marry, no end of your wealth, sir, God decrease it.   20

VOLTORE

Mistaking knave! What, mock'st thou my misfortune?

VOLPONE

His blessing on your heart, sir, would 'twere more.

                            [*Exit* VOLTORE]

Now to my first again, at the next corner.

---

6   *fingering* manipulation, how to handle it (playing off the reference to 'learned hands')

8   *out of reparations* needing repairs

10   *Piscaria* Fish-market

12   *customed* well supplied with customers (or, possibly, permitted, either because bribes have been paid as 'customs', or because it has been established by custom) *bawdy-house* house of prostitution

13   *none dispraised* not to say anything bad of the others (Kernan)

16–17   *Why . . . done* Well, if your honoured self will just give me your handshake (or handwriting) promising me first refusal on the property, I won't ask any more favours

18   *toy* trifle
       candle-rents rents from deteriorating property

20   *decrease* A deliberate slip for 'increase'; Volpone plays the sergeant like a Shakespearean comic constable, such as the malapropist Dogberry.

22   *would 'twere more* Under the guise of politely wishing Voltore's fortune were even greater, Volpone can tauntingly wish that Voltore's misfortune were even greater.

ACT 5, SCENE 8

[*Enter*] CORBACCIO, CORVINO; MOSCA [*walking across the stage dressed as a clarissimo*]

CORBACCIO
See, in our habit! See the impudent varlet!

CORVINO
That I could shoot mine eyes at him, like gunstones.

[*Exit* MOSCA]

VOLPONE
But, is this true, sir, of the parasite?

CORBACCIO
Again, to afflict us? Monster!

VOLPONE   In good faith, sir,
I'm heartily grieved a beard of your grave length   5
Should be so over-reached. I never brooked
That parasite's hair, methought his nose should cozen:
There still was somewhat, in his look, did promise
The bane of a *clarissimo*.

CORBACCIO   Knave –

VOLPONE   Methinks
Yet you, that are so traded i' the world,   10
A witty merchant, the fine bird, Corvino,
That have such moral emblems on your name,
Should not have sung your shame, and dropped your cheese,
To let the fox laugh at your emptiness.

---

1   *in our habit* dressed like us (despite his lower birth)
5–6   *a beard ... over-reached* that someone of your advanced age has been so
        outsmarted
6   *brooked* could tolerate
8   *still* always
9   *bane* poison
10   *traded* experienced (playing on Corvino's occupation)
12–14   *That have ... emptiness* Volpone here refers explicitly to one of the Aesop's fables
        that have informed the entire play: the fox who flatters the crow into dropping his
        cheese. Horace (*Satires*, II.v.55–7) alludes to this tale when describing a legacy-
        hunter much like Corvino: one who married his daughter to an old man, but was
        left out of the old man's will anyway.
14   *emptiness* the now-empty beak, but also the empty head that made it so

CORVINO

Sirrah, you think the privilege of the place,   15
And your red saucy cap, that seems, to me,
Nailed to your jolt-head with those two chequins,
Can warrant your abuses. Come you, hither:
You shall perceive, sir, I dare beat you. Approach.

VOLPONE

No haste, sir, I do know your valour, well,   20
Since you durst publish what you are, sir.

CORVINO   Tarry,
I'd speak with you.

VOLPONE   Sir, sir, another time –

CORVINO

Nay, now.

VOLPONE   O God, sir! I were a wise man,
Would stand the fury of a distracted cuckold.

CORBACCIO

What! Come again?

MOSCA *walks by 'em*

VOLPONE   [*Aside*] Upon 'em, Mosca: save me.   25

CORBACCIO

The air's infected where he breathes.

CORVINO   Let's fly him.
[*Exeunt* CORVINO *and* CORBACCIO]

VOLPONE

Excellent basilisk! Turn upon the vulture.

15   *place* either his role as a court official or the physical proximity to the high court
      Sirrah implies that the speaker outranks the person spoken to
17   *jolt-head* block-head
      chequins probably coin-like gold medallions on the cap
20–1 *I do know ... sir* I don't doubt your courage, since you were brave enough to
      announce publicly that you are a cuckold
23–4 *I were ... cuckold* I'd have to be very wise to stand still and endure the fury of an
      insane cuckold (spoken sarcastically)
27   *basilisk* a mythical serpent that could kill with just its glance

ACT 5, SCENE 9

[*Enter*] VOLTORE

VOLTORE
Well, flesh-fly, it is summer with you now;
Your winter will come on.

MOSCA   Good advocate,
'Pray thee, not rail, nor threaten out of place, thus:
Thou'lt make a solecism (as Madam says).
Get you a biggin more: your brain breaks loose.   5

VOLTORE
Well, sir.

VOLPONE   Would you have me beat the insolent slave?
Throw dirt upon his first good clothes?

VOLTORE   This same
Is, doubtless, some familiar!

VOLPONE   Sir, the court,
In troth, stays for you. I am mad a mule,
That never read Justinian, should get up,   10
And ride an advocate. Had you no quirk
To avoid gullage, sir, by such a creature?
I hope you do but jest; he has not done't.
This's but confederacy, to blind the rest.
You are the heir?

VOLTORE   A strange, officious,   15
Troublesome knave! Thou dost torment me.

VOLPONE   I know –
It cannot be, sir, that you should be cozened:

---

1   *flesh-fly* the meaning of 'Mosca' – a fly that plants its eggs in dead flesh (OED)
4   *Madam* Lady Would-Be (cf. 4.2.43)
5   *biggin* lawyer's cap
8   *familiar* evil spirit (renewing the theme of demonic possession)
9   *I am mad* It drives me crazy
9–11 *a mule ... advocate* Lawyers traditionally rode mules; Justinian wrote the great Roman code of law.
11   *quirk* trick
12   *gullage* being made a fool of
14   *confederacy* a conspiratorial subterfuge (with Mosca – but Volpone himself is dangerously blind to the possibility that he no longer has such a conspiracy with Mosca)

'Tis not within the wit of man, to do it;
You are so wise, so prudent – and 'tis fit
That wealth and wisdom still should go together –   20

                                                    [*Exeunt*]

ACT 5, SCENE 10

[*Enter four*] AVOCATORI, NOTARIO, COMMANDATORI
[*including the disguised*] VOLPONE], BONARIO, CELIA,
                    CORBACCIO, CORVINO

1st AVOCATORE
    Are all the parties here?
NOTARIO   All but the advocate.
2nd AVOCATORE
    And here he comes.

                    [*Enter* VOLTORE]

1st AVOCATORE   Then bring 'em forth to sentence.
VOLTORE
    O, my most honoured fathers, let your mercy
    Once win upon your justice, to forgive –
    I am distracted –
VOLPONE   [*Aside*] What will he do now?
VOLTORE   O,   5
    I know not which t' address myself to first,
    Whether your fatherhoods, or these innocents –
CORVINO
    [*Aside*] Will he betray himself?
VOLTORE   Whom, equally,
    I have abused, out of most covetous ends –

---

2   *And here he comes* Here and at line 20, F gives the speech to 'AVO', Q to 'AVOC',
    which might indicate the lines are spoken by several of the judges together; but
    editorial tradition has reasonably assigned these lines to individual judges.
    'em Celia and Bonario
4   *win upon* take precedence over
5   *distracted* mad, out of his wits
9   *out of most covetous ends* because of extremely greedy motives

CORVINO
    [*Aside*] The man is mad!
CORBACCIO   [*Aside*] What's that?
CORVINO   [*Aside*] He is possessed.   10
VOLTORE
    For which, now struck in conscience, here I prostrate
    Myself, at your offended feet, for pardon. [*Throws himself down*]
1st, 2nd AVOCATORI
    Arise.
CELIA   O heaven, how just thou art!
VOLPONE   [*Aside*] I'm caught
    I' mine own noose –
CORVINO [*Aside to* CORBACCIO] Be constant, sir: nought now
    Can help but impudence.
1st AVOCATORE   Speak forward.
COMMANDATORE   Silence.   15
VOLTORE
    It is not passion in me, reverend fathers,
    But only conscience – conscience, my good sires –
    That makes me, now, tell truth. That parasite,
    That knave hath been the instrument of all.
1st AVOCATORE
    Where is that knave? Fetch him.
VOLPONE   I go.   [*Exit*]
CORVINO   Grave fathers,   20
    This man is distracted, he confessed it now;
    For, hoping to be old Volpone's heir,
    Who now is dead –
3rd AVOCATORE   How?
2nd AVOCATORE   Is Volpone dead?
CORVINO
    Dead since, grave fathers –
BONARIO   O, sure vengeance!
1st AVOCATORE   Stay –
    Then he was no deceiver?
VOLTORE   O, no, none;   25
    The parasite, grave fathers –
CORVINO   He does speak

---

15   *impudence* shamelessness (in sticking to their earlier lie)
16   *passion* frenzy

Out of mere envy, 'cause the servant's made
The thing he gaped for. Please your fatherhoods,
This is the truth; though, I'll not justify
The other, but he may be somewhere faulty.   30
VOLTORE
Ay, to your hopes, as well as mine, Corvino;
But I'll use modesty. Pleaseth your wisdoms
To view these certain notes, and but confer them:
                        [*Gives papers to the* AVOCATORI]
As I hope favour, they shall speak clear truth.
CORVINO
The devil has entered him!
BONARIO   Or bides in you.   35
4th AVOCATORE
We have done ill, by a public officer
To send for him, if he be heir.
2nd AVOCATORE   For whom?
4th AVOCATORE
Him that they call the parasite.
3rd AVOCATORE   'Tis true:
He is a man of great estate now left.
4th AVOCATORE
[*To* NOTARIO] Go you, and learn his name; and say, the court   40
Entreats his presence here, but to the clearing
Of some few doubts.
                        [*Exit* NOTARIO]
2nd AVOCATORE   This same's a labyrinth!
1st AVOCATORE
Stand you unto your first report?
CORVINO   My state,
My life, my fame –
BONARIO   Where is't?
CORVINO   Are at the stake

32   *modesty* restraint, moderation
33   *certain* particular, or, offering reliable proof
      but confer simply compare them, or confer about them
35   *bides* abides, remains
40   *you* the Notario, a more decorous emissary
41   *but to* only for
43   *Stand you unto* Do you hold to
      state estate
44   *fame* reputation

157

1st AVOCATORE

[To CORBACCIO] Is yours so too?

CORBACCIO   The advocate is a knave: 45

And has a forkèd tongue –

2nd AVOCATORE   Speak to the point.

CORBACCIO

So is the parasite, too.

1st AVOCATORE   This is confusion.

VOLTORE

I do beseech your fatherhoods, read but those –

CORVINO

And credit nothing the false spirit hath writ:

It cannot be, my sires, but he is possessed.   50

                                                    [*Exeunt*]

ACT 5, SCENE 11

[*Enter*] VOLPONE

VOLPONE

To make a snare for mine own neck! and run

My head into it, wilfully! with laughter!

When I had newly 'scaped, was free, and clear!

Out of mere wantonness! O, the dull devil

Was in this brain of mine, when I devised it;   5

And Mosca gave it second: he must now

Help to sear up this vein, or we bleed dead.

[*Enter* NANO, ANDROGYNO, *and* CASTRONE]

49   *credit* believe
50   *It cannot be . . . but* There is no possible explanation except that
0   This brief scene is evidently set on a street. The next scene (5.12) picks up right
      where 5.10 left off – in fact, in Q that next scene is again numbered 5.10 – and
      presumably the courtroom set and actors were not rushed off and rushed back on
      twenty-two lines later, so they are often frozen in a darkened tableau while this
      scene occurs downstage.
1   *snare* noose; but the same term would have been used for a fox-trap.
4   *wantonness* playful enthusiasm, careless self-indulgence
6   *gave it second* seconded the idea
7   *sear* cauterize

How now! Who let you loose? Whither go you, now?
What? To buy gingerbread? Or to drown kitlings?

NANO

Sir, Master Mosca called us out of doors,   10
And bid us all go play, and took the keys.

ANDROGYNO   Yes.

VOLPONE

Did Master Mosca take the keys? Why, so!
I am farther in. These are my fine conceits!
I must be merry, with a mischief to me!
What a vile wretch was I, that could not bear   15
My fortune soberly? I must ha' my crotchets!
And my conundrums! Well, go you, and seek him;
His meaning may be truer than my fear.
Bid him, he straight come to me, to the court;
Thither will I, and, if't be possible,   20
Unscrew my advocate, upon new hopes:
When I provoked him, then I lost myself.

                                                          [*Exeunt*]

ACT 5, SCENE 12

[*Enter*] AVOCATORI, [NOTARIO, COMMANDATORI,
BONARIO, CELIA, VOLTORE, CORBACCIO, CORVINO]

1st AVOCATORE

[*Studying* VOLTORE's *notes*] These things can ne'er be
   reconciled. He here
Professeth, that the gentleman was wronged;

9   *kitlings* kittens; Volpone suggests the pastimes of naughty or cruel children.
13   *farther in* in even more trouble than I realized; Volpone now suspects Mosca's true
     intentions, so the remainder of the line is spoken sarcastically.
     conceits schemes
14   *I must . . . to me* I had to enjoy myself with something that would do me harm
16   *My fortune soberly* My wealth, or my good luck in court, wisely
16–17 *my crochets . . . my conundrums* my perverse and clever whims
18   *truer* more honest and loyal
19   *Bid* Instruct, or Ask
21   *Unscrew* Reverse the course of, or perhaps, Calm the fierce resolution of *upon* by
     offering him
1   *He* Voltore

And that the gentlewoman was brought thither,
Forced by her husband; and there left.

VOLTORE   Most true.

CELIA

How ready is heaven to those that pray!

1st AVOCATORE   But, that   5
Volpone would have ravished her, he holds
Utterly false, knowing his impotence.

CORVINO

Grave fathers, he is possessed; again I say,
Possessed; nay, if there be possession
And obsession, he has both.

3rd AVOCATORE   Here comes our officer.   10

[*Enter* VOLPONE, *still disguised*]

VOLPONE

The parasite will straight be here, grave fathers.

4th AVOCATORE

You might invent some other name, sir varlet.

3rd AVOCATORE

Did not the notary meet him?

VOLPONE   Not that I know.

4th AVOCATORE

His coming will clear all.

2nd AVOCATORE   Yet it is misty.

VOLTORE

May't please your fatherhoods –

VOLPONE *whispers* [*to*] *the advocate* [VOLTORE]

VOLPONE   Sir, the parasite   15
Willed me to tell you that his master lives;
That you are still the man; your hopes the same;
And this was only a jest –

VOLTORE   How?

VOLPONE   Sir, to try

---

5   *ready* promptly responsive
10   *obsession* a devil's assault on a person from the outside (as opposed to possession, which is from the inside)
12   *invent* find, choose (because Mosca's wealth makes him suddenly worthy of a nobler term)
14   *Yet it is misty* Still, up to this moment, it remains unclear

If you were firm, and how you stood affected.

VOLTORE
Art sure he lives?

VOLPONE   Do I live, sir?

VOLTORE   O me!   20
I was too violent.

VOLPONE   Sir, you may redeem it.
They said you were possessed; fall down, and seem so:

                    VOLTORE *falls*

I'll help to make it good. [*Aloud*] God bless the man!
[*Aside to* VOLTORE] Stop your wind hard, and swell.
      [*Aloud*] See, see, see, see!
He vomits crooked pins! His eyes are set,   25
Like a dead hare's, hung in a poulter's shop!
His mouth's running away! Do you see, Signor?
Now 'tis in his belly!

CORVINO   Ay, the devil!

VOLPONE
Now, in his throat.

CORVINO   Ay, I perceive it plain.

VOLPONE
'Twill out, 'twill out: stand clear. See, where it flies!   30
In shape of a blue toad, with a bat's wings!
Do not you see it, sir?

CORBACCIO   What? I think I do.

CORVINO
'Tis too manifest.

VOLPONE   Look! He comes t' himself!

---

19   *stood affected* truly felt (about Volpone)
20   *Do I live* This normally means something like, 'as surely as I am here talking to you', with an added irony in this situation; but Volpone may also lift off his disguise momentarily for Voltore here, which would explain Voltore's instant change of tactics, though it does not explain how he would hope to inherit anytime soon from such a radically revived man.
23   *good* convincing
24   *Stop your wind* Hold your breath
25–31 *He vomits . . . bat's wings* Similar phenomena were reported during Jacobean exorcisms (of which King James became a prominent debunker).
26   *poulter* seller of poultry and small game such as hares
27   *running away* moving wildly – perhaps twitching side to side, perhaps silently imitating rapid speech

VOLTORE
　Where am I?
VOLPONE　　　Take good heart, the worst is past, sir.
　You are dispossessed.
1st AVOCATORE　　　What accident is this?　　　　　　　　35
2nd AVOCATORE
　Sudden, and full of wonder!
3rd AVOCATORE　　　　　　　If he were
　Possessed, as it appears, all this is nothing.
CORVINO
　He has been, often, subject to these fits.
1st AVOCATORE
　Show him that writing. [*To* VOLTORE] Do you know it, sir?
VOLPONE
　[*Aside to* VOLTORE] Deny it, sir, forswear it, know it not.　　40
VOLTORE
　Yes, I do know it well, it is my hand;
　But all that it contains is false.
BONARIO　　　　　　　　　　O practice!
2nd AVOCATORE
　What maze is this!
1st AVOCATORE　　Is he not guilty, then,
　Whom you there name the parasite?
VOLTORE　　　　　　　　　　　Grave fathers,
　No more than his good patron, old Volpone.　　　　　45
4th AVOCATORE
　Why, he is dead!
VOLTORE　　　　O no, my honoured fathers,
　He lives –
1st AVOCATORE How! Lives?
VOLTORE　　　　　　　Lives.
2nd AVOCATORE　　　　　　This is subtler yet!
3rd AVOCATORE
　You said he was dead!
VOLTORE　　　　　　Never.

34　*Take good heart* Cheer up, be encouraged
35　*accident* unforeseen event
37　*this* Probably indicating Voltore's notes to the court.
41　*hand* handwriting
42　*O practice!* This is a treachery!
47　*subtler* trickier

3rd AVOCATORE [*To* CORVINO] You said so!

CORVINO   I heard so.

4th AVOCATORE

Here comes the gentleman, make him way.

[*Enter* MOSCA]

3rd AVOCATORE   A stool.

4th AVOCATORE

A proper man! And, were Volpone dead,   50

A fit match for my daughter.

3rd AVOCATORE   Give him way.

VOLPONE

[*Aside to* MOSCA] Mosca, I was almost lost, the advocate

Had betrayed all; but now it is recovered:

All's on the hinge again – say I am living.

MOSCA

What busy knave is this! Most reverend fathers,   55

I sooner had attended your grave pleasures,

But that my order for the funeral

Of my dear patron did require me –

VOLPONE   [*Aside*] Mosca!

MOSCA

Whom I intend to bury like a gentleman –

VOLPONE

[*Aside*] Ay, quick, and cozen me of all.

2nd AVOCATORE   Still stranger!   60

More intricate!

1st AVOCATORE And come about again!

4th AVOCATORE

It is a match, my daughter is bestowed.

MOSCA

[*Aside to* VOLPONE] Will you gi' me half?

---

50 *proper* handsome
53 *recovered* revived, repaired, or covered up again
54 *on the hinge* working properly
55 *busy* meddling, officious
56 *sooner ... pleasures* would have responded sooner to the summons from you important men
60 *quick* alive
61 *come about* reversed (because Volpone is reported dead after all)

VOLPONE	First I'll be hanged.

MOSCA   [*Aside to* VOLPONE I know,
    Your voice is good, cry not so loud.

1st AVOCATOREM   Demand
    The advocate. Sir, did not you affirm   65
    Volpone was alive?

VOLPONE   Yes, and he is;
    This gent'man told me so. [*Aside to* MOSCA] Thou shalt have
      half.

MOSCA
    Whose drunkard is this same? Speak, some that know him:
    I never saw his face. [*Aside to* VOLPONE] I cannot now
    Afford it you so cheap.

VOLPONE [*Aside to* MOSCA] No?

1st AVOCATORE [*To* VOLTORE] What say you?   70

VOLTORE
    The officer told me.

VOLPONE   I did, grave fathers,
    And will maintain he lives with mine own life,
    And that this creature told me. [*Aside*] I was born
    With all good stars my enemies.

MOSCA   Most grave fathers,
    If such an insolence as this must pass   75
    Upon me, I am silent; 'twas not this
    For which you sent, I hope.

2nd AVOCATORE [*Indicating* VOLPONE] Take him away.

VOLPONE
    [*Aside to* MOSCA] Mosca.

3rd AVOCATORE   Let him be whipped.

VOLPONE   [*Aside to* MOSCA] Wilt thou betray me?
    Cozen me?

3rd AVOCATORE   And taught to bear himself
    Toward a person of his rank.

4th AVOCATORE   Away.   80

       [*Officers begin to drag* VOLPONE *away*]

---

64   *cry* shout; Mosca is apparently warning Volpone that his exasperated reply in the
        previous line was dangerously audible.

72   *And will . . . lives* I would bet my life he is alive (repeating the joke from line 20)

74   *With all good stars my enemies* Under a bad astrological sign; hence, unlucky

75–6   *pass / Upon me* will be tolerated against me

80   *his* Mosca's

MOSCA
    I humbly thank your fatherhoods.
VOLPONE   Soft, soft. [*Aside*] Whipped?
    And lose all that I have? If I confess,
    It cannot be much more.
4th AVOCATORE [*To* MOSCA] Sir, are you married?
VOLPONE
    They'll be allied, anon: I must be resolute;
    The fox shall, here, uncase.

                He puts off his disguise

MOSCA [*Aside to* VOLPONE] Patron.
VOLPONE   Nay, now,   85
    My ruins shall not come alone. Your match
    I'll hinder sure; my substance shall not glue you,
    Nor screw you, into a family.
MOSCA   [*Aside to* VOLPONE] Why, patron!
VOLPONE
    I am Volpone, and this [*Indicating* MOSCA] is my knave;
    This, his own knave; this, avarice's fool;   90
    This [*Indicating* CORVINO], a chimera of wittol, fool, and
        knave;
    And, reverend fathers, since we all can hope
    Nought but a sentence, let's not now despair it.
    You hear me brief.
CORVINO   May it please your fatherhoods –
COMMANDATORI   Silence.
1st AVOCATORE
    The knot is now undone, by miracle!   95
2nd AVOCATORE
    Nothing can be more clear.

---

81   *Soft* Take it easy, wait a minute
84   *allied, anon* made allies (by marriage) soon
85   *uncase* drop his disguise, and perhaps also (like a hunted fox) break from his cover,
        or, possibly, (like a captured fox) have his coat flayed off
86–8   *Your . . . family* I'll never let you use my wealth to marry into the aristocracy
89   *knave* low-ranking servant, with a connotation of low ethics
90   *avarice's fool* a person duped by greed; the 'knave' is probably Voltore and the 'fool'
        Corbaccio, as some editors stipulate, but it could be the other way around.
91   *chimera* a mythical beast combining lion, goat, and serpent
93   *let's . . . despair it* don't disappoint us (spoken with bitter irony)
94   *brief* keeping my remarks brief (to get this over with)

3rd AVOCATORE	Or can more prove

These innocent.

1st AVOCATORE   Give 'em their liberty.

BONARIO

Heaven could not, long, let such gross crimes be hid.

2nd AVOCATORE

If this be held the high way, to get riches,
May I be poor.

3rd AVOCATORE   This's not the gain, but torment.   100

1st AVOCATORE

These possess wealth, as sick men possess fevers,
Which, trulier, may be said to possess them.

2nd AVOCATORE

Disrobe that parasite.

CORVINO, MOSCA   Most honoured fathers –

1st AVOCATORE

Can you plead aught to stay the course of justice?
If you can, speak.

CORVINO, VOLTORE   We beg favour.

CELIA   And mercy.   105

1st AVOCATORE

You hurt your innocence, suing for the guilty.
Stand forth; and, first, the parasite. You appear
To have been the chiefest minister, if not plotter,
In all these lewd impostures; and now, lastly,
Have, with your impudence, abused the court,   110
And habit of a gentleman of Venice,
Being a fellow of no birth or blood;
For which, our sentence is, first thou be whipped;
Then live perpetual prisoner in our galleys.

VOLPONE

I thank you, for him.

MOSCA   Bane to thy wolfish nature.   115

---

100   *This's ... torment* This one gained nothing but torment, or, This is not profit but torment

109   *lewd impostures* wicked falsehoods

115   VOLPONE F and Q give the bitter thanks to Voltore, but – considering Mosca's immediate response, and the vengeful parallel with line 81 – it fits better spoken by Volpone. This is particularly true if the scene is staged with each miscreant led offstage immediately after his sentencing.
    Bane Mosca is cursing Volpone; wolf's-bane was a powerful poison

1st AVOCATORE

>Deliver him to the *Saffi*. Thou, Volpone,
>By blood and rank a gentleman, canst not fall
>Under like censure; but our judgement on thee
>Is, that thy substance all be straight confiscate
>To the hospital of the *Incurabili*;   120
>And, since the most was gotten by imposture,
>By feigning lame, gout, palsy and such diseases,
>Thou art to lie in prison, cramped with irons,
>Till thou be'st sick and lame indeed. Remove him.

VOLPONE

>This is called mortifying of a fox.   125

1st AVOCATORE

>Thou, Voltore, to take away the scandal
>Thou hast giv'n all worthy men of thy profession,
>Art banished from their fellowship, and our state.
>Corbaccio, bring him near. We here possess
>Thy son of all thy estate; and confine thee   130
>To the monastery of *San' Spirito*;
>Where since thou knew'st not how to live well here,
>Thou shalt be learned to die well.

CORBACCIO   Ha! What said he?

COMMANDATORE

>You shall know anon, sir.

1st AVOCATORE   Thou Corvino, shalt

>Be straight embarked from thine own house, and rowed   135
>Round about Venice, through the Grand Canal,

116   *Saffi* bailiffs
119   *substance* wealth, material goods
120   *Incurabili* incurables – mostly victims of venereal disease
125   *mortifying* a quintuple pun – the word means not only 'humiliation' and 'bringing
      toward death', but also 'tenderizing animal meat', 'teaching sinners, by punishment,
      to overcome their worldly appetites', and even 'disposing of property for charitable
      purposes' (Parker).
126–7 *the scandal . . . profession* the disgrace you have brought on all honourable lawyers;
      the Dedication and Epistle suggest that Jonson was aiming his play at an audience
      which included many legal scholars.
133   *die well* The arts of dying well – the *ars moriendi* – were a central religious practice
      throughout the Renaissance.
135   *embarked* sent out on a boat

Wearing a cap, with fair, long ass's ears,
Instead of horns; and so to mount, a paper
Pinned on thy breast, to the *Berlino* –
CORVINO   Yes,
And have mine eyes beat out with stinking fish,   140
Bruised fruit and rotten eggs – 'Tis well. I'm glad
I shall not see my shame, yet.
1st AVOCATORE   And to expiate
Thy wrongs done to thy wife, thou art to send her
Home, to her father, with her dowry trebled;
And these are all your judgements –
ALL   Honoured fathers.   145
1st AVOCATORE
Which may not be revoked. Now you begin,
When crimes are done, and past, and to be punished,
To think what your crimes are; away with them.
Let all that see these vices thus rewarded
Take heart, and love to study 'em. Mischiefs feed   150
Like beasts, till they be fat, and then they bleed.

                                              [*Exeunt*]

[*Enter*] VOLPONE [*as* EPILOGUE]

The seasoning of a play is the applause.
Now, though the fox be punished by the laws,
He yet doth hope there is no suff'ring due
For any fact which he hath done 'gainst you.
If there be, censure him; here he doubtful stands.   5
If not, fare jovially, and clap your hands.

THE END

137–8   *ass's ears . . . horns* Because Corvino behaved like an ass but was never actually a
        cuckold.
138   *so to mount* to climb in that costume
139   *Berlino* the pillory, where malefactors were exposed to public humiliation
142   *I shall not see my shame, yet* I still won't be forced to witness my own humiliation,
        not even such a prominent humiliation (since my eyes will be smashed by the
        garbage that people throw at those in the pillory)
150   *Take heart . . . study 'em* Be encouraged, and love to practice those vices (spoken
        ironically)
4   *fact* crime
6   *fare jovially* be cheerful; Jonson here translates a standard closing plea for applause
        from classical comedies, and alters the familiar phrase 'farewell' to invoke the
        supposedly happy planetary influence of Jupiter.

TO

THE MOST

NOBLE AND

MOST EQVALL

SISTERS

THE TWO FAMOVS

VNIVERSITIES

FOR THEIR LOVE

AND

ACCEPTANCE

SHEW'N TO HIS POEME IN THE

PRESENTATION

BEN. IONSON

THE GRATEFVLL ACKNOWLEDGER

DEDICATES

BOTH IT AND HIMSELFE.

EQUAL equal to each other in quality, and fair (equitable) in their judgements; Jonson was granted honorary degrees from both Oxford and Cambridge, partly perhaps in appreciation of this play.
UNIVERSITIES Oxford and Cambridge
POEM *Volpone*, which was performed at Oxford and Cambridge between its early 1606 London premiere and its early 1607 Quarto printing.

Jonson's dedicatory letter to Oxford and Cambridge Universities defends litera-ture (Jonson uses the term 'poetry' broadly) against its accusers (including, implicitly, Puritans), though it concedes that sloppy and slanderous writers have recently injured literature's ancient prestige. The Epistle draws its didactic justifi-cation of literary art from Jonson's own 'Apologetical Dialogue' in *Poetaster* five years earlier, as well as from Erasmus, Minturno, and Jonson's perennial favourite, Horace.

Jonson strives for an erudite elegance of style in addressing his university audi-ence, which makes for interesting but difficult reading for more modern audi-ences. His rich and varied sentences provide some sense of how the best literary minds of Jacobean England chose ceremoniously to communicate their beliefs. The Epistle is so convoluted in syntax and so mannered in diction, however, that a single modern paraphrase – here presented on left-hand pages facing the relevant original text – seems preferable to dozens of piecemeal glosses, and I have added footnotes only where they add substance, not where they merely provide translation.

The sense of the Epistle is:

Since no writer is great enough to succeed without favourable circumstances, including admirers, writers should especially defend themselves when that entails defending their admirers also. So, while the endorsement of you great universities should be enough in itself, further justification is called for in an era when writers are so widely condemned.

Undisciplined writers have certainly damaged the reputation of literature; otherwise these accusations would be completely outrageous. Good writers have to be good men, and anyone who can provide the benefits true literature provides should be spared snobbish, ill-informed accusations. But the accusers will object that modern writers hardly correspond to the high dignity traditionally associated with literature; many people claim the title of author, while (especially in drama) producing only stupid and offensive works. I cannot deny that, but it is unfair to

9   *the bounty of your act* your generous patronage (which Jonson is trying to repay by explaining to the world why support of literature is justified)

15   *their mistress* poetry; 'poetasters' are weak, pretentious, dilettante poets, whose failings oblige true poets to defend their profession.

34–7   *especially ... practised* Jonson here echoes some of the Puritans' principal objections to the English theatre.

38   *features* plays, though it also suggests a condemnation of the authors' faces

THE EPISTLE

Never, most equal Sisters, had any man a wit so presently
excellent, as that it could raise itself; but there must come both
matter, occasion, commenders, and favourers to it. If this be
true, and that the fortune of all writers doth daily prove it, it
behooves the careful to provide well towards these accidents; and,   5
having acquired them, to preserve that part of reputation most
tenderly, wherein the benefit of a friend is also defended. Hence
is it that I now render myself grateful, and am studious to justify
the bounty of your act; to which, though your mere authority
were satisfying, yet, it being an age wherein poetry and the   10
professors of it hear so ill on all sides, there will a reason be looked
for in the subject.

It is certain, nor can it with any forehead be opposed, that the
too much licence of poetasters in this time hath much deformed
their mistress; that, every day, their manifold and manifest igno-   15
rance doth stick unnatural reproaches upon her. But for their
petulancy, it were an act of the greatest injustice, either to let the
learned suffer, or so divine a skill – which indeed should not be
attempted with unclean hands – to fall under the least contempt.
For, if men will impartially, and not asquint, look toward the   20
offices and function of a poet, they will easily conclude to themselves the impossibility of any man's being the good poet, without
first being a good man. He that is said to be able to inform young
men to all good disciplines, inflame grown men to all great virtues,
keep old men in their best and supreme state, or, as they decline to   25
childhood, recover them to their first strength; that comes forth
the interpreter and arbiter of nature, a teacher of things divine no
less than human, a master in manners; and can alone, or with a
few, effect the business of mankind: this, I take him, is no subject
for pride and ignorance to exercise their railing rhetoric upon. But   30
it will here be hastily answered, that the writers of these days are
other things; that not only their manners, but their natures, are
inverted; and nothing remaining with them of the dignity of poet,
but the abused name, which every scribe usurps; that now, especially in dramatic, or (as they term it) stage-poetry, nothing but   35
ribaldry, profanation, blasphemy, all licence of offence to God and
man is practised. I dare not deny a great part of this, and am sorry
I dare not, because in some men's abortive features – and would
they had never boasted the light – it is over-true. But, that all are

judge all writers by these bad pretenders. I have always tried to avoid blasphemy or bawdiness; and though my satires are considered biting, what society have I offended, what public person have I insulted? My works are licensed, because I avoid excessive or personal criticisms, attacking only bad kinds of people, who richly deserve it. Any text can be wilfully misinterpreted, and it is unfair to blame me if malicious commentators try to interpret my works as attacks on individuals (whom the commentators themselves want to attack indirectly).

Those writers who seek popularity by recklessly slandering people will get no competition from me: I would rather go unread than become famous that way. Nor can I blame the authorities who, recognizing the damage slander can do, would rather see stupid, old-fashioned slapstick comedies and morality plays than satires on individuals, leaders, or nations. As Horace writes,

'Everyone is afraid of satires, even if personally uninjured, and hates them'.

41–5   Jonson's rowdy conduct throughout his life – including persistent drunkenness, nasty insults, censored plays, brawling, killing a fellow-actor, and fathering illegitimate children – makes this claim that he 'can – and from a most clear conscience – affirm that I have ever trembled to think toward the least profaneness' seem like a wildly self-serving falsehood. If it were not for the context of a serious defence of poetic morality, it would be tempting to read it as a self-deprecating in-joke designed to elicit mocking whoops of laughter from an audience.

52   *entirely mine* Jonson must make an exception for collaborations such as *The Isle of Dogs, Eastward Ho!* and perhaps the first version of *Sejanus*, which landed Jonson in serious trouble with the authorities.

53   *particular* aiming at a specific person; satirists traditionally defended themselves by claiming they were attacking the faults, not any actual individual person; and that for anyone to complain of slander was foolishly to confess to the vices the satires depicted.

61   *Application* Interpretation designed to apply the satire to specific persons or events, the seeking out of personal allusions and political allegories; Volpone himself was apparently taken as a caricature of the wealthy Thomas Sutton.

70–1   *whose living faces . . . petulant styles* what actual persons' public image they mutilate with their writing (punning on 'stiles', meaning pens); writers convicted of slandering royalty sometimes had their faces scarred in punishment, and Jonson himself had been in danger of that disfigurement, though he here insists he would never compete with such gossip-columnists.

74   *providing* foreseeing; Jonson here provisionally sides with those who, for the good of the society, prefer old-fashioned entertainments to the current trends in satire.

80   *Sibi . . . odit* Horace, *Satires*, II.1.23, which Jonson translates (in *Poetaster*, 3.5.41) as 'In satires, each man, though untouched, Complains/As he were hurt; and hates such biting strains'.

embarked in this bold adventure for hell, is a most uncharitable   40
thought, and, uttered, a more malicious slander. For my particular,
I can (and from a most clear conscience) affirm, that I have ever
trembled to think toward the least profaneness; have loathed the
use of such foul and unwashed bawdry, as is now made the food of
the scene. And, howsoever I cannot escape, from some, the impu-   45
tation of sharpness, but that they will say, I have taken a pride, or
lust, to be bitter, and not my youngest infant but hath come into
the world with all his teeth; I would ask of these supercilious politics, what nation, society, or general order or state I have provoked?
What public person? Whether I have not in all these preserved   50
their dignity, as mine own person, safe? My works are read, allowed,
(I speak of those that are entirely mine). Look into them: what
broad reproofs have I used? where have I been particular? where
personal? except to a mimic, cheater, bawd, or buffoon – creatures,
for their insolencies, worthy to be taxed? Or to which of these so   55
pointingly, as he might not either ingenuously have confessed, or
wisely dissembled his disease? But it is not rumour can make men
guilty, much less entitle me to other men's crimes. I know that
nothing can be so innocently writ or carried, but may be made
obnoxious to construction; marry, whilst I bear mine innocence   60
about me, I fear it not. Application is now grown a trade with
many; and there are that profess to have a key for the deciphering
of every thing: but let wise and noble persons take heed how they
be too credulous, or give leave to these invading interpreters
to be over-familiar with their fames, who cunningly, and often,   65
utter their own virulent malice, under other men's simplest
meanings.

As for those that will – by faults which charity hath raked up, or
common honesty concealed – make themselves a name with the
multitude, or, to draw their rude and beastly claps, care not whose   70
living faces they entrench with their petulant styles, may they do it
without a rival, for me: I choose rather to live graved in obscurity,
than share with them in so preposterous a fame. Nor can I blame
the wishes of those grave and wiser patriots, who providing the
hurts these licentious spirits may do in a state, desire rather to see   75
fools and devils, and those antique relics of barbarism retrieved,
with all other ridiculous and exploded follies, than behold the
wounds of private men, of princes and nations: for, as Horace
makes Trebatius speak, in these,

– *Sibi quisque timet, quanquam est intactus, & odit.*   80

Some writers seem to enjoy that; but all worthy observers already abhor it, as they abhor the chaotic practices of the popular theatre, and the ugly, incorrect, nonsensical writing that offends anyone who cares about language, morality, or Christianity.

I am naturally concerned when my own reputation, and that of many virtuous scholars, is at risk; when the traditionally noble title of author is made scornful by these bad imitators; when those traditionally honoured by monarchs must endure the insults of every loud-mouthed, self-appointed preacher. That is what compels me to write this defence, and what always made me careful to distinguish myself from those bad writers. Therefore, in this new play *Volpone*, which you have honoured me by approving, I have tried to teach them all a lesson by copying the virtues of ancient literature: the structure, the style, the decorum, and finally the moral instruction, which is the principal purpose of literature – to teach people how to live, and why.

And though the ending of the play may be criticized as diverging from the traditions of comedy, strictly defined, I ask the knowledgeable and generous reader to recognize that it was done deliberately (except that I do not want to seem boastful, I could show here how easily I could have followed those traditional rules). But, because I was especially concerned to stifle those who claim that plays never punish sin, I took some liberty (though even my variations have precedents in the classics, where comedies often end with some characters appropriately punished, about which I will write more adequately soon).

94	*vernaculous* ill-bred, probably also implicating those who accuse in the vernacular language because they (and their low-class audience) lack the ability to use Latin
100	*to my crown* to my credit and glory (playing on the laureate crown granted to great poets)
101	*reduce* restore; Jonson often claims to be reviving the forms and mores of the classics.
105	*catastrophe* denouement, final act; Jonson concedes that *Volpone* lacks the happy ending traditional to the genre.
109	*his scale* the traditional measurements used by a learned critic (with a pun on the variations that can be played on a musical scale)
115	*mulcted* punished; the classical precedents Jonson broadly claims here for his harsh ending have been hard for modern scholars to find.

And men may justly impute such rages, if continued, to the writer, as his sports. The increase of which lust in liberty, together with the present trade of the stage, in all their miscellane interludes, what learned or liberal soul doth not already abhor, where nothing but the garbage of the time is uttered, and that with such impropriety 85 of phrase, such plenty of solecisms, such dearth of sense, so bold prolepses, so racked metaphors, with brothelry able to violate the ear of a pagan, and blasphemy to turn the blood of a Christian to water?

I cannot but be serious in a cause of this nature, wherein my 90 fame, and the reputation of diverse honest and learned are the question; when a name so full of authority, antiquity, and all great mark, is, through their insolence, become the lowest scorn of the age; and those men subject to the petulancy of every vernaculous orator, that were wont to be the care of kings and happiest 95 monarchs. This it is that hath not only rapt me to present indignation, but made me studious heretofore, and by all my actions, to stand off from them; which may most appear in this my latest work, which you, most learned arbitresses, have seen, judged, and to my crown, approved; wherein I have laboured for their instruc- 100 tion and amendment, to reduce not only the ancient forms, but manners of the scene, the easiness, the propriety, the innocence, and last, the doctrine, which is the principal end of poesy, to inform men in the best reason of living.

And though my catastrophe may, in the strict rigour of comic 105 law, meet with censure, as turning back to my promise, I desire the learned and charitable critic to have so much faith in me to think it was done of industry: for, with what ease I could have varied it nearer his scale (but that I fear to boast my own faculty) I could here insert. But my special aim being to put the snaffle in their 110 mouths, that cry out, We never punish vice in our interludes, etc., I took the more liberty; though not without some lines of example, drawn even in the ancients themselves, the goings-out of whose comedies are not always joyful, but oft-times the bawds, the serv- ants, the rivals, yea, and the masters are mulcted; and fitly, it being 115 the office of a comic poet to imitate justice, and instruct to life, as well as purity of language, or stir up gentle affections; to which, upon my next opportunity toward the examining and digesting of my notes, I shall speak more wealthily, and pay the world a debt.

Meanwhile, since I have been careful to show my gratitude for your support, and to show the world, in this epistle, why your support was justified, I hope I can count on that patronage continuing, which will give me time to complete even better works, which will restore the great ancient reputation of literature which has lately been besmirched.

As for those nasty and lazy commentators who have never tried to do anything positive, or who know themselves so sinful that they fear literature's ability to reveal truth, and therefore, as a precaution, defend themselves by long-winded attacks on it: they will find that literature's servants (whose feelings are easily aroused) will throw some ink at them that will disfigure their reputations more deeply than acid would disfigure their bodies; and not even a skilful plastic surgeon will be able to remove the scars, which will remain until death, announcing their unworthiness.

136   *Cinnamus* cf. Martial, *Epigrams* VI, 24–6; barbers were surgeons in the Renaissance, and Jonson, whose thumb had been branded for killing a fellow-actor, would have had reason to ponder the permanence of such marks of disgrace.

In the meantime, most reverenced Sisters, as I have cared to be 120
thankful for your affections past, and here made the understanding
acquainted with some ground of your favours, let me not despair
their continuance, to the maturing of some worthier fruits;
wherein, if my muses be true to me, I shall raise the despised head
of poetry again, and stripping her out of those rotten and base rags 125
wherewith the times have adulterated her form, restore her to her
primitive habit, feature, and majesty, and render her worthy to be
embraced and kissed of all the great and master-spirits of our
world.

As for the vile and slothful, who never affected an act worthy of 130
celebration, or are so inward with their own vicious natures as they
worthily fear her, and think it a high point of policy to keep her in
contempt, with their declamatory and windy invectives: she shall
out of just rage incite her servants (who are *genus irritabile*) to
spout ink in their faces, that shall eat farther than their marrow 135
into their fames; and not Cinnamus the barber, with his art, shall
be able to take out the brands; but they shall live, and be read, till
the wretches die, as things worst deserving of themselves in chief,
and then of all mankind.

From my House in the Black-Friars, this 11th of February, 1607.